Fast Access/Lotus 1-2-3 (Release 3.1+)

Rhyder McClure
Mary Abdill

Brady Publishing

New York London Toronto Sydney Tokyo Singapore

Brady Publishing

A Divison of Simon & Schuster, Inc.
15 Columbus Circle
New York, NY 10023

Manufactured in the United States of America

10 9 8 7 6 5 4 3 2 1

Library of Congress Cataloging-in-Publication Data

McClure, Rhyder.
    Fast access/Lotus 1-2-3 (release 3.1+) / Rhyder McClure. Mary Abill.
       p.   cm.
    Includes index.
    1. Lotus 1-2-3 (Computer program) 2. Business--Computer programs.
I. Abdill, Mary, 1947-   . II. Title. III. Title: Fast access/Lotus one-two-three
(release 3.1+)
HF5548.4.L67M329 1991
650'.285'5369--dc20
                                                      91-26553
                                                          CIP

ISBN 0-13-307109-x

Limits of Liability and Disclaimer of Warranty

The authors and publisher of this book have used their best efforts in preparing this book and the programs contained in it. These efforts include the development, research, and testing of the theories and programs to determine their effectiveness. The authors and publisher make no warranty of any kind, expressed or implied, with regard to these programs or the documentation contained in this book. The authors and publisher shall not be liable in any event for incidental or consequential damages in connection with, or arising out of, the furnishing, performance, or use of these programs.

Registered Trademarks

Lotus, 1-2-3 and Visicalc are registered trademarks of the Lotus Development Corporation.

IBM, IBM Personal Computer, and PC-DOS are a registered trademarks of International Business Machines Corporation.

MS-DOS, Word, Windows, and Windows 3.0 are registered trademarks of Microsoft Corporation.

WordStar is a registered trademark of MicroPro International.

WordPerfect is a registered trademark of the WordPerfect Corporation.

Ashton-Tate, MultiMate, dBASE, dBASE III , dBASE III PLUS and dBASE IV are registered trademarks of Ashton-Tate Corporation.

AT&T is a registered trademark of AT&T. AT&T 6300 is a trademark of AT&T.

The Norton Utilities is a registered trademark of Peter Norton Computing, Inc.

SideKick is a registered trademark of Borland Corporation.

EPSON is a registered trademark of EPSON Corporation.

Bernoulli Box is a registered trademark of the IOMEGA Corporation.

FAST ACCESS is a registered trademark of RMI Microcomputer Consulting.

TABLE OF CONTENTS

Preface

Do you have a spreadsheet or database you want to computerize? Do you need a graph to enhance your statistics? Then *Fast Access/Lotus 1-2-3 (Release 3.1+)* is for you. This book gives *fast access* to 1-2-3's spreadsheet, database, and graphic capabilities. Users with little or no experience can quickly locate and use those portions of this software package that apply to a desired application while ignoring irrelevant portions.

Most users of 1-2-3 are not full-time users. They use 1-2-3 as a tool just a few times a week or month, and they need a book that quickly translates ideas into meaningful worksheets. They need to become productive instantly and to continue being productive with each new worksheet. When they need to know how to do something, they look it up; they don't need to memorize everything.

Fast Access/Lotus 1-2-3 is designed for this user. It is a tutorial and a quick reference and refresher manual, not just to commands, but also to errors, basic designs, and potential dangers. This book presents the most commonly used and abused commands and is designed to lay flat and open while you work at your computer.

Chapter 1—The Basics—guides the user through the creation and use of a basic spreadsheet.

Chapter 2, the largest chapter, is an alphabetical reference to worksheet enhancements, including spreadsheet appearance, protecting desired areas, handling very large worksheets, saving, and printing. It includes file management, database management, graphics, mouse movements, printing, Wysiwyg, transferring data between 1-2-3 and other software, such as your word processor, and so on.

Have you ever made a spreadsheet mistake? The biggest frustration of users is discovering that an error exists. Sometimes little or no warning is given when you make an error, and sometimes the machine just beeps and won't let you continue. Chapter 3—Problems and Solutions—may be the most important chapter in the book, for your sanity.

Perhaps you are wondering about upgrading to Release 3.1+. Release 3.1 and 3.1+ have several major benefits over Release 3.0:

- Wysiwyg (a sophisticated screen and report formatting add-in).

- Mouse support.
- Runs under all three modes of Windows 3.0.
- Auditor feature to fix problematic formulas (Release 3.1+ only).
- Backsolver feature when you know the answer and need the formula to get it. (Release 3.1+ only).
- Solver feature to find answers to sophisticated "what-if" questions (Release 3.1+ only).
- Viewer feature—a Magellan-like feature—that allows you to easily find and view any file on your disk (Release 3.1+ only).

In addition, Release 3.1 and 3.1+ have the following advantages over Release 2.2:

- Directly access a dBASE database and bring into your worksheet selected information from the database without translating it first.
- Link several files together, using formulas, not just single cell addresses.
- Create three-dimensional spreadsheets containing multiple layers.
- Manage and print graphs with much less grief.

Reasons not to upgrade to Release 3.1 or 3.1+:

- You need at least 1 megabyte of memory (RAM).
- You need at least an 80286 or 80386 CPU chip.
- You need a hard disk.
- Release 3.0 runs under either DOS or OS/2. Release 3.1 and 3.1+ only run under DOS.

Fast Access/Lotus 1-2-3 (Release 3.1+) is written specifically for 1-2-3 Release 3.1 and 3.1+ users. Wysiwyg is integrated into examples throughout the book because Wysiwyg completely changes how you can best use this Release of 1-2-3.

There is a *Fast Access/Lotus 1-2-3 (Release 3)* book written just for Release 3.0 users. It integrates the use of three dimensional spreadsheets throughout the book because 3-D spreadsheets can completely change how you design and use spreadsheets.

There is a *Fast Access/Lotus 1-2-3 (Release 2.2)* book written just for Release 2.2 users. Release 2.2 was released in July 1989, and is directed to the DOS user who cannot, or chooses not to, upgrade to Release 3 or higher.

Users of 1-2-3 Release 2 and 2.01 are encouraged to use the original *Fast Access/Lotus 1-2-3* book.

Chapter 1

The Basics

Worksheet Concepts and Uses

Spreadsheets are used for financial applications, such as budgets, income and expense reporting, invoicing, taxes, accounting, projections, sales analysis, vouchers, as well as for statistical analysis, salary and overtime payments, and other information gathering and data reporting.

I frequently use a spreadsheet instead of a calculator. While others may punch numbers into a calculator, I type the numbers, formulas, and commentary into a spreadsheet. If a price or discount changes, I type just the changed value, and a new total is instantly and automatically recalculated. With a calculator, you usually enter all the numbers again, not just the changes.

Worksheets hold your spreadsheets, databases, and the information for your graphs.

A spreadsheet is a large grid of columns and rows in which you enter information, such as numbers, commentary, and formulas for calculations. Each intersection of a row and column forms a small box that is called a *cell*; information is placed in the cells.

The figure below on the left shows what you actually type—the labels, numbers, and special formulas for calculations—and the one on the right shows what you actually see on the spreadsheet.

What you type:

	A	B
1	ITEM	"COST
2		
3	Desk	199.95
4	Chair	49.95
5	Lamp	12.55
6		
7	TOTAL	+B3+B4+B5

What you see:

	A	B
1	ITEM	COST
2		
3	Desk	199.95
4	Chair	49.95
5	Lamp	12.55
6		
7	TOTAL	262.45

The keystrokes **+B3+B4+B5** illustrate an example of a formula. This formula tells 1-2-3 to add together the contents of cell B3 (199.95) plus the contents of cell B4 (49.95) plus the contents of cell B5 (12.55). The resulting sum appears in cell B7 because that is where the formula exists. When you type a formula into your spreadsheet, the resulting value—262.45, not the formula, appears. The contents of a cell can be different from the appearance of that cell.

Notice the " (quote) in front of COST. That makes it right aligned instead of left aligned in its cell. Although the quote is in the cell, it isn't displayed.

The wonderful aspect to spreadsheets is the ability to recalculate numbers. If you change the cost of a desk from 199.95 to 299.95, your total instantly becomes 362.45.

Now you know everything there is to know about spreadsheets—except for printing, saving, formatting, graphing, editing, databases, cell protection, and a few other things.

Please note that although grid lines may or may not appear on your screen, the remaining figures in this book show grid lines, as follows, for readability:

	A	B
1	ITEM	COST
2		
3	Desk	199.95
4	Chair	49.95
5	Lamp	12.55
6		
7	TOTAL	262.45

Page Layout for This Book

FEATURE   NAME

Command:	Command(s) used to implement this feature.
@Function:	Function(s) used to implement this feature.
Note:	Information and an overview the examples that follow.
Related:	A list of related features. One of these alternative features may be the one you need.
Tip:	Useful tips.
Warning:	Possible traps and pitfalls.

Example:	Describes what you accomplish in the following step-by-step walk-through.
You:	Describes what you do. Words in italics explain the meaning of the often cryptic keystrokes.
1-2-3:	Describes or shows what should happen or appear as a result of your action.
Result:	Describes the overall accomplishment.

Keys and Terminology Used in This Book

TAP   Like a woodpecker. Tap a key and remove your finger as fast as possible.

HOLD   Put your finger on the designated key and hold it down. Do not release it, until you have tapped another key. There are only three keys you hold: **Ctrl**, **Alt**, and **Shift**.

↑   The **Up** arrow key

↓   The **Down** arrow key

→   The **Right** arrow key

←   The **Left** arrow key (contrast this with the **Backspace** key)

←┘   The **Enter** key, which is sometimes called the **Return** key

⇆   The **Tab** key

Ø   The number zero. Ø is often used to differentiate zero from the letter O

\\   The Backslash key, which is different than the slash (/) key

¦   The broken bar key, which is the shifted backslash on most keyboards. On some monitors and printers, this appears as a vertical bar (|).

Backspace Key

This key is located above the ←┘ key. On some keyboards, it looks exactly like the left arrow but it acts very differently in Lotus 1-2-3.

Positioning Keys

Any of the following keys or key combinations:

↑ ↓ → ← **PgUp** **PgDn** ⇆ **Shift**⇆ **Ctrl**→ **Ctrl**←

Disk   Disk is used as a general term in this book to refer to floppy disks (diskettes), hard (permanent, nonremovable) disks, Bernoulli Boxes, and so on.

If your computer does not have function keys (**F1** through **F10**) and an **Alt** key, refer to your 1-2-3 documentation for the keys to use for these functions: Help, Edit, Name, Absolute, GoTo, Window, Query, Table, Calc, and Macro.

Getting Started

INSTALLING LOTUS 1-2-3

Fast Access/Lotus 1-2-3 assumes that 1-2-3 has already been installed according to the documentation provided by Lotus.

If you need to install 1-2-3, follow the detailed instructions provided in the Lotus 1-2-3 documentation. The install program asks about your computer hardware, and stores this information on disk. Install also copies many files to your disk.

STARTING LOTUS 1-2-3

There are a variety of ways to start up 1-2-3, depending on how it was installed. You should follow your own instructions; however, two sample methods are described below.

Tip: If you start Lotus 1-2-3 by typing **123** (rather than by typing **LOTUS**), you can build slightly larger spreadsheets and avoid the Lotus 1-2-3 Access Menu.

Example 1:   One way to start Lotus 1-2-3 from the DOS prompt, which may look like **C:\>**

You: Type **C:** ←┘   *if 1-2-3 is on another drive, use that letter instead*

Type **CD \123R3** ←┘   *if 1-2-3 is in another directory, use that name instead*

Type **123** ←┘

Example 2:   Another way to start Lotus 1-2-3 from the DOS prompt.

You: Type **C:** ←┘   *if 1-2-3 is on another drive, use that letter instead*

Type **CD \123R3** ←┘   *if 1-2-3 is in another directory, use that name instead*

Type **123** ←┘

1-2-3: **Lotus 1-2-3 Access Menu**

You: Tap ←┘   *to choose the 1-2-3 option*

Moving around the Worksheet

KEYBOARD VERSUS MOUSE

This chapter first teaches you to create spreadsheets using keyboard commands. Later you are introduced to Wysiwyg and alternative mouse methods.

SCREEN LAYOUT

When 1-2-3 starts, you will see a worksheet similar to the following:

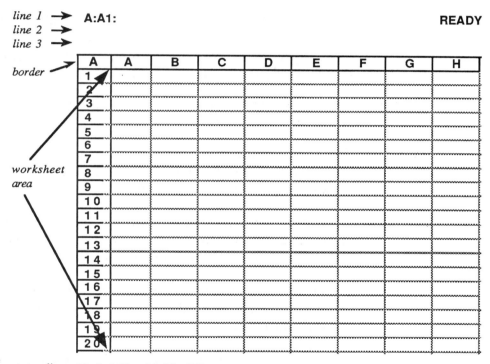

Control
Panel

Lines 1 through 3, shown in the preceding diagram, are the control panel.

Line 1   shows the address of the highlighted cell (**A:A1**) and, sometimes, other information. The upper-right corner shows the mode, which, in this example, is **READY**. (For more information, see **Control Panel** in Chapter 2.)

Line 2   is usually blank. When you type new information or edit existing information, it appears on this line until after you tap ←⟶ , when it then appears in the cell. When using commands, the command choices appear here.

Line 3   is also usually blank. If you start a command, the subcommands and descriptions appear here.

Worksheet Area   Your spreadsheet and database information appear here. The worksheet area consists of one or more sheets (layers), each with many columns and rows. The worksheet is much larger than the portion actually displayed on the screen.

Border   Letters and numbers indicating which sheets, columns, and rows are displayed on the monitor.

Column   Columns are indicated with letters. All the boxes below the letter B are cells in column **B**. There are 256 columns. Try tapping the → to see what happens after column letter Z.

Row   The numbers indicate the rows. All the boxes to the right of the number **3** are cells in row 3. There are 8,192 rows. Tap the **PgDn** key and watch what happens to the row numbers.

Sheet   The first letter on the left indicates the sheet. It is possible to have multiple layers of information. (For more information, refer to **Multiple Sheets** in Chapter 2.)

Cell   The box at the intersection of a column and row in a particular sheet is a cell. Cells are named by the sheet, column, and row they are in. Cell **A:B3** is the cell in sheet **A**, column **B**, and row **3**, shown below. The sheet letter can be omitted when referring to the current sheet. Cell B3, in the example below, contains the value 456. Because this cell is the one highlighted (in reverse video), its contents also appear on line 1 of the panel.

Line 1:   **A:B3**   **456**

A	A	B	C	D
1				
2				
3		456		
4				

Status Line The status line is at the bottom of the screen. It may display the date and time or the current file name. Sometimes indicator messages appear here, such as **CAP** (indicating the **Caps Lock** key has been tapped).

Date and Time The date and time may appear at the bottom of the screen. If the date or time is incorrect, your computer's battery-powered internal clock/calendar is incorrectly set. See **Dates, Example 1** in Chapter 2 to correct it.

File Name When a file name appears in the lower-left corner, the displayed worksheet exists on disk, although not necessarily with the most recent changes. See **Clock** in Chapter 2 to customize this display.

RESCUE KEYS

There are two rescue keys to get you out of trouble: **Home** and **Esc**. They can't hurt, and using them can be helpful.

Home causes the upper-left corner of your worksheet (usually cell A1) to appear. Tap the **Home** key if your spreadsheet suddenly disappears.

Esc erases any unentered typing and also backs out of partially completed commands. If your screen suddenly goes blank, tap the **Esc** key. You may need to tap multiple times until **READY** appears in the upper-right corner.

NUM Tap the **Num Lock** key several times. Do you see the word **NUM** appear and disappear at the bottom of your screen? Now look at your keyboard. Do you have arrow keys in addition to those on your number pad keys? If so, **NUM** should appear at the bottom of the screen. If not, remove **NUM** from the bottom of the screen.

To move from cell to cell—also specified as highlighting a cell

> **You:**   Tap any of the positioning keys (such as ↑ ↓ → ←). Notice how the highlighted cell changes. Mouse instructions are covered later.

> **Tip:**   Always highlight the desired cell prior to entering information.

To move faster

> **You:**   Tap the **PgDn** or **PgUp** key to move up or down one screen.
>
> Hold the **Ctrl** key and tap → or ← to move a full screen right or left.
>
> Tap the ⇆ (**Tab**) key to move a full screen right.
>
> Hold the **Shift** key and tap ⇆ to move a full screen left.

To go to a specific cell using the GoTo function key

> **You:**   Tap the **F5** key *the GoTo key*

> *1-2-3:*   **Enter address to go to:**

> **You:**   Type the column letter and row number (for example, **G77**).
>
> Tap ←┘

> *1-2-3:*   The specified cell appears on the screen, highlighted.
>
> If the specified cell was not already on the screen, the cell will appear in the upper-left corner of the worksheet area. If the cell was already on the screen, the cell becomes highlighted, but the worksheet does not move.

Highlight cell(s)

Tap any of the positioning keys to highlight the desired cell(s). "Position the cursor" and "highlight cell(s)" are similar in meaning and sometimes people use them interchangeably. Highlighted information is in reverse video or in a different color. The cursor is a small underscore either in a cell or in the panel lines above the worksheet. When entering or editing information, the cursor appears on the second line above the worksheet. Within the worksheet, moving the cursor determines which cell(s) is highlighted. Even when many cells are highlighted simultaneously, the cursor is only in one of those cells, usually the lower-right cell.

In this example there are six cells highlighted, but only the upper-left cell has the cursor in it (the short white line).

	A	B	C	D
1				
2				
3				
4				
5				

See **Highlighting Cells** in Chapter 2 for more information.

Entering Information—The Basics

OVERVIEW OF STEPS

- Make sure **READY** appears in the upper-right corner.

- Highlight the correct cell. That is, move the cursor to the cell where the information is to appear.

- Type the information.

Note: Lotus 1-2-3 has a marvelous editing feature. When typing new information into a cell with existing information, the new information COMPLETELY REPLACES the old. It is gone! So, a word to the wise: look at your cell position before typing.

Example: Entering information into cells.

You: Look for **READY** in the upper-right corner.

Using the arrow keys, highlight cell B3.

Type   **Eggs**   *don't tap* ← *yet*

1-2-3: The following is displayed:

line 1   **A:B3:**   **LABEL**
line 2   **Eggs**
line 3

A	A	B	C	D	E	F	G	H
1								
2								
3								
4								
5								

Note: Notice **Eggs** on line two. It has not yet been transferred into the cell. The word **LABEL** in the upper-right corner indicates we are entering textual information.

You: Tap ←   *to transfer the information into the cell*

1-2-3:   The following is displayed:

line 1   **A:B3:   'Eggs**   **READY**
line 2
line 3

A	A	B	C	D	E	F	G	H
1								
2								
3		Eggs						
4								
5								

Note: **Eggs** appears in cell B3. And **READY** appears again, replacing **LABEL**. **Eggs** appears on line 1 because cell B3 is highlighted.

Notice the apostrophe before **Eggs** on line 1. Lotus 1-2-3 puts a code (' or " or ^) at the beginning of all textual information to distinguish it from numbers. This code also indicates alignment (' for left, ^ for centering, and " for right alignment within the cell).

If your worksheet doesn't look like this (that is, **Eggs** is in the wrong cell, or something like that) turn to the section on **Command Basics** on page 17 and then to the section called **Correcting Typing Mistakes** on page 21 and fix your typo.

You: Tap →

1-2-3:   Cell C3 is highlighted.

You: Type **1.19** ↵

1-2-3:   The following is displayed:

line 1   **A:C3:   1.19**   **READY**
line 2
line 3

A	A	B	C	D	E	F	G	H
1								
2								
3		Eggs	1.19					
4								
5								

Note: Notice that the number 1.19 does not have an apostrophe. Numbers are always right aligned. You can't center or left align a number without losing its value.

You: Finish filling in your worksheet so that it looks like this:

A	A	B	C	D
1				
2				
3		Eggs	1.19	
4		Milk	0.89	
5		Bread	1.49	
6				
7		SubTotal		
8		Tax		
9				
1 0		TOTAL		

Now we need to calculate the subtotal, the tax, and the total.

You: Highlight cell C7.
Type **@SUM(C3..C5)** ↵

Note: This is a formula. Be careful not to type any spaces.

The **@** (pronounced "at") is the symbol 1-2-3 uses to designate a function. Functions are built-in calculations and other processes. **@SUM** (pronounced "at sum") is the function used to add all the numbers in a range.

C3..C5 is an example of a range; in this case, the cells C3 through C5. When designating a range, two periods (also called full stops) separate the end points of the range. Ranges are frequently used in 1-2-3; many more examples are given in this book.

The formula **@SUM(C3..C5)** means add together all the numbers contained in cells C3, C4, and C5.

1-2-3:   **A:C7   @SUM(C3..C5)**   **READY**

A	A	B	C	D
1				
2				
3		Eggs	1.19	
4		Milk	0.89	
5		Bread	1.49	
6				
7			**3.57**	
8				
9				
10				

Notice that line 1 of the control panel shows the formula, while cell C7 shows the calculated result: 3.57.

You: Highlight cell C3.

Type   **2.09** ←┘   *The price of eggs just increased*

1-2-3:   **A:C7   @SUM(C3..C5)**   **READY**

A	A	B	C	D
1				
2				
3		Eggs	2.09	
4		Milk	0.89	
5		Bread	1.49	
6				
7		SubTotal	**4.47**	
8		Tax		
9				
10		TOTAL		

Notice the subtotal just changed to 4.47, reflecting the price change.

You: Highlight cell C8.

Type   **+C7*.05** ←┘

Note: This formula means take the subtotal and multiply (* means multiply) by .05 (assuming 5 percent tax).

You: Highlight cell C10.

Type   +C7+C8 ↵

Note: This formula means add the subtotal and the tax together.

Result:

A	A	B	C	D
1				
2				
3		Eggs	2.09	
4		Milk	9.89	
5		Bread	1.49	
6				
7		SubTotal	4.47	
8		Tax	.2235	
9				
1 0		TOTAL	4.6935	

You: Are the four decimal places in TOTAL acceptable? If you think four decimal places for currency is unsatisfactory, keep reading. The next step is to learn about commands; then you can format these cells to your liking using a Format command.

Tip: Always test your worksheets. Look for reasonableness in the answers.

Command Basics

Commands   Many operations on your worksheet require the use of commands. Examples of commands are File Save, File Retrieve, Print, Format, Erase, and so on. Chapter 2 is full commands and examples.

READY Mode   You start commands and enter data from **READY** mode. If **READY** does not appear in the upper-right corner of the screen, tap **Esc** repeatedly until **READY** appears.

To start a command, tap   /

This causes a menu of the main commands to appear on the second line of your monitor. Often, commands lead to subcommands, which don't appear until after you choose a command.

When you are in **READY** mode, type /. The / does not go into a cell; instead it starts the command mode.

To back out of a command instead of completing it

Tap the **Esc** key repeatedly until **READY** appears.

Free Advice   Tap the forward slash "/" and not the backslash "\" to start a command. If you tap the wrong key, tap **Esc** to get back to **READY** mode, then start again with /.

Range   A range is a rectangular group of one or more cells. Many commands use ranges as part of the command. A range name address specifies the cell names in two diagonal corners of the range. For example B3..D4 (or B4..D3 or D3..B4 or D4..B3) specifies the range of the six cells highlighted below.

A	A	B	C	D	E
1					
2					
3					
4					
5					

In 1-2-3 Release 3 and up, ranges frequently begin with the sheet letter. So this range can also be written as: A:B3..A:D4

Example: Let's try a command. (Don't worry if information is still displayed in your worksheet from before.)

You: Tap the **Home** key to highlight cell A1.

Tap **/**   *The slash starts commands. Do not tap* ←⏎

1-2-3:   Lines 1, 2, and 3 at the top of your screen should look like this:

line 1	A:A1:						MENU	
line 2	Worksheet Range Copy Move File Print Graph Data System Quit							
line 3	Global Insert Delete Column Erase Titles Window Status Page Hide							

A	A	B	C	D	E	F	G	H
1								

Line 1 shows the address of the cell currently highlighted and the word **MENU**. Line 2 shows the main commands. Line 3 shows the subcommands of the first command (Worksheet).

Tip: You could mess up your worksheet or erase files, so be reasonable when experimenting. Read messages. If a message on the screen indicates 1-2-3 will do something unpleasant, tap the **Esc** key.

Selecting Commands—two ways

Slow Way   Tap → to highlight the command you want. Note that the long prompt (the third line) changes, giving you a hint about what the highlighted command does. Tap ←⏎ when the desired command is highlighted.

Fast Way   Just type the first letter of the command. For example, type **W** for Worksheet, **R** for **R**ange. Do *not* tap ←⏎ after the letter.

You: Using either method, select **Range**.

1-2-3:

line 1	A:A1:						MENU	
line 2	Format Label Erase Name Justify Prot Unprot Input Value Trans Search							
line 3	Fixed Sci Currency , General +/- Percent Date Text Hidden Other Reset							

A	A	B	C	D	E	F	G	H
1								

Note: Line 2 shows the subcommands of Range. Line 3 shows the
subcommands of the first subcommand—Format.

You: Tap **E**   *to Erase*

1-2-3:

line 1   **A:A1:**   **POINT**
line 2   **Enter range to erase: A:A1..A:A1**
line 3

A	A	B	C	D	E	F	G	H
1								

The system suggests a range to be erased.

POINT in the upper-right corner indicates we can point (paint) with
the positioning keys.

You: Tap ↓ ↓ ↓ →   *but do not tap* ↵

1-2-3:

line 1   **A:A1:**   **POINT**
line 2   Enter range to erase: A:A1..A:B4
line 3

A	A	B	C	D
1				
2				
3		Eggs	1.19	
4		Milk	0.89	
5		Bread	1.49	
6				
7		SubTotal	3.57	
8		Tax	0.1785	
9				
1 0		TOTAL	3.7485	

It's okay if you have different information in the cells. What is
important here is that you have the same eight cells in reverse video.

Range Tips: When a command asks for a range and is simultaneously showing a
sample range, you can tap positioning keys to "paint" the desired
range.

What if the command does not give me a range?
If the command only gives you a single cell address, such as A:B5, you can change that to a range by tapping a period (don't type the word period, just tap .). A:B5 becomes A:B5..A:B5

What if the command gives me a range I don't want?
You can always type in the desired range. For example, you can type **A1..B4** to specify the range you painted on the previous page. Your typing will replace the range displayed on line 2 of the control panel.

More information on managing ranges
Refer to the section called **Ranges** in Chapter 2 for many more examples and tips.

Backing Out: In this example, we are going to back out and not complete this command. If you don't want to complete a command you can frequently back out, as long as you are not yet back to **READY** mode. Just keep tapping **Esc** until **READY** appears. Alternately, hold the **Ctrl** key and tap the **Break** key (**Break** is printed on the *front,* not the top, of the key). Either technique brings you back to **READY** mode.

You: Tap the **Esc** key four times.

1-2-3:   Each time you tap **Esc** the command backs out one level.

Result: **READY** appears in the upper-right corner. Because you backed out and did not complete the command, no information was erased.

Tip: **Ctrl+Break** is like a "mega" escape. It taps **Esc** as many times as necessary to return to **READY** mode.

College Marketing Group
50 Cross Street
Winchester, MA 01890

ATT: **Cheryl Read**

Correcting Typing Mistakes

Fixing mistakes before ↵ is tapped

> Tap the **Backspace** key to erase the last character typed. The **Backspace** key is the key (often dark grey) above the ↵ key.
>
> Or, tap the **Esc** key to remove all the text on line 2.

Fixing mistakes already in a cell

> *Highlight* the cell first, then do one of the following:
>
> Type your new entry, then tap ↵   *This replaces the old entry*
>
> Or, type **/ R E** ↵   *Range Erase. This erases the cell*
>
> Or, edit the cell contents using the **F2** key. (See **Edit** in Chapter 2.)

Warning: Do *not* replace the contents of a cell with spaces because spaces in cells affect calculations differently than do empty cells. Averages and counts may give the wrong results.

Example: Let's make two mistakes and then correct them.

You: Highlight cell E3.

> Type **New York Stateeeee** *this is our first mistake*
>
> Tap the **Backspace** key four times   *to remove the extra e's*
>
> Tap ↵

Result: **New York State** is correctly entered into cell E3.

You: Highlight cell E5.

> Type **This is junk in my worksheet** ↵   *another mistake*
>
> Type **/ R E** ↵

Result: Cell E5 is now empty.

Basic File Saving and Retrieving

Everything you type will be lost if you do not save it. There is *no* automatic save, although 1-2-3 usually warns you if you forget to save. Save frequently. Save before experimenting. If disaster occurs, at least you will have a recent copy on disk.

SAVE EVERY 15 MINUTES.

Save stores your current worksheet on disk. If you use a new diskette, be sure it is formatted. (See **Formatting Diskettes** in Chapter 2.)

Example 1:   Save a worksheet for the first time (creates a new file on disk).

You: If **READY** is not in the upper-right corner, tap **Esc** until it is.

You: Type **/ F S**   *for the command File Save*

1-2-3:   **Enter name of file to save: C:\123R3\FILEØØØ1.WK3**

Note: 1-2-3 provides a sample name you can use if you wish. The name includes a drive (**C:**), directory (**\123R3** on the C: disk), file name (**FILEØØØ1**), and file extension (**WK3**).

You: Type **GROCERY** ←┘

Warning: If **Cancel Replace Backup** appears, then GROCERY already exists on the disk. Choose **C** for Cancel and repeat this save example using a different name, such as GROCERY2.

Note: You may type any one- to eight-character file name. Do not leave blank spaces. I recommend using only letters and numbers, even though DOS permits other characters. It doesn't matter whether you use upper- or lowercase letters in the file name.

1-2-3:   **WAIT** then **READY** appear in the upper-right corner.

Result: Your worksheet (on the screen) is now saved to disk. In other words, the information is now in two places—disk and memory.

Example 2: Save changes to a file already existing on disk.

You: Type **/ F S** *File Save*

1-2-3: **Enter name of file to save: C:\123R3\xxx.WK3** *where xxx is your file name*

Note: The file name is already there, so there is no need to retype it. .WK3 is the extension added by 1-2-3 Release 3 (and up).

You: Tap ⏎

1-2-3: **Cancel   Replace   Backup**

This appears on the second line. 1-2-3 is asking whether you want the disk file replaced with the current file seen on the screen.

You: Type   **R**   *to replace the disk file with the newest version*

Note: Backup puts two versions of your worksheet on disk: the latest, ending in **.WK3,** and the second latest, ending in **.BAK**. Cancel backs out of this save operation and does *not* save your file to disk.

1-2-3: **WAIT** then **READY** appear in the upper-right corner.

Result: Your updated worksheet is now on both disk and memory.

Example 3: Retrieve (load) an existing file from disk.

You: Type **/ F R** *File Retrieve*

1-2-3: **Enter name of file to retrieve: C:\123R3*.WK***

You: Tap the **F3** key *the Name key*

1-2-3: All the 1-2-3 files in the current directory are displayed.

You: Tap → *or* ↓ until the desired file name is highlighted.

You: Tap ⏎ *this selects the highlighted file and loads it from disk*

1-2-3: **WAIT** then **READY** appear in the upper-right corner.

Basic Printing

Wysiwyg is presented in a few pages, and it has a much better print command. If you choose to use Wysiwyg, then skip this page altogether. Chapter 2 has a variety of printing using different options and printers.

Example: Print your current worksheet.

You: Turn on your printer, and be sure it is ready. If you use continuous feed paper, align the perforation just above the print head, even with the top of the ribbon.

You: Tap / **P P** *for the command Print Printer*

1-2-3: **Range Line Page Options Clear Align Go Image Sample Hold Quit** *the Main Print Menu*

You: Tap **R** *Range*

1-2-3: **Enter Print range:**

You: Type A1..F15 ⏎ *or any range you want printed. If text overlaps into adjoining cells, include them in the range.*

1-2-3: **Range Line Page Options Clear Align Go Image Sample Hold Quit** *the Main Print Menu*

You: Tap **A G P Q** *Align Go Page Quit*

If your printer has continuous feed paper, tap **A G P P Q** *Align Go Page Page Quit* instead of **A G P Q.** Page informs the printer to print the last line and eject the sheet of paper. With continuous feed paper, tapping **P** twice ejects the paper so the next perforation is accessible.

1-2-3: The printer prints the specified range of your worksheet.

You: Do *not* adjust the printer; just remove the printed worksheet.

Start a New Worksheet

Command: / **Worksheet Erase**

Note: When you are finished using a worksheet, you can erase the entire worksheet and start on a new one by using the **Worksheet Erase** command.

Warning: *SAVE FIRST,* or you may loose the worksheet you were currently working on, especially any changes since the last time you saved.

Free Advice: There are many different Erase commands. You now know two: **Range Erase** and **Worksheet Erase.** Eventually you will learn **File Erase.** Be careful because they erase differently. Do not use **Worksheet Erase** when you just mean to erase the contents of a few cells (a range). Use **Range Erase.**

Note: **Worksheet Erase** returns your worksheet to its initial settings: empty cells, column width of 9, cell format of General, and label alignment of left. This command does not affect files on disks.

Example: Erase the current worksheet and start a new worksheet.

You: Save your worksheet if you wish to keep the changes.

Type / **F S** *File Save*

Type the name of your worksheet file, or use the one appearing on the top line of the screen.

Tap ↵

If **Cancel Replace Backup** appears, tap **R** to replace the file on disk. If you don't wish to replace it, tap **C** *Cancel.* Tap **B** *Backup* to put two copies on disk (see **Basic Saving and Retrieving**).

Type / **W E Y** *Worksheet Erase Yes*

Result: An empty worksheet appears, like the one shown on page 7.

Quitting 1-2-3

Command: **/ Quit Yes**

Note: First, *save your worksheet!*

Although it is not necessary to quit 1-2-3 before turning off the power, it is a good practice. If you run 1-2-3 under Windows, first quit 1-2-3, then exit from Windows.

Example: Quit 1-2-3.

You: Look in the upper-right corner of your screen, If it does not show **READY**, tap the **Esc** key several times until **READY** appears.

You: Save your worksheet now, if you want a current version on disk. The command starts: **/ F S**

You: Type **/ Q** *Quit*

1-2-3:   **No   Yes**

You: Type **Y** *Yes*

1-2-3:   **No   Yes**
WORKSHEET CHANGES NOT SAVED! End 1-2-3 anyway?
You only get this message if your current worksheet was not saved.

You: To exit without saving changes, you type **Y** *Yes*

To stay in 1-2-3, type **N**   *No*.
Then, use **/ File Save** to save your file.

1-2-3:   **1-2-3 Access Menu**
You only get this message if you started 1-2-3 by typing **LOTUS**

You: To exit from the Lotus 1-2-3 Access Menu appears, tap **E** *for Exit*

Starting Wysiwyg

Note: Wysiwyg has so much to offer that I recommend you always use it.

This book is about fast access, fast access to your data, results, reports, and printouts. If you truly want fast access, get a mouse and always use Wysiwyg.

Throughout this book, you will see the not so subliminal message— Wysiwyg is better, Wysiwyg is better. Older methods are included, in case you haven't installed Wysiwyg yet.

This example shows how to make Wysiwyg start automatically, every time you start 1-2-3. Once you do this example, you will never have to start Wysiwyg again. 1-2-3 will do it for you.

Example: Make Wysiwyg start automatically whenever you start 1-2-3.

You: Hold the **Alt** key and tap **F10**
Type **S S S**   *Setting System Set*
Tap **F3**

1-2-3: A list of files appears.

You: If you see **WYSIWYG.PLC**
　　Highlight **WYSIWYG.PLC**
　　Tap ←⏎

If you do not see **WYSIWYG.PLC**
　　Tap **Backspace**
　　Highlight **ADDINS**
　　Tap ←⏎   *hopefully you now see WYSIWYG.PLC*
　　Highlight **WYSIWYG.PLC**
　　Tap ←⏎

If you still do not see **WYSIWYG.PLC**
　　Try another directory, or another drive.
　　Or, perhaps you need to install it. Add-ins are installed separately from the main 1-2-3 software.

You: Type **Y N U Q L**   *Yes No-key Update Quit Load*

Tap **F3**

1-2-3:   A list of files appears.

You: If you see **WYSIWYG.PLC**
Highlight **WYSIWYG.PLC**
Tap ⏎

If you do not see **WYSIWYG.PLC**
Tap **Backspace**
Highlight **ADDINS**
Tap ⏎   *hopefully you now see WYSIWYG.PLC*
Highlight **WYSIWYG.PLC**
Tap ⏎

1-2-3:   The worksheet turns white.

You: Type **N Q**   *No-key Quit*

Note: The Wysiwyg screen differs from the usual screen. If your mouse is correctly set up, you can see an arrow in the screen, which you can move with your mouse. Also, on the left side of the screen there are seven little pictures (icons) of triangles, arrows, and a question mark.

Result: Wysiwyg is now active. From now on, every time you start 1-2-3, Wysiwyg will also start.

Wysiwyg and Main Menus

Note: Be sure Wysiwyg is active before trying this example (see the previous page). If the worksheet isn't white, you probably don't have Wysiwyg loaded. Try the previous section again.

With 1-2-3, you have a main menu which appears if you type a slash.

When Wysiwyg is active, you have another menu, which appears if you type a colon.

The next section shows how to choose these different menus using your mouse.

Example: Look at the two menus.

You: If **READY** doesn't appear in the upper-right corner, tap **Esc**
Tap **/**

1-2-3: The 1-2-3 main menu appears, as follows:
Worksheet Range Copy Move File Print Graph Data System Quit Global Insert Delete Column Erase Titles Window Status Page Hide

You: Tap **Esc** *to back out of this menu*

1-2-3: **READY** appears in the upper-right corner.

You: Tap **:**

1-2-3: The Wysiwyg menu appears, as follows:
Worksheet Format Graph Print Display Special Text Named-Style Quit Column Row Page

You: Tap **Esc** *to back out of this menu*

1-2-3: **READY** appears in the upper-right corner.

Wysiwyg and the Mouse

Note: If you don't have a mouse skip this section. But go out and buy a mouse and come back to this section.

Be sure Wysiwyg is active before trying these examples (see the previous pages). Move the mouse around on the desk. Do you see an arrow moving around on the screen? If not, perhaps Wysiwyg is not loaded (see **Wysiwyg** in chapter 2) or your mouse doesn't have the proper driver (see **Config.sys** in chapter 2).

Example 1: Basic mouse mechanics.

You: Using either hand, take hold of the mouse so that the cord goes away from you. Take care not to rotate the mouse.

Rest your index and middle fingers lightly over the buttons.

Move the mouse, keeping it in contact with the surface of your desk.

1-2-3: An arrow moves about on the screen corresponding to your mouse movements.

Note: The mouse contains a rolling ball that translates your hand movements into screen movements. Only about 5 or 6 inches are needed to move the mouse, although initially it will seem like a lot more is needed, as you will constantly be running off the edge of the desk or banging into the keyboard.

You: If your mouse reaches the edge of the desk before the arrow reaches the desired screen destination, lift the mouse into the air and put it down on the other side of the available surface space.

Note: At first you may feel uncoordinated, but it is worth the effort to make friends with your mouse. Soon you won't want to give it up.

Tip: When entering lots of information, keep your hands on the keyboard and use the keys for data entry, cursor movements, and choosing commands. But when you do a lot of copying, selecting cells, formatting, or graphics work, use the mouse.

Example 2:   Selecting a cell with the mouse and entering information.

You: Move the mouse so that the arrow on the screen is over cell C2.

Click the left mouse button.

1-2-3:

A	A	B	C	D
1				
2			████	
3				

You: Type **SALES** ←┘

1-2-3:

A	A	B	C	D
1				
2			**SALES**	
3				

Example 3:   Choosing commands with the mouse, then "escaping" back out.

You: Move the mouse about a half inch above the worksheet area.

1-2-3:   A menu appears.

You: Click the right mouse button.

1-2-3:   A different menu appears.

Note: Click the right mouse button to switch back and forth between the 1-2-3 main menu and the Wysiwyg menu.

You: Click the right mouse button until the 1-2-3 main menu (shown on the next line) appears.

1-2-3:   **Worksheet Range Copy Move File Print Graph Data System Quit**
Global Insert Delete Column Erase Titles Window Status Page Hide

You: Using the left mouse button, click on the word **Range**

1-2-3:   **Format Label Erase Name Justify Prot Unprot Input Value Trans Search Fixed Sci Currency , General +/- Percent Date Text Hidden Other Reset**

You: Using the left mouse button, click on the word **Label**

1-2-3:   **Left Right Center**
            Left-align labels in cells

You: The following commands will allow you to escape out of this command in order to not complete it.

You: With your fingers off the buttons, move the mouse arrow down over the worksheet area.

            Click the right mouse button three times.

Note: The number of times you click depends on how far you got into the command.

Result: Nothing happened because you escaped from the command.

Example 4:   Erasing one cell, using the mouse.

You: Create the following spreadsheet (see example 2):

A	A	B	C	D
1				
2			SALES	
3				

1-2-3:

You: Highlight cell C2 (which is the cell to be erased).

            Move the mouse about a half inch above the worksheet area.

            If the main menu doesn't appear, click the right mouse button until it does.

1-2-3:   **Worksheet Range Copy Move File Print Graph Data System Quit Global Insert Delete Column Erase Titles Window Status Page Hide**

You: Using the left mouse button, click on the word **Range**

1-2-3: **Format Label Erase Name Justify Prot Unprot Input Value Trans Search Fixed Sci Currency , General +/- Percent Date Text Hidden Other Reset**

You: Using the left mouse button, click on the word **Erase**

1-2-3: **Enter range to erase: A:C2..A:C2**

You: Keeping the mouse arrow on the phrase "Enter range to erase" click the left mouse button once more.

Result: The cell contents are erased.

Example 5: Copy a cell using the mouse.

You: Using left mouse button, click in cell A2.

Type 50000 ↵

A	A	B	C	D
1				
2	50000			
3				

1-2-3:

You: Move the mouse about a half inch above the worksheet area.

If you don't see the 1-2-3 main menu, click the right mouse button.

1-2-3: **Worksheet Range Copy Move File Print Graph Data System Quit Global Insert Delete Column Erase Titles Window Status Page Hide**

You: Click the left mouse button on the word **Copy**

1-2-3: **Enter range to copy FROM: A:A2 .. A:A2**

You: With the mouse arrow over that phrase, click the left mouse button.

1-2-3: **Enter range to copy TO: A:A2**

You: Move the mouse arrow over cell A2.

Click the left mouse button and drag the mouse pointer to cell D2.

Release mouse button.

1-2-3:   **Enter range to copy TO: A:A2 .. D2**

A	A	B	C	D
1				
2	50000			
3				

You: Click the left mouse one more time (it is similar to tapping ←⏎).

A	A	B	C	D
1				
2	50000	50000	50000	50000
3				

1-2-3:

Example 6:   Erase a range of cells using the mouse.

You: Create the following spreadsheet (see example 5):

A	A	B	C	D
1				
2	50000	50000	50000	50000
3				

1-2-3:

You: Hold down the **Ctrl** key.

Move the mouse arrow over cell A2.

Click the left mouse button and drag the mouse pointer to cell D2.

A	A	B	C	D
1				
2	50000	50000	50000	50000
3				

1-2-3:

You: Move the mouse about a half inch above the worksheet area.

If you don't see the 1-2-3 main menu, click the right mouse button.

1-2-3:   **Worksheet Range Copy Move File Print Graph Data System Quit Global Insert Delete Column Erase Titles Window Status Page Hide**

You: Click the left mouse button on the word **Range**

1-2-3:   **Format Label Erase Name Justify Prot Unprot Input Value Trans Search Fixed Sci Currency , General +/- Percent Date Text Hidden Other Reset**

You: Click the left mouse button on the word **Erase**

Result: The cell contents are erased.

Example 7:   Alternate (longer) method of erasing a range of cells with the mouse. This method doesn't preselect the range to be erased.

You: Move the mouse about a half inch above the worksheet area.

If you don't see the 1-2-3 main menu, click the right mouse button.

1-2-3:   **Worksheet Range Copy Move File Print Graph Data System Quit Global Insert Delete Column Erase Titles Window Status Page Hide**

You: Click the left mouse button on the word **Range**

1-2-3:   **Format Label Erase Name Justify Prot Unprot Input Value Trans Search Fixed Sci Currency , General +/- Percent Date Text Hidden Other Reset**

You: Click the left mouse button on the word **Erase**

1-2-3:   **Enter range to erase: A:A1..A:A1** *or some other range*

You: With your finger off the buttons, move the mouse over cell C2 (or some cell containing unwanted information).

Holding the left mouse button, drag to D3, then release the button.

1-2-3:   **Enter range to erase: A:C3..A:D4**

	A	B	C	D
1				
2			████	████
3			████	████

You: Click the left mouse button once.

Result: The cell contents of C2 through D3 are erased.

Example 8:   Entering formulas with the mouse.

You: Create this
worksheet:

	A	B	C
1	BUDGET		
2			
3	Income	50000	
4	Expense	20000	
5			
6	Net		

You: Move the mouse over cell B6 and click once with the left button.

1-2-3:

	A	B	C
1	BUDGET		
2			
3	Income	50000	
4	Expense	20000	
5			
6	Net	████	

You: Type   **+**   *a plus sign*

Move the mouse over cell B3 and click once with the left button.

Note: If B6 appears, click again.
If B3 . . B3 appears, click with the right button to remove one B3.

1-2-3:   **A:B3:   50000**
+A : B3

You: Type –   *a minus sign*

Move the mouse over cell B4 and click once with the left button.

Tap ←┘

1-2-3:   **A:B6: +B3-B4**   **READY**

A	A	B	C
1	BUDGET		
2			
3	Income	50000	
4	Expense	20000	
5			
6	Net	**30000**	

You: If your top line doesn't contain +B3-B4, then erase cell B6 and try again. Be sure just the tip of the mouse arrow is over the cell before clicking.

Example 9:   Retrieving a file with the mouse.

Warning: Before you retrieve a new file, be sure to save the one you are working on because you may lose your current file without warning.

You: Move the mouse about a half inch above the worksheet area.

If you don't see the 1-2-3 main menu, click the right mouse button.

1-2-3:   **Worksheet Range Copy Move File Print Graph Data System Quit Global Insert Delete Column Erase Titles Window Status Page Hide**

You: Click the left mouse button on the word **File**

1-2-3:   **Retrieve Save Combine Xtract Erase List Import Dir New Open Admin Replace the current file with a file from disk**

You: Click the left mouse button on the word **Retrieve**

1-2-3: **List .. ◄ ► ▲ ▼   A: B: C: D:**

Enter the name of file to retrieve: C:\123R3*.WK*

ACCTG.WK3   **ACME_SLS.WK3**   **CONSOL.WK3**   *etc.*

You: Click the left mouse button on the word **List** in the upper left corner

1-2-3: Four columns of file names appear.
At the bottom of the list are **ADDINS** and **WYSIWYG**
These are directory names, because they end in a slash.

You: If you wish to see files on a different disk, click on the appropriate letter—A: B: C: D:

If you wish to see files in a different directory, click on the appropriate directory name (directory names end in a \).

If you wish to see files on the parent directory, click on ..

Click on the name of the file you wish to retrieve.

Note: See **Directories** in Chapter 2 for more information.

1-2-3: The spreadsheet is loaded from disk and appears on the screen.

Printing with Wysiwyg

Note: Wysiwyg makes printing so much easier. Wysiwyg supports many different printers, which means never needing to set the page length or the setup string for the particular printer you have.

Be sure Wysiwyg is active before trying these examples. Depending on whether or not you have a mouse, do the first or the second example.

Example 1: Printing with Wysiwyg without a mouse.

You: Tap **:** *a colon (a shifted semicolon) brings up the Wysiwyg menu*

1-2-3: This is the Wysiwyg menu:
Worksheet Format Graph Print Display Special Text Named-Style Quit Column Row Page

You: Tap **P R S** *Print Range Set*

1-2-3: **Range to Print:**

You: Type **A1..F15** ↵ *or any range you want printed. If text overlaps into adjoining cells, include them in the range*

1-2-3: The range A1..F15 is printed.

Example 2: Printing with Wysiwyg using the mouse.

You: Hold the **Ctrl** key.

You: Using the left button, click in cell A1 and drag to cell F15.

1-2-3: The range A1 .. F15 is highlighted *If text overlaps into adjoining cells, include them in the range*

You: Move the mouse about a half inch above the worksheet area.

You: Click the right mouse button until the Wysiwyg menu appears.

1-2-3:   This is the Wysiwyg menu:
           Worksheet Format Graph Print Display Special Text Named-Style Quit
           Column Row Page

You: Move the mouse over **Print** and click with the left button.

1-2-3:   The print options screen appears.

You: Move the mouse over **Range** and click with the left button.

You: Move the mouse over **Set** and click with the left button.

1-2-3:   The range you highlighted is now chosen.

You: Move the mouse over **Go** and click with the left button.

1-2-3:   The range A1..F15 is printed.

Chapter 2

Managing Worksheets

Where Do I Go from Here?

This chapter is the bulk of the book, containing over 100 topics in alphabetical order. Many of these will not be needed right away, whereas some you will use frequently, and some not so often. Following this chapter is a chapter on problems and solutions. At the end of the book is an extensive index.

Let me emphasize that this chapter is best used as a reference guide. It is not a chronological series of exercises. Start with the topics you have the most need and interest in exploring.

Wysiwyg offers many commands that are alternatives to the 1-2-3 main menu commands. Where there is a choice, I recommend using the Wysiwyg commands. If you haven't already done so, do the **Starting Wysiwyg** section in Chapter 1, page 27.

- If you can't decide where to start, I suggest starting with the following topics:
  Column Width
  Formatting Numbers
  Aligning Labels
  Printing—Basics
  Copy
  Formulas

- For help designing:
  A spreadsheet, refer to **Designing Spreadsheets**.
  A database, refer to **Database 1—Input Area,** or **Sort**.
  Data for a graph, refer to **Graphs**.

- Type the text and values into your worksheet, as shown in the previous chapter, or refer to **Label (Text) Entries**, or **Numeric Entries**.

- To align decimal points, add dollar signs, or add commas to your numbers, refer to **Formatting Numbers**. Did you type 5.00 and lose the .00 part of the number? Again, refer to Formatting Numbers.

- To widen or narrow columns (especially if a cell contains *************), refer to **Column Width**.

- To center or right align your text, refer to **Aligning Labels**.

- For help with calculations, refer to **Formulas, Designing Spreadsheets**, or **Functions**.

- For dates, refer to **Dates** or to **Printing—Date and Time**.

- To repeat formulas or information, refer to **Copy**.

- Did something end up in the wrong place. Refer to **Move, Insert a Row, Insert a Column, Delete a Row**, or **Delete a Column**.

- To print a worksheet, refer to the various **Printing** topics. To print a graph, refer to **Graphs**.

- To start a new worksheet, refer to **Erase Worksheet**, or **New Worksheet**.

- To bring data from dBASE see **Database**, then **Database 9—dBASE Input**.

- Do you have a word processor? Look up **Translate Data to Word processors**. You can insert spreadsheets and 1-2-3 databases directly into your reports and documents.

- Look up **Database, Protecting Cells, Insert Column, Large Worksheets** and so on. Each feature is carefully described and illustrated to help you become instantly productive.

The features in this chapter are designed to be quick references for the work you want to do. Many features refer to other features, and, where necessary, suggest a specific order in which to read them.

This book is designed as a quick, step-by-step reference to the Lotus 1-2-3 features and commands that, based on my experience as a consultant and teacher, 95 percent of us use 95 percent of the time. If you don't find the feature you're looking for here, try 1-2-3's terrific on-line help feature (see **Help**). If that doesn't do it, open the manual.

When working with commands, you may occasionally be confused with Worksheet versus Range versus File commands. Here is a hint: Range commands, such as **Range Erase,** affect part of the worksheet—they affect a range of cells. Worksheet commands, such as **Worksheet Erase**, usually affect the entire worksheet. File commands, such as **File Save, File Retrieve,** and **File Erase**, work with files on disk.

Now—have fun expressing your ideas in spreadsheets, databases, graphs, and graphics.

Add-Ins

Note: Add-ins are probably the reason you upgraded to Release 3.1+. Add-ins provide sophisticated enhancements to 1-2-3's basic capabilities.

Some examples of add-ins are:
Wysiwyg—customize screen and printed appearance
Solver—answers sophisticated "what-if" questions
Backsolver—when you know the answer and need a formula
Auditor—used to fix problematic formulas
Viewer—Magellan-like feature used to find and view files

Add-ins are different from the regular 1-2-3 commands since you need to perform some extra steps to make them work. When you start 1-2-3, the regular commands automatically load. Add-ins need to be loaded separately. Also, they use additional memory, which reduces the memory available for very large spreadsheets.

STEPS TO USE AN ADD-IN

1. Hold down **Alt** and tap **F10**   *add-in menu appears*

2. Select **Load**   *to load the add-in feature into memory*

3. Select the actual add-in you want   *may need to change directories. See **Directories** in Chapter 2 for what a directory is.*

4. Sometimes you have the opportunity to assign a function key.

5. Sometimes you select **Invoke**   *to activate the add-in and often to bring up the selected add-in's menu*

6. Refer to each specific add-in for the steps to use the add-in.

Related: **Auditor**
Backsolver
Solver
Viewer
Wysiwyg
See these individual Wysiwyg commands: **Worksheet, Format, Graph, Print, Display, Special, Text,** and **Named-Style**

Aligning Labels

Command: **/ Range Label**

Note: If you have Wysiwyg, I recommend the next section—**Aligning Labels with Wysiwyg**—instead of this section.

The **Range Label** command can center, right align, or left align a label (text) within a cell. It does not affect numbers or labels that overlap into the next cell. Numbers always right align.

Every label (text information) begins with a special label prefix character. These are:

' (apostrophe) to left align the text in the cell
" (quote) to right align the text in the cell
^ (caret) to center align the text in the cell
\ (backslash) to repeat the label in the cell

Tip: When you specify the range for aligning text, do not include cells with the repeating text prefix (the **Backslash**) or the **Broken bar** because the align command will replace the \ or ¦ with a new label prefix: ' (for left alignment), " (for right alignment), or ^ (for centering).

Related: **Label (Text) Entries**
Aligning Labels with WYSIWYG

Example: In the following worksheet, right align "AMT", center "ITEM" and "Desk", and underline "ITEM" and "AMT" with equal signs.

You: Create the following worksheet:

A	A	B	C
1		ITEM	AMT
2			
3		Desk	30

You: Highlight cell C1 *the cell containing AMT*

Type **/ R L R** ↵ *Range Label Right*

1-2-3:

A	A	B	C
1		ITEM	AMT
2			
3		Desk	30

You: Highlight cell B1 *the cell containing ITEM*

Type **/ R L C** ↓ ↓ ↵ *Range Label Center*

1-2-3:

A	A	B	C
1		ITEM	AMT
2			
3		Desk	30

You: Highlight cell B2 *the cell under ITEM*

Type **\ =** ↵

Highlight cell C2 *the cell under AMT*

Type **\ =** ↵

1-2-3:

A	A	B	C
1		ITEM	AMT
2		========	========
3		Desk	30

Aligning Labels with Wysiwyg

Command: : Text Align

Note: This command can center, right or left align, or evenly justify a label (text) within a cell or across cells. Numbers always right align.

Tip: Avoid aligning text beginning with a **Backslash** or **Broken bar** because the align command will replace it with a new label prefix: ' (left align), " (right align), ^ (center), or '| (evenly justify).

When Wysiwyg aligns, it marks the cell with the {Text} attribute, which appears in the upper-left when the cell is highlighted.

Related: **Label (Text) Entries**
Aligning Labels

Example 1: Right align AMT and center ITEM and Desk (use your mouse where appropriate).

You: Create the following worksheet: (reminder: first, save your current worksheet, then use / **W E Y** to erase the screen version):

A	A	B	C
1		ITEM	AMT
2			
3		Desk	30

You: Type : **T A R C1** ↩ *Text Align Right, to align "AMT"*

1-2-3:

A	A	B	C
1		ITEM	AMT
2			
3		Desk	30

Note: Highlight cell C1 and notice the {Text} in the upper-left corner.

You: Type : **T C C1** ↩   *Text Clear, to clear the {Text} so that the next Text command will work.*

You: Type : **T A C B1..B3** ↵   *Text Align Center , to center*
                                              "ITEM" and "Desk"

1-2-3:

A	A	B	C
1		ITEM	AMT
2			
3		Desk	30

Example 2:   Center text across several columns.

You: Create the following worksheet for illustrating this command (see
New Worksheet in Chapter 2):

	A	B	C	D
1	Annual Expenses			
2				

You: Type : **T A C A1 . . D1** ↵   *Text Align Center*

1-2-3:

	A	B	C	D
1			Annual Expenses		
2				

Result: The title is centered across columns A, B, C, and D, and all four
cells, A1, B1, C1, and D1, have a text attribute.

Example 3:   Remove the text attribute. You may need to remove the text attribute
in order to realign text differently.

You: Use the worksheet created in Example 2.

Highlight cells A1, B1, C1, and D1. Notice that they all have the
text attribute, shown in the upper-left corner of the screen.

Type : **T C A1 . . D1** ↵   *Text Clear*

1-2-3:

	A	B	C	D
1	Annual Expenses			
2				

Result: The text is no longer aligned. The {Text} attributes are removed.

Annotating Values with Hidden Comments

Note: You may include an explanatory note with any number or formula in your worksheet. The note is not visible on the printed or displayed worksheet. It is only visible on line 1 of the control panel when you highlight the cell.

To enter hidden comments, type the number (or formula) followed immediately by a **;** (semicolon) and then the desired commentary. Do not precede the **;** with a space.

Related: **Label (Text) Entries**

Example: Add a comment to the value 30, as shown below:

A	A	B	C
1		ITEM	AMT
2			
3		Desk	30

You: Highlight cell C3 *the cell containing 30*

Tap the **F2** key *starts Edit mode*

Type **; Down payment** ↵ *the semicolon indicates a comment*

1-2-3:   *line 1*   **A:C3   30; Down payment**

A	A	B	C
1		ITEM	AMT
2			
3		Desk	**30**

The comment—**Down payment**—appears in the control panel but not in the cell display.

Auditor

Note: Auditor is an add-in to help you check formulas in your worksheet for accuracy. Use Auditor to display information about specific formulas, to identify all formulas that depend on a particular cell, or to display cells involved in a circular reference.

An add-in must be loaded before it can be used. After starting 1-2-3, hold **Alt** and tap **F10,** select **Load,** and select **AUDITOR.PLC.** See **Add-Ins** in Chapter 2 for details and alternatives.

OVERVIEW OF STEPS

1. Create or load your worksheet.

2. Load the Auditor add-in.

3. Invoke the Auditor add-in.

4. Use the Auditor menu to check out your formulas.

5. Reset the highlights set by the Auditor.

6. Quit the Auditor add-in.

TERMS YOU SHOULD KNOW

Circ—A circular reference. Usually an error. It means that a formula either directly or indirectly refers to itself. Example 1 creates three circular references.

Precedents—These are the cells that a formula refers to.

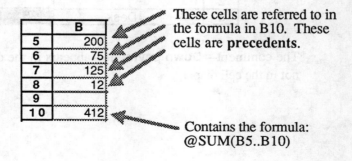

These cells are referred to in the formula in B10. These cells are **precedents.**

Contains the formula: @SUM(B5..B10)

Dependents—These are the cells that contain formulas. Formulas depend on the contents of other cells.

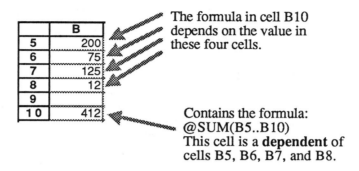

The formula in cell B10 depends on the value in these four cells.

Contains the formula:
@SUM(B5..B10)
This cell is a **dependent** of cells B5, B6, B7, and B8.

Audit range—The range of cells you are analyzing. It is usually best to leave the audit range alone and let it refer to all the cells in all the loaded worksheets.

Related: **Add-Ins**

Example 1:   Create a sample worksheet with some mistakes in the formulas. We will use this worksheet in the subsequent examples.

You: Start with an empty spreadsheet (see **New Worksheet** in Chapter 2 for details, if necessary).

Move cursor to A1. Type   **/ W C S 18** ← *set width to 18*

Type in the information shown in the following figure:

	A	B	C	D
1	Office Expenses			
2				
3				
4				
5	Depreciation	200	210	220
6	Telephone	75	88	92
7	Supplies	125	155	144
8	Subscriptions	12	15	14
9				
10	Total			
11				
12	GRAND TOTAL			
13				
14	Number of people			15
15				
16	Expenses / person			

Highlight cell B3.   Type **"01-Jan** ↵   *enter column headers*
Highlight cell C3.   Type **"01-Feb** ↵
Highlight cell D3.   Type **"01-Mar** ↵

Highlight cell B10.   Type **@SUM(B5..B10)** ↵   *a bad formula*
Highlight cell C10.   Type **@SUM(C5..C10)** ↵   *a bad formula*
Highlight cell D10.   Type **@SUM(D5..D10)** ↵   *a bad formula*
Highlight cell D12.   Type **@SUM(B10..B12)** ↵ *a bad formula*
Highlight cell D16.   Type **+D12/D14** ↵

1-2-3: You have created the worksheet shown on the next page. The
numbers from row 8 down may be different due to the intentional
formula errors. Notice the CIRC at the bottom of your screen. It
means you have a circular formula somewhere.

	A	B	C	D
1	Office Expenses			
2				
3				
4				
5	Depreciation	200	210	220
6	Telephone	75	88	92
7	Supplies	125	155	144
8	Subscriptions	12	15	14
9				
10	Total	412	468	470
11				
12	GRAND TOTAL			1350
13				
14	Number of people			15
15				
16	Expenses / person			90

> Your spreadsheet could contain different values
> since this spreadsheet contains circular references.

Example 2: Load Auditor from the **C:\ADDINS** directory.

You: Hold the **Alt** key and tap **F10**. Release the **Alt** key.

Type **L** *Load*

1-2-3: The following appears:
Specify an add-in to read into memory: C:\123R3*.PLC

You: Tap **F3**

1-2-3: A list of files appears.

You: If you see **AUDITOR.PLC**
      Highlight **AUDITOR.PLC**
      Tap ←⏎

If you do not see **AUDITOR.PLC**
      Tap **Backspace**
      Highlight **ADDINS**
      Tap ←⏎   *hopefully you now see AUDITOR.PLC*

Highlight **AUDITOR.PLC**
Tap ↵

If you still do not see **AUDITOR.PLC**
Try another directory, or another drive.
Or, perhaps you need to install it.   Add-ins are installed
separately from the main 1-2-3 software.

1-2-3: **No-Key 1 2 3**

You: If these choices appear, you can type a **1**, **2**, or **3** so that later you
will be able to activate this add-in with a function key.

Or, if you don't wish to use functions keys, tap **N**   *for No-Key*

Note: Activating an add-in key with a function key is convenient if you
will be using it repeatedly. Otherwise, choose No-Key.

You: **Q**   *Quit*

Result: It may look like nothing happened, but now you are ready to Invoke
Auditor. Continue with Example 3.

Note: Once you have loaded an add-in, do not load it again, unless you
quit 1-2-3. You can make an add-in load automatically when 1-2-3
is started. See Example 6 below.

Example 3:   Invoking and using the Auditor add-in for circular references.

You: Invoke Auditor as follows:

If you assigned a function key to Auditor:

Hold **Alt** and tap that function key

Otherwise:

Hold the **Alt** key and tap **F10**
Type **I**   *Invoke*
Tap **F3**   *to show the list of loaded add-ins*
Highlight **AUDITOR**
Tap ↵

1-2-3:   The Auditor menu and Auditor settings box appear:

Precedents Dependents Formulas Recalc-List Circs Options Quit
Identify all cells that provide data for specified formula cell

```
┌──────────────────── Auditor  Settings ────────────────────┐
│ Audit all files in memory              Audit Mode: HIGHLIGHT │
└─────────────────────────────────────────────────────────────┘
```

You: Type   **O T Q**   *Options Trace Quit*

1-2-3:   The audit mode changed to TRACE.

Precedents Dependents Formulas Recalc-List Circs Options Quit
Identify all cells that provide data for specified formula cell

```
┌──────────────────── Auditor  Settings ────────────────────┐
│ Audit all files in memory              Audit Mode: TRACE     │
└─────────────────────────────────────────────────────────────┘
```

You: Type **C**   *Circs*

1-2-3:   The three circular references are listed:
Select a cell at the beginning of a circular path:
A:B10   A:C10   A:D10

Note: If the computer beeps here, it probably means you have no CIRC references. See the note on the bottom of the screen.

You: Tap →   to highlight A:C10 on line three of the screen.

Tap ←┘

Tap **F** or **B**   *to highlight cellsl involved in the CIRC references*

1-2-3:   The computer beeps because there are no other cells involved in this **CIRC**. If there were other formulas involved, they would be highlighted now. The beeping indicates the error is entirely in cell C10 and involves no other cells. Likewise for cells B10 and D10.

You: **Q O R H Q Q**   *Quit Options Reset Highlight Quit Quit*

Note: If you forget **Options Reset Highlight Quit**, your circular reference cell will remain green or bright because it is marked with a U for Unprotected.

You: Fix these formulas as follows:

Highlight cell **B10.**   Type   @SUM(B5..B8) ↵   *corrected*
Highlight cell **C10.**   Type   @SUM(C5..C8) ↵   *corrected*
Highlight cell **D10.**   Type   @SUM(D5..D8) ↵   *corrected*

Example 4:   Invoking and using the Auditor add-in for precedent references.

You: Create the worksheet described in Example 1 and fix three of the bad formulas as described at the end of Example 2.

You: Invoke Auditor as follows:

If you assigned a function key to Auditor:

    Hold **Alt** and tap that function key

Otherwise:

    Hold the **Alt** key and tap **F10**
    Type **I**   *Invoke*
    Tap **F3**   *to show the list of loaded add-ins*
    Highlight **AUDITOR**
    Tap ↵

You: Type **O H Q**   *Options Highlight Quit*

1-2-3:   **Precedents Dependents Formulas Recalc-List Circs Options Quit**
Identify all cells that provide data for specified formula cell

```
──────────────── Auditor  Settings ────────────────
Audit all files in memory              Audit Mode: HIGHLIGHT
```

You: Type **P**   *Precedents*

Highlight cell **D16**   *we are looking for the cells that affect the formula in cell D16*

Tap ↵

1-2-3:   The following appears. The precedent cells (B5, B6, B7, B8, B10, B12, and B14) appear bold or green on your worksheet.

	A	B	C	D
1	Office Expenses			
2				
3				
4				
5	Depreciation	**200**	210	220
6	Telephone	**75**	88	92
7	Supplies	**125**	155	144
8	Subscriptions	**12**	15	14
9				
10	Total	**412**	468	470
11				
12	GRAND TOTAL			**412**
13				
14	Number of people			**15**
15				
16	Expenses / person			27.4667

Notice that for some reason cells C10 and D10 are not bold. That means that they have been left out of the grand total. Let's check it out.

You: Type **P ↑ ↑ ↑ ↑** *Precedents for the Grand Total in cell D12*

Look at the formula in cell D12:
It is   @SUM(B10..B12)
It should be   @SUM(B10..D10)

Note: You need to quit Auditor to fix the this misbehaving formula.

You: Type **← O R H Q Q ←** *Options Reset Highlight Quit Quit*

Note: If you forget **Options Reset Highlight Quit**, your circular reference cell will remain green or bright because it is marked with a U for Unprotected.

You: If any cells remain green (or bright), highlight each green cell, then type **/ R P ←** *for Range Protect*

You: Fix this formula as follows:

Highlight cell **D12**. Type **@SUM(B10..D10) ←** *corrected*

Example 5:   Invoking and using the Auditor add-in for dependent references.

You: Create the worksheet described in Example 1 and fix three of the bad formulas as described at the end of Example 2 and Example 3.

You: Invoke Auditor as follows:

If you assigned a function key to Auditor:

> Hold **Alt** and tap that function key

Otherwise:

> Hold the **Alt** key and tap **F10**
> Type **I**   *Invoke*
> Tap **F3**   *to show the list of loaded add-ins*
> Highlight **AUDITOR**
> Tap ←⏎

You: Type   **O L Q**   *Options List Quit*

1-2-3:   **Precedents Dependents Formulas Recalc-List Circs Options   Quit**
Identify all cells that provide data for specified formula cell

```
┌──────────────── Auditor Settings ────────────────┐
│ Audit all files in memory          Audit Mode: LIST │
└─────────────────────────────────────────────────────┘
```

You: Type   **D**   *Dependents*

Highlight cell **B5**   *we are looking for the cells that affect the formula in cell D16*

Tap ←⏎

1-2-3:   **Enter target range for list: A:xxx**

You: Type   **F5..F20** ←⏎   *Or any place that is not important*

Type **Q**   *Quit*

1-2-3:   The following appears. The cells that are dependent on cell B5 are B10, D12, and D16, as shown in the list.

	F	G	H
5	Dependents of cell		
6	A:B10: @SUM(B5..B8)		
7	A:D12: @SUM(B10..D10)		
8	A:D16: +D12/D14		

You: Change the value in cell B5.

Notice that the values in cells B10, D12, and D16 also change, but no other cell is affected, because no other cell is dependent on B5.

Example 6: Customize 1-2-3 so that Auditor automatically loads whenever you start 1-2-3.

You: Start 1-2-3 as usual.

Hold the **Alt** key and tap **F10**

Type **S S S** *Settings System Set*

Tap **F3**

Note: The aim of these next key strokes is to find **AUDITOR.PLC**. It could be in any of several directories.

You: If you see **AUDITOR.PLC**
  Highlight **AUDITOR.PLC**
  Tap ←┘

If you don't see **AUDITOR.PLC**
  Tap **Backspace**
  Highlight **ADDINS**   Tap ←┘
  Highlight **AUDITOR.PLC**   Tap ←┘

Note: If you want to assign a function key to Auditor, type 1, 2, or 3 instead of N in the following line.

You: Type **Y N U Q Q** *Yes No-key Update Quit Quit*

Result: From now on, every time you start 1-2-3, Auditor will also start. You just need to wait a few seconds longer.

Example 7:   Remove Auditor from memory and prevent it from automatically loading when you start 1-2-3.

You: Hold the **Alt** key and tap **F10**

Type **S S C**   *Setting System Cancel*

Highlight **AUDITOR**   *unloads it*

Tap ←┘

Type **U Q R**   *Update Quit Remove*

Highlight **AUDITOR**   *remove it from the automatic load list*

Tap ←┘

Type **Q**   *Quit*

Result: From now on, when you start 1-2-3, Auditor will not automatically start.

Automatically Loading 1-2-3 Worksheets

Note: To create a worksheet that loads just by starting 1-2-3, save your worksheet with the name AUTO123 in the directory where 1-2-3 normally stores your files (the default directory). See **Directories** for more information.

If this AUTO123 file contains a macro (precoded instructions and commands) named **\Ø** (**Backslash** zero), the macro will be automatically started when the worksheet is loaded.

OVERVIEW OF STEPS

- Create your worksheet.

- For automatically starting macros, create a macro named \Ø (see **Macros**).

- Save your worksheet as AUTO123 (see below).

- Quit 1-2-3.

- Next time you start 1-2-3, your worksheet will automatically appear on the screen.

Related: **Directories**
Macros

Example 1: Create a worksheet that is to be automatically loaded when Lotus 1-2-3 is started.

You: Create (or retrieve) a worksheet (see Chapter 1).

Type / **F S AUTO123** ↵ *File Save*

You are saving this worksheet with a special name—**AUTO123**

If **Cancel Replace Backup** appears, tap **R** to replace the file AUTO123 on disk. If you don't want to replace it, tap **C** *Cancel* or **B** *Backup*.

1-2-3:   **READY**   appears in the upper-left corner.

Result: The next time you start Lotus 1-2-3, this worksheet will automatically be loaded. There is no need to type / **F R** *File Retrieve.*

Example 2:   Stop the automatic loading of a worksheet whenever 1-2-3 is started.

You: Save your current worksheet. Reminder: / **F S** *File Save* etc. See **Save** in Chapter 2 for details.

Type / **W E Y** *Worksheet Erase Yes to clear the screen*

Type / **S** *System*

1-2-3:   This message appears:
(Type EXIT and press [ENTER] to return to 1-2-3) followed by other system and copyright messages and the system prompt. You are now in DOS.

You: Type **RENAME   AUTO123.WK3   NOAUTO.WK3** ←⏎

If AUTO123.WK3 is in another directory or drive, then this command won't work. If so, retype the command with the correct drive and directory. For example:
RENAME   D:\JAN\AUTO123.WK3   NOAUTO.WK3 ←⏎

This worksheet now has a new name, NOAUTO, and will no longer be automatically loaded.

Type **EXIT** ←⏎

1-2-3:   **READY**   appears in the upper-left corner.

Result: The next time you start 1-2-3, this worksheet will not automatically load. To load it, type / **F R NOAUTO** ←⏎

Backsolver

Note: Backsolver is an add-in to determine a variable value in a formula when you know what you want the answer to be. For example, you have a desired profit margin in mind, and you want to know what the total sales must be to reach than desired value.

Backsolver answers "what-if" questions by working backwards. You know the answer, and you know the formula. Backsolver determines a specific value necessary to achieve your answer.

An add-in must be loaded before it can be used. After starting 1-2-3, hold **Alt** and tap **F10**, select **Load,** and select **BSOLVER.PLC**. See **Add-Ins** in Chapter 2 for details and alternatives.

OVERVIEW OF STEPS

1. Create or load your worksheet.

2. Load the Backsolver add-in.

3. Invoke the Backsolver add-in.

4. Use the Backsolver menu.

5. Quit the Backsolver add-in.

TERMS YOU SHOULD KNOW

Value—This is the desired value. In our example, it is the desired profit margin. In the example we want a profit margin of $222,000.

Formula cell—This is the cell that contains a formula that you want to display the desired value. In our example, it is the cell containing the formula that computes profit margin.

Adjustable cell—This is the cell that contains a value that Backsolver will change until the formula cell displays the desired value. Obviously the adjustable cell must be one of the components of the formula. In our example, the adjustable cell is the total sales amount. Backsolver will replace whatever is in this cell with another amount, so save the original contents if you need them.

Adjustable cell. The one that Backsolver will change.

	A	B
1	Widget Inc - one year plan	
2		
3	INCOME	
4	sales	0
5	dividends	2000
6	total income	2000
7		
8	EXPENSES	
9	salaries	98000
10	rent	44000
11	other	77000
12	total expenses	219000
13		
14	NET PROFIT	-217000

Formula cell. The one that we want to have equal $222,000, which is our "value."

Related: **Add-Ins**

Example 1: Create a sample worksheet to use with Backsolver in the subsequent examples.

You: Start with an empty spreadsheet (see **New Worksheet** in Chapter 2 for details, if necessary).

Move cursor to A1. Type **/ W C S 18** ↵ *set width to 18*

Type in the information shown below:

	A	B
1	Widget Inc - one year plan	
2		
3	INCOME	
4	sales	439000
5	dividends	2000
6	total income	
7		
8	EXPENSES	
9	salaries	98000
10	rent	44000
11	other	77000
12	total expenses	
13		
14	NET PROFIT	

Highlight cell B6. Type **@SUM(B4..B5)** ↵
Highlight cell B12. Type **@SUM(B9..B11)** ↵
Highlight cell B14. Type **+B6-B12** ↵

1-2-3: You have created the following worksheet:

	A	B
1	Widget Inc - one year plan	
2		
3	INCOME	
4	sales	0
5	dividends	2000
6	total income	2000
7		
8	EXPENSES	
9	salaries	98000
10	rent	44000
11	other	77000
12	total expenses	219000
13		
14	NET PROFIT	-217000

Example 2: Load Backsolver from the **C:\ADDINS** directory.

You: Hold the **Alt** key and tap **F10**. Release the **Alt** key.

Type **L** *Load*

1-2-3:   The following appears:
            Specify an add-in to read into memory: C:\123R3*.PLC

You: Tap **F3**

1-2-3:   A list of files appears.

You: If you see **BSOLVER.PLC**
               Highlight **BSOLVER.PLC**
               Tap ←

            If you do not see **BSOLVER.PLC**
            Tap **Backspace**
            Highlight **ADDINS**
            Tap ←   *hopefully you now see BSOLVER.PLC*
            Highlight **BSOLVER.PLC**
            Tap ←

            If you still do not see **BSOLVER.PLC**
               Try another directory, or another drive.
               Or, perhaps you need to install it.   Add-ins are installed
               separately from the main 1-2-3 software.

1-2-3:   **No-Key 1 2 3**

You: If these choices appear, you can type a **1**, **2**, or **3** so that later you
            will be able to activate this add-in with a function key.

            Or, if you don't wish to use functions keys, tap **N**   *for No-Key.*

Note: Activating an add-in key with a function key is convenient if you
            will be using it repeatedly. Otherwise, choose No-Key.

You: **Q**←   *Quit*

Result: It may look like nothing happened, but now you are ready to Invoke
            Backsolver—see Example 3.

Note: Once you have loaded an add-in, do not load it again, unless you
            quit 1-2-3. You can make an add-in load automatically when 1-2-3
            is started. See Example 4 below.

Example 3: Invoking and using the Backsolver add-in to determine the necessary sales to have a net profit of $222,000.

You: Invoke Backsolver as follows:

If you assigned a function key to Backsolver:

Hold **Alt** and tap that function key

Otherwise:

Hold the **Alt** key and tap **F10**
Type **I**   *Invoke*
Tap **F3**   *to show the list of loaded add-ins*
Highlight **BSOLVER**
Tap ↵

1-2-3: The Backsolver menu appears:

Formula-Cell   Value   Adjustable   Solve Quit
Specify the formula cell to be set to the target value

You: Type   **F B14** ↵   *Formula-Cell*

Type   **V 222000** ↵   *Value—this is your desired profit margin*

Type   **A B4** ↵   *Adjustable—this is the cell that will be changed by 1-2-3*

Type   **S**   *Solve—in a flash, you have your necessary sales*

1-2-3: $439,000 in sales is needed to have a net profit of $222,000.

The adjustable cell now contains $439.000, which is the amount of sales needed to generate a profit of $222,000.

	A	B
1	Widget Inc - one year plan	
2		
3	INCOME	
4	sales	439000
5	dividends	2000
6	total income	441000
7		
8	EXPENSES	
9	salaries	98000
10	rent	44000
11	other	77000
12	total expenses	219000
13		
14	NET PROFIT	222000

Example 4:   Customize 1-2-3 so that Backsolver automatically loads whenever you start 1-2-3.

You: Start 1-2-3 as usual.

Hold the **Alt** key and tap **F10**

Type **S S S**   *Settings System Set*

Tap **F3**

Note: The aim of these next key strokes is to find **BSOLVER.PLC**. It could be in any of several directories.

You: If you see **BSOLVER.PLC**
   Highlight **BSOLVER.PLC**
   Tap ←

If you don't see **BSOLVER.PLC**
   Tap **Backspace**
   Highlight **ADDINS**   Tap ←
   Highlight **BSOLVER.PLC**   Tap ←

Note: If you want to assign a function key to Backsolver, type **1**, **2**, or **3** instead of **N** in the following line.

You: Type **Y N U Q Q**   *Yes No-key Update Quit Quit*

Result: From now on, every time you start 1-2-3, Backsolver will also start. You just need to wait a few seconds longer.

Example 5: Remove Backsolver from memory and prevent it from automatically loading when you start 1-2-3.

You: Hold the **Alt** key and tap **F10**

Type **S S C**   *Setting System Cancel*

Highlight **BSOLVER**   *to remove it from memory*

Tap ⏎

Type **U Q R**   *Update Quit Remove*

Highlight **BSOLVER**   *to remove it from the automatic load list*

Tap ⏎

Type **Q**   *Quit*

Result: From now on, when you start 1-2-3, Backsolver will not automatically start.

Backups

Note: Make backup copies of all important worksheets—worksheets that took a while to write and you plan to use again.

Backing up files means copying them from your hard disk to another place. The second place can be a diskette, a tape cartridge, etc.

Lotus 1-2-3 doesn't provide an adequate backup procedure. You can use the DOS BACKUP command or buy a utility package that backs up files. The **Backup** option in / **File Save** is not a substitute for backing up important files.

Example 1: Use the DOS BACKUP command to backup your entire 123R3 directory. (Example 2 is a much faster backup.)

You: Exit from 1-2-3 and get to the DOS prompt.

DOS: **C>** or **C:\123R3>** or similar prompt

You: Put a formatted diskette in drive A: (see **Formatting Diskettes**).

Type **BACKUP   C:\123R3*.*   A:** ←┘

DOS: The machine will beep at you and display:

> **Warning! Files on the target**
> **drive A:\ root directory will be erased.**
> **Strike any key when ready**

You: Tap ←┘ *to proceed with the backup*

Result: This backs up all files in the 123R3 directory, including .WK3 files for spreadsheets, .FM3 files for Wysiwyg, PCX and .CGM files for graphs, .PRN files for printer files, etc. This also backs up all your LOTUS 1-2-3 program files, which may not be such a good ideas.

Important: A backed up file is now in two places, on your hard disk and also on a diskette. Access the file on your hard disk in the usual way, with / **File Retrieve**. If you accidentally destroy your hard disk file, you will want to use the copy on your diskette. If you used the DOS BACKUP command, the only way to retrieve files from your diskette is with the DOS RESTORE command (see **Restore**).

Example 2: Use the DOS BACKUP command to backup just your worksheets and associated Wysiwyg files.

You: Exit from 1-2-3 and get to the DOS prompt.

DOS: **C>** or **C:\123R3>** or similar prompt

You: Put a formatted diskette in drive A: (see **Formatting Diskettes**).

Type   **BACKUP   C:\123R3*.WK***   **A:**   ⏎

DOS: The machine will beep at you and display:

**Warning! Files on the target
drive A:\ root directory will be erased.
Strike any key when ready**

You: Tap ⏎ *to proceed with the backup*

Type   **BACKUP   C:\123R3*.FM***   **A:/A**   ⏎

DOS: The machine will beep at you and display:

**Insert last backup diskette in drive A:
Strike any key when ready**

You: Tap ⏎ *to proceed with the backup*

Result: This backs up all files in the 123R3 directory that end in .WK3 (worksheets) or .FM3 (format for Wysiwyg). The second backup command needs the /A at the end, or it needs to be to a separate diskette.

Clock

Command: **/ Worksheet Global Default Other Clock**

Note: This command sets the display in the lower-left corner of your screen to one of the following choices:

Filename Switches between filename and clock display depending on whether the current file exists on disk. This does not mean that the disk version is current.

Clock The current date and time is always in the lower-left corner.

None Nothing appears in the lower-left corner.

Related: **Status**

Example: Set the display to show the current **Filename** in the lower-left corner. When there is no current file, the date and time will appear.

You: Start with an empty worksheet.

To save the current worksheet, type **/ F S** *etc.* ←

To erase the current worksheet, type **/ W E Y** *Worksheet Erase Yes*

You: Type **/ W G D O C F U Q** ← *Worksheet Global Default*
Other Clock Filename Update Quit

1-2-3: The current date and time appear in the lower-left corner.

You: Type anything into several cells.

1-2-3: The current date and time still appear in the lower-left corner, because the file isn't saved to disk yet.

You: Type **/ F S JUNK** ←   *this saves the worksheet*

1-2-3: **JUNK.WK3** appears in the lower-left corner because the file now exists on disk.

Column Width

Command: / **Worksheet Column Set-Width**
/ **Worksheet Column Reset-Width**
/ **Worksheet Column Column-Range Set-Width**
/ **Worksheet Column Column-Range Reset-Width**
/ **Worksheet Global Column-Width**

Note: If you have Wysiwyg, I recommend the next section—**Column Width with Wysiwyg**—instead of this section.

Use these commands to make the column width visually pleasing.

The last command, **Worksheet Global Column-Width**, sets the width of all 256 columns, *except for* columns already set with the first or third command. The column width set with this command is called the **global width**. If you don't use this command, then the global width is nine.

The first command, **Worksheet Column Set-Width**, sets the width of just *one* column.

The second command, **Worksheet Column Reset-Width**, resets the width of *one* column to the global width.

The third command, **Worksheet Column Column-Range Set-Width**, allows you to set the width of a *range* of columns.

The fourth command, **Worksheet Column Column-Range Reset-Width**, resets the width of a *range* of columns to the global width.

Tips: If you want to set many contiguous columns to the same width, use the command / **W G C** or / **W C C S**

If the last command won't set a column, use a reset command— / **W C R** or / **W C C R**—to reset the obstinate column.

If cells in a column suddenly fill with ********** (asterisks), it is usually because the column is too narrow.

Example: In your worksheet, set column widths as follows:
Column A   20 characters wide
All other columns   12 characters wide

You: Highlight cell A1 *or any cell in column A*

Type **/ W C S** *Worksheet Column Set-Width*

1-2-3: **Enter column width (1..240): 9** *might not be 9*

You: Tap → until the column is 20 characters wide.

Note: You could just type 20 ←⟂ but then you lose the flexibility of watching the column width as it is adjusted.

1-2-3: **Enter column width (1..240):   20**

You: Tap ←⟂

1-2-3: **A:A1**   **READY**

A	A	B	C	D	E	F
1	███████					
2						

We set the width of *one* column—column A. Look for **READY** in the upper-right corner to be sure you are finished. A frequent error is to forget the ←⟂ at the end of the command.

Note: Note that every cell in column A is 20 positions wide.

You: Type **/ W G C** *Worksheet Global Column-Width*
Tap → until a global column width of 12 appears.
Tap ←⟂

Result: **A:A1**   **READY**

	A	B	C	D	E
1	██████				
2					

We set the width of *all* the columns except column A to 12.

Column Width with Wysiwyg

Command: : **Worksheet Column Set-Width**
: **Worksheet Column Reset-Width**
Mouse control

Note: Use these commands to adjust the width to be visually pleasing.

Tip: If cells in a column suddenly fill with ********** (asterisks), it is usually because the column is too narrow.

Example 1: In your worksheet, set column A to a width of 20.

You: Type **: W C S** *Worksheet Column Set-Width*

Highlight cell A1 *or any cell in column A*

1-2-3: **Enter range for column-width change: A:A1**

You: Tap ⏎

1-2-3: **Enter column width (1..240): 9** *might not be 9*

You: Tap → until the column is 20 characters wide.

Note: You could just type 20, but then you lose the flexibility of watching the column width as it is adjusted.

1-2-3: **Enter column width (1..240): 20**

You: Tap ⏎

1-2-3: **A:A1**   **READY**

A	A	B	C	D	E	F
1						
2						

Look for **READY** in the upper-right corner to be sure you are finished. If it isn't there, you forgot the ⏎ to end the command.

Example 2: Use the mouse to change the width of a column by dragging.

You: Move the mouse arrow so that the point is between the A and B column names, as shown in this diagram:

	A	B	C	D
1				
2				

Click and hold down the left mouse button.

1-2-3: The mouse arrow becomes like a cross.

You: Keep holding down the mouse button and drag to the right. Release the button.

1-2-3: Column A is larger.

Combining 1-2-3 Files

Command: / **File Combine Add**
/ **File Combine Subtract**
/ **File Combine Copy**

Note: **File Combine** is useful when you want to combine information from different worksheets coming from other people. See **Multiple (Linked) Files** or **Multiple Sheets** for alternative ideas.

With **File Combine**, values in a worksheet on disk are added to (/ **File Combine Add**), subtracted from (/ **File Combine Subtract**), or copied over (/ **File Combine Copy**) a range of cells in your current worksheet.

Related: **Multiple Sheets**
Multiple (Linked) Files
Database 9—dBASE Input
File Choices (a list of cross-references)
Designing Spreadsheets—Balance Brought Forward

Example: Add the monthly sales that are in separate files named **EAST3** and **WEST3** into a column called **YTD SALES** (year to date sales) in the current worksheet. To illustrate this we need to create the files **EAST3**, **WEST3**, and **YTD3**.

Create EAST3

You: Create the following worksheet:

	A	B
1	MARCH	EAST SALES
2		
3	WIDGETS	12.34
4	TOYS	123.45
5	KITS	1.23
6	THINGS	234.56

You: Type / **F S EAST3** ↵ *to save this worksheet*

If **Cancel Replace Backup** appears, tap **R** to replace the file on disk. If you don't want to replace it, tap **C** *Cancel* or **B** *Backup*.

Create WEST3

You: Create the following worksheet:

	A	B
1	MARCH	WEST SALES
2		
3	WIDGETS	54.32
4	TOYS	543.21
5	KITS	4.32
6	THINGS	765.43

You: Type **/ F S WEST3** ←┘ *to save this worksheet*

If **Cancel Replace Backup** appears, tap **R** to replace the file on disk. If you don't want to replace it, tap **C** *Cancel* or **B** *Backup*.

Create YTD3

You: Create the following worksheet:

	A	B	C
1		SPECIALITY CORPORATION	
2			
3	MARCH	YTD SALES	
4			
5	WIDGETS		
6	TOYS		
7	KITS		
8	THINGS		

You: Type **/ F S YTD3** ←┘ *to save this worksheet*

If **Cancel Replace Backup** appears, tap **R** to replace the file on disk. If you don't want to replace it, tap **C** *Cancel* or **B** *Backup*.

Combine the sales figures from EAST3 and WEST3 into YTD3

You: Type **/ F R YTD3** ←┘ *to retrieve the YTD3 file*

Highlight cell B5   *This is where the sales figures from EAST3 and WEST3 will be combined*

Type **/ F C C N** *File Combine Copy Named/Specified-Range*

1-2-3: **Enter range name or coordinates:**

You: Type **B3..B6** ←┘   *to choose the range in EAST3 containing sales figures*

Tip: Make sure you know the range in the disk worksheet before starting the File Combine command. You can't point to these cells B3..B6.

1-2-3: **Name of file to combine: C:\123R3*.wk?**

You: Type **EAST3** *or highlight the name EAST3*

Tap ←┘

1-2-3:

	A	B	C
1		SPECIALITY CORPORATION	
2			
3	MARCH	YTD SALES	
4			
5	WIDGETS	12.34	
6	TOYS	123.45	
7	KITS	1.23	
8	THINGS	234.56	

The sales figures from EAST3 are now *copied* into the range B5..B8 in the current worksheet, YTD3.

You: Highlight cell B5   *this is where the sales figures from WEST3 will be added*

Type **/ F C A N** *File Combine Add Named/Specified-Range*

1-2-3: **Enter range name or coordinates:**

You: Type **B3..B6** ←┘   *to choose the range in WEST3 containing sales figures*

1-2-3: **Name of file to combine: C:\123R3*.wk?**

You: Type **WEST3** *or highlight the name WEST3*

You: Tap ↵

1-2-3:

	A	B	C
1		SPECIALITY CORPORATION	
2			
3	MARCH	YTD SALES	
4			
5	WIDGETS	66.66	
6	TOYS	666.66	
7	KITS	5.55	
8	THINGS	999.99	

Save your changes to YTD3

You: Type **/ F S YTD3** ↵   *to save this worksheet*

If **Cancel Replace Backup** appears, tap **R** to replace the file on disk. If you don't want to replace it, tap **C** *Cancel* or **B** *Backup*.

Result: The sales figures from **EAST3** and **WEST3** have been added together.   Their sum is in the range **B5..B8** of the current worksheet, which is called **YTD3**.

Conditions

A condition is a specialized formula that compares one value with another. For example: +D6=100 means, "Does the value in cell D6 equal 100?" Lotus 1-2-3 uses conditions to decide the course of action to take.

Conditions, also called logical expressions, are used in **@IF** functions, in / **Data Query Criteria**, and in macro {IF} statements. Refer to these two related features, then use this section as a reference for different types of conditions.

Symbols for comparing two values

=	equal to
<	less than
>	greater than
<=	less than or equal
>=	greater than or equal
<>	not equal to

Testing a single condition

+D6>250 *tests whether the contents of cell D6 are greater than 250*

Testing multiple conditions

#AND#	tests if both conditions must be true
#OR#	tests if either condition will suffice

+D6>250#AND#D6<500 *determines whether the number in cell D6 is greater than 250 and less than 500*

Related: **Functions (especially @IF)**
Database 2—Criteria Area
Macros (especially {IF})

Example 1: Calculate employee overtime hours (hours over 40 hours).

You: Create the following worksheet:

A	A	B	C	D
1		Employee	Hours	Overtime
2		Name	worked	hours
3				
4		Jones	40	
5		Smith	32	
6		Andrews	55	

You: Highlight cell D4.

You: Type   @IF(C4>40,C4-40,0) ↵

The **@IF** statement has three arguments (parameters). The first is the condition (**C>40**) and the second and third are the possible computations. If the condition is true, the second parameter is calculated. If the condition is false, the third parameter is calculated. In this case, C contains 40, so the condition becomes: "Is 40 greater than 40?" It is false, so the third parameter—Ø (zero)—is put into cell D4.

1-2-3:

A	A	B	C	D
1		Employee	Hours	Overtime
2		Name	worked	hours
3				
4		Jones	40	0
5		Smith	32	
6		Andrews	55	

You: Type / C ↵ . ↓ ↓ ↵   *to copy the formula down column D*

Result:

A	A	B	C	D	
1		Employee	Hours	Overtime	
2		Name	worked	hours	
3					
4		Jones	40	0	← *zero hours overtime*
5		Smith	32	0	← *also zero hours*
6		Andrews	55	15	← *55-40 gives 15 hours*

Example 2: Mark the rows that paid between January 1 and December 1, 1988 okay, as shown below. This will use a compound condition.

	A	B	C
1	Name	Date Paid	Mark
2			
3	Hankins	05/03/87	
4	Simons	01/11/88	OK
5	Adams	05/03/88	OK
6	Hadden	05/03/89	

You: Enter information in column A and row 1 as shown above.

You: Highlight cell B3 and type **5/3/87** ←⟂
Highlight cell B4 and type **1/11/88** ←⟂
Highlight cell B5 and type **5/3/88** ←⟂
Highlight cell B6 and type **5/3/89** ←⟂

Type **/ W C S 10** ←⟂ *to widen the column to 10*

Highlight cell B3.

Type **/ R F D 4 ↓ ↓ ↓** ←⟂ *to format as dates*

Highlight cell C3.

Type **@IF(B3>=@DATE(88,1,1)#AND#**
B3<=@DATE(88,12,31),"OK"," ") ←⟂

The condition B3>=@DATE(88,1,1)#AND#B3<=@DATE(88,12,31) has two parts: The first part, B3>=@DATE(88,1,1), checks whether the date in cell B3 is on or after January 1, 1988. The second part, B3<=@DATE(88,12,31), checks whether the date in cell B3 is on or before December 31, 1988. The #AND# checks whether both parts are true. If both parts are true, then **OK** is put into cell C3. If both parts are not true, then " " is put into cell C3. It doesn't matter whether or not you put a space between the quotes.

You: Type **/ C** ←⟂ **. ↓ ↓ ↓** ←⟂ *to copy the formula down column C*

Config.sys

Note: In order for the mouse to work, you usually need a line in the config.sys file saying:

DEVICE=C:\DOS\MOUSE.SYS

DEVICE = specifies a device driver. A driver is a program that extends DOS. Drivers can be used to support nonstandard hardware, such as the mouse, which DOS doesn't usually expect you to have on your computer.

Some mouse drivers (from Microsoft) are loaded with MOUSE.COM, which would go in your AUTOEXEC.BAT file as follows:

C:\DOS\MOUSE.COM

In addition, your CONFIG.SYS needs the following lines:

BUFFERS=20

FILES=20   *or 40 if you plan to open more than 10 worksheets simultaneously*

Either number could be higher, especially if ;you have over 1 M RAM (memory).

Control Panel

The control panel is the top three lines displayed on your screen.

Line 1 contains information about the highlighted cell and the mode indicator (see **Mode** for more information). Line 2 may show possible commands, subcommands, or cell information being entered or edited. Line 3 may show subcommands or descriptions of the command highlighted on line 2. Lines 2 and 3 are usually blank. Wysiwyg has additional attributes that it can add to a cell.

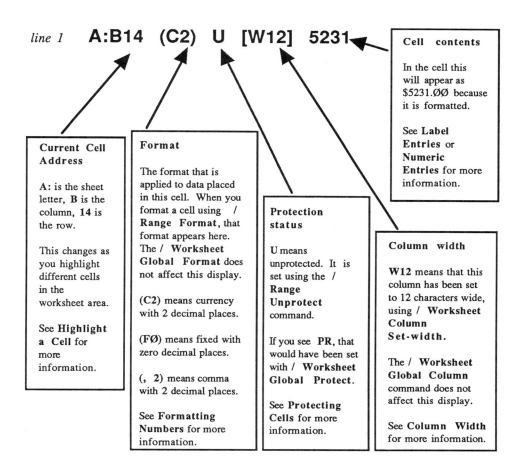

line 1 **A:B14 (C2) U [W12] 5231**

Cell contents

In the cell this will appear as $5231.ØØ because it is formatted.

See **Label Entries** or **Numeric Entries** for more information.

Current Cell Address

A: is the sheet letter, **B** is the column, **14** is the row.

This changes as you highlight different cells in the worksheet area.

See **Highlight a Cell** for more information.

Format

The format that is applied to data placed in this cell. When you format a cell using / **Range Format**, that format appears here. The / **Worksheet Global Format** does not affect this display.

(C2) means currency with 2 decimal places.

(FØ) means fixed with zero decimal places.

(, 2) means comma with 2 decimal places.

See **Formatting Numbers** for more information.

Protection status

U means unprotected. It is set using the / **Range Unprotect** command.

If you see **PR**, that would have been set with / **Worksheet Global Protect**.

See **Protecting Cells** for more information.

Column width

W12 means that this column has been set to 12 characters wide, using / **Worksheet Column Set-width**.

The / **Worksheet Global Column** command does not affect this display.

See **Column Width** for more information.

Copy

Command: / **Copy**
                / **Range Transpose**
                / **Range Value**

Note: **Copy** is used to duplicate information and associated formatting from one cell or cells to another cell or cells. This command has four distinct steps:

1. Specify the *FROM* cell(s)—often only *one* cell, it contains information or formulas.

2. Tap ←⏐ *to end the "from" part*

3. Specify the *TO* cell(s)—the cells receiving information.

4. Tap ←⏐ *to end the "to" part*

The examples illustrate five types of copying:

1. Copying information (text or numbers)
2. Copying formulas with relative cell addresses
3. Copying formulas with absolute cell addresses
4. Copying a vertical list and making it horizontal
5. Converting formulas to values

What is *relative*?

Copying formulas containing *relative* cell addresses is a common form of copying. In the following figure, we type a formula into cell A4, then copy it down into cells B4 and C4. This way we only type the formula once. 1-2-3 can do this copy because it is a *relative* copy.

The term *relative* refers to a cell address in a formula that changes relative to the cell the formula is copied or moved to. It means the copied formulas are similar, not identical. Look at the formulas in the worksheet below:

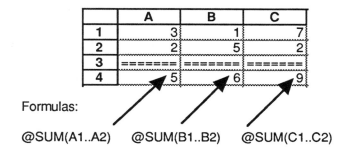

Formulas:

@SUM(A1..A2)   @SUM(B1..B2)   @SUM(C1..C2)

In this example the formulas **@SUM(A1..A2)   @SUM(B1..B2)** and **@SUM(C1..C2)** are similar because they add together the numbers above them, but they are not identical because the first adds numbers in column A, the second in column B, and the third in column C.

What is *absolute*?

Absolute cell references are not so commonly used, but they save a lot of time in some situations.

The term *absolute* refers to a cell address in a formula that never changes when the formula is copied or moved. You indicate to 1-2-3 that a cell address is absolute by inserting a $ in front of the column and also in front of the row. **B9** is a **relative** cell address; **$B$9** is the same cell address written as an **absolute** cell address. (See **Multiple Sheets** for an absolute sheet address.) Look at the formulas in the worksheet below:

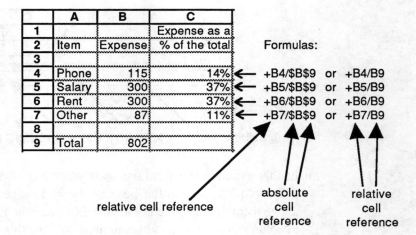

The expenses in rows 4 through 7 are each divided by the total expense in row 9 to give the percent of expense. Therefore, while the numerator changes (a relative reference), the denominator is always **B9** (or **$B$9**). The formulas are given in two ways for the cells in column C. Use the first column of formulas if you want to type the formula in once and copy it down the column. Use the second column of formulas if you want to type each formula separately and not use the **Copy** command.

Absolute cell references only affect the copies of formulas because the cell references in the copies are identical to the original formula, and not just similar, as they are with relative cell references.

Copy a vertical list and make it horizontal

Range Transpose allows you to copy data listed vertically and produce a horizontal list, or vice versa.

Convert formulas permanently into values

Range Value allows you to copy formulas and convert them to values in the "TO" range. In other words, the displayed values are copied, not the formulas underlying them. If you copy a range on top of itself (i.e., if the "FROM" and "TO" ranges are the same), 1-2-3 converts your formulas to values. However, you will lose your original formulas.

Related: **Formulas**
           Functions
           Move
           Relative and Absolute Cell References

Example 1: Copy ======== across several cells.

You: Create the following worksheet:

	A	B	C
1	3	1	7
2	2	5	2

You: Highlight cell A3.

Type \=   ⟵

1-2-3:

	A	B	C
1	3	1	7
2	2	5	2
3	=======		

You: Tap **/ C** *Copy*

1-2-3: **Enter range to copy FROM: A:A3..A:A3**

You: Tap ⟵

1-2-3: **Enter range to copy TO: A:A3**   *1-2-3 does not show a range; you need to make it into a range*

You: Tap .   *the period changes A:A3 to A:A3..A:A3, which is a range*

1-2-3: **Enter range to copy TO: A:A3..A:A3** *now you have a range*

You: Tap → →   *to paint the range*

1-2-3: **Enter range to copy TO: A:A3..A:C3**

You: Tap ⟵

Result: The following appears:

	A	B	C
1	3	1	7
2	2	5	2
3	=======	=======	=======

Example 2:   Copy a formula in one cell across several cells.

You: Create the following worksheet:

	A	B	C
1	3	1	7
2	2	5	2
3	=======	=======	=======
4			

You: Highlight cell A4.

You: Type   **@SUM(A1..A2)** ⟵ *to add the numbers in A1 through A2*

1-2-3:

	A	B	C
1	3	1	7
2	2	5	2
3	=======	=======	=======
4	5		

You: Tap **/ C** *Copy*

1-2-3:   **Enter range to copy FROM: A:A4..A:A4**

You: Tap ⟵

1-2-3:   **Enter range to copy TO: A:A4**

You: Tap   **. → →**   *don't forget the period*

1-2-3:   **Enter range to copy TO: A:A4..A:C4**

You: Tap ⟵

Result: The following appears:

	A	B	C
1	3	1	7
2	2	5	2
3	=======	=======	=======
4	5	6	9

The sum of each column of numbers appears in row 4.

If you highlight each of these cells in turn, you will see the following formulas in the upper-left corner:

A4:   @SUM(A1..A2)
B4:   @SUM(B1..B2)
C4:   @SUM(C1..C2)

Example 3:   Copy a formula with absolute cell references across several cells.

You: Create the following worksheet:

	A	B	C
1	3	1	7
2	2	5	2
3	=======	=======	=======
4	5	6	9
5			
6			

You: Highlight cell A6.

You: Type +A4/@SUM($A$4..$C$4) ↵

This formula divides each number in the fourth row by the sum of all the numbers in the fourth row, giving the fraction of the total that each number represents.

1-2-3:

	A	B	C
1	3	1	7
2	2	5	2
3	=======	=======	=======
4	5	6	9
5			
6	Ø.25		

You: Type **/ C** *Copy*

Tap ↵

Tap **.** → → *don't forget the period*

Tap ↵

Result: The following appears:

	A	B	C
1	3	1	7
2	2	5	2
3	=======	=======	=======
4	5	6	9
5			
6	Ø.25	Ø.3	Ø.45

The ratio of each total appears in row 6. You can format row 6 as percent (to show the percent of the total for each column) by typing **/ R F P 2** ↵ **A6..C6** ↵

If you highlight each cell in turn you will see the following formulas in the upper-left corner of the screen:

A6:	+A4/@SUM($A$4..$C$4)
B6:	+B4/@SUM($A$4..$C$4)
C6:	+C4/@SUM($A$4..$C$4)

Note that while the numerator changed from A4 to B4 to C4, the denominator, @SUM($A$4..$C$4), remained the same.

Example 4: Copy a list of names, writing them horizontally on row 8.

You: Enter the following list of names:

	A
1	JONES
2	SMITH
3	ZAK
4	ABDILL
5	McCLURE

You: Tap the **Home** key   *to highlight the first name*

Type **/ R T ↓ ↓ ↓ ↓ ↩ A8 ↩**   *Range Transpose*

Result: The following appears:

	A	B	C	D	E
1	JONES				
2	SMITH				
3	ZAK				
4	ABDILL				
5	McCLURE				
6					
7					
8	JONES	SMITH	ZAK	ABDILL	McCLURE

If you wish, erase A1..A5 by typing **/ R E A1..A5 ↩**

Example 5:   Enter a formula and then replace it with its calculated value.

You: Highlight cell A2   and type   **+33+44+55 ↩**
Highlight cell B2   and type   **+11+22 ↩**
Highlight cell C2   and type   **+22+33+55+66+77+88   ↩**

1-2-3:   **A:C2   +22+33+55+66+77+88**

	A	B	C
1			
2	132	33	341

A2..C2 contain formulas that are recalculated each time the worksheet is recalculated. Let's replace these formulas with their calculated value.

You: Highlight cell A2.

Type **/ R V ↩ → → ↩**   *Range Value*

1-2-3:   **A:C2   341**

	A	B	C
1			
2	132	33	341

You: Highlight cells A2, B2, then C2 and look at the top line. The top line shows that each cell now contains a value, not a formula. This is one less formula for 1-2-3 to recalculate.

For just one cell, you could instead tap **F2** (Edit), **F9** (Calc) ↵

Database

Databases are collections of information about employees, clients, equipment, inventory, library books, audio tape collections, expenses, sales history, and so on.

Setting up a Lotus 1-2-3 database has many steps.   An advantage of a 1-2-3 database is that it is on a worksheet and uses the same commands as do 1-2-3 spreadsheets.

A **database** in Lotus 1-2-3 is a rectangular table of information in columns and rows, such as the following:

	A	B	C	D	E	F	G
1			EMPLOYEE DATA BASE				
2							
3	NAME	STREET	CITY	ST	ZIP	PHONE	SALARY
4	Smith, Jane	44 Park	New York	NY	10022	212-222-1234	200.55
5	Rosa, Joe	117 Jay	Brooklyn	NY	11217	718-444-3333	355.85
6	Ward, Sue	21 Main	Stamford	CT	06926	203-555-1234	390.25
7		*etc*					

Each *column* of information is called a **field** (for example, the STREET field). A column must contain all values or all label information. Do not mix numbers and labels. In this example, columns A—F contain all label information. Column G contains only numbers starting in row 4 down.

Each *row* of information is called a **record** (Row 4 contains Jane Smith's record).

Row 3, the top row of the database, contains **field names** (for example, NAME, STREET, CITY, etc.).

With 1-2-3 Release 3, databases can be relational, that is, you can create two databases and relate them on a common field. You can also simulate a simple relation with the **@VLOOKUP, @HLOOKUP,** or **@CHOICE** function.

Before creating your database, decide what you want to do with it, that is, what you want from it. For instance:

• SORT listings (*sort* means to put all the rows in order, for example, the phone book in order by last name).

• FIND a row of information (*find* the phone number for SMITH).

- EXTRACT rows of information, such as produce a list of the people living in New York City.

- Compute subtotals or subaverages, and so on (like how many people are in marketing, or what is the average salary of the employees working in NYC).

To sort data records—refer to the section on **Sort**, unless you wish to do other operations. In this case refer to the section on **Database 1—Input Area**, as the database rules are more restrictive than the Sort rules.

To find or extract data—refer to the section on **Database 1—Input Area** or **Database 9—dBASE Input**. Then follow the Overview of Steps in **Database 4—Data Query Find Specified Records**, **Database 5— Data Query Extract Specified Records**, or in **Database 6—Data Query Unique Records Extracted**. An example in the **Multiple Sheets** section illustrates an extract using three sheets.

A quick alternative to find—see **Search**.

To extract information from a dBASE III or III Plus database—refer to the section **Database 9—dBASE Input**.

To compute totals, subtotals, and so on—refer to the section on **Database 1— Input Area**, skipping the Data Query references, then refer to **Database 8—Database Functions**.

       Related: **Multiple Sheets**
                 Sort
                 Search

Database 1—Input Area

In databases, the input area is your database information. In this section, you will create an input area on your worksheet. The input area is used by / **Data Query** commands and in database functions. It is similar to the Data-Range used in the / **Data Sort** command. (Remember, *sorting* means put all the rows in order, whereas *searching* means find specific rows.)

OVERVIEW OF STEPS

- Create an input area (see examples below), or use dBASE (see **Database 9**).
- Create a criteria area (see **Database 2**).
- To extract data and create an output area, see **Database 3,** then **Databases 5 or 6.**
- To find particular row(s) of data, see **Database 4.**
- To delete particular row(s) of data, see **Database 7.**
- To use database functions, see **Database 8.**

DESIGN OF DATABASE

The design of the database is very important. You decide the information for each column of your database. Each column is called a *field*. Worksheets have a physical limitation of 256 columns, which is also the maximum number of fields. However, memory limitations will often considerably restrict the database size. Here are some other considerations.

- dBASE databases may be used as input. (See **Database 9—dBASE Input.**)

- Sometimes you might want to divide a field into two fields. If you have people's names in the database, and you want to search on last names, but you want to display first then last name, put first and last names in separate columns:

	A	B
1	FIRST	LAST
2	Mary	Smith
3	Joe	Rosa

- You may not want to divide a field into two. If you do not need to sort on street names, put street numbers and names in the same column.

  While you can search for a string that is embedded in a longer string, it does require a more complicated condition. You may also consider dividing a field into two columns for search purposes. See **Search** for a quick alternative to find.

	C
1	STREET
2	111 Main
3	20 West Drive

- As your worksheet becomes fragmented into more and more fields, it uses more memory and disk space and also requires more keystrokes to enter information.

- Try to bunch the information toward the upper-left corner of your worksheet.

- With large databases, put your input and output areas on separate sheets (see **Multiple Sheets**).

FIELD NAMES

The first row of the input area contains field names (column names). Avoid using more than one row for field names. No two names may be the same. The second row of the input area is the first row of your information (i.e., the first record). Do not leave blank rows.

DATABASE SIZE

While the maximum capacity of your database is 8,192 rows and 256 columns, the RAM size of your computer will limit your actual database size. One way to determine if you have enough room is to type one line of your database, then copy it down the worksheet however many times your expected number of rows will be. Then check your worksheet status to see how much space is left (type / **W S**).

Related: **Database**
          Database 9—dBASE Input
          Sort

Example 1:   Set up an input area for an address database with Name, Street, City, State, Zip, Phone, and Salary columns. Note that until you make a criteria area and issue a Data Query command or use a database function, the input area does nothing for you.

You: Highlight cell C1.

Type **EMPLOYEE DATA BASE** ←⌐

Enter field names

You: Highlight cell A3.

Type	**NAME**	Tap →	
Type	**STREET**	Tap →	
Type	**CITY**	Tap →	
Type	**ST**	Tap →	*abbreviation for STATE*
Type	**^ZIP**	Tap →	*the ^ is for centering*
Type	**^PHONE**	Tap →	
Type	**"SALARY**	Tap ←⌐	*the " is for right alignment*

Set the column widths

You: Highlight cell A4.
Type **/ W C S 13** ←⌐ *Worksheet Column Set-Width to 13*

You: Highlight cell B4.   Type **/ W C S 15** ←⌐
        Highlight cell C4.   Type **/ W C S 14** ←⌐
        Highlight cell D4.   Type **/ W C S 3** ←⌐
        Highlight cell E4.   Type **/ W C S 6** ←⌐
        Highlight cell F4.   Type **/ W C S 12** ←⌐

1-2-3:

	A	B	C	D	E	F	G
1			EMPLOYEE DATA BASE				
2							
3	NAME	STREET	CITY	ST	ZIP	PHONE	SALARY

Format the cells that will contain labels that may begin with numbers

You: Highlight cell B4.
      Type **/ R F O L**   *Range Format Other Label*
      Tap the **End** key.
      Tap ↓   *paint column B from row 4 to row 8192*
      Tap ↵

You: Highlight cell E4.
      Type **/ R F O L**
      Tap the **End** key.
      Tap ↓   *paint column E from row 4 to row 8192*
      Tap ↵

You: Highlight cell F4.
      Type **/ R F O L**
      Tap the **End** key.
      Tap ↓   *paint column F from row 4 to row 8192*
      Tap ↵

Enter the rows of data

You: Highlight cell A4.

You: Type **Smith, Jane**   Tap →
      Type **44 Lexington**   Tap →   *the ' is unnecessary*
                                              because column B is
                                              formatted as Other Label.

      Type **New York City**   Tap →
      Type **NY**   Tap →
      Type **10022**   Tap →
      Type **212-222-1234**   Tap →
      Type   **200.55**   Tap ↵   *no apostrophe is used*
                                              because this is a value

1-2-3:

	A	B	C	D	E	F	G
1			EMPLOYEE DATA BASE				
2							
3	NAME	STREET	CITY	ST	ZIP	PHONE	SALARY
4	Smith, Jane	44 Park	New York	NY	10022	212-222-1234	200.55

You: Enter some more employee records (i.e., rows).

Warning: If you did not format columns B, E, and F as **Other Label**, then all entries in these columns need to begin with an apostrophe; otherwise, your future sorts, finds, and extracts won't work.

1-2-3:

	A	B	C	D	E	F	G
1			EMPLOYEE DATA BASE				
2							
3	NAME	STREET	CITY	ST	ZIP	PHONE	SALARY
4	Smith, Jane	44 Park	New York	NY	10022	212-222-1234	200.55
5	Rosa, Joe	117 Jay	Brooklyn	NY	11217	718-444-3333	355.85
6	Ward, Sue	21 Main	Stamford	CT	06926	203-555-1234	390.25
7		*etc*					

You: Save this worksheet.

Example 2: To make life a little easier, give your input area a range name.

You: Highlight cell A3.
Type **/ R N C** *Range Name Create*

1-2-3: **Enter name:**

You: Type **INPUT1** ↵ *you may choose any name for this range*

1-2-3: **Enter name: INPUT1 Enter range:** *some range appears*

You: Tap the **Backspace** key.

1-2-3: **Enter name: INPUT1 Enter range: A:A3**

You: Tap **.** *tap the period to change the single cell A3 into a range*

1-2-3: **Enter name: INPUT1 Enter range: A:A3..A:A3**

You: Tap the **End** key.
Tap ↓
Tap the **End** key.
Tap →

1-2-3:   The entire range of your input area is painted. If your entire input range is not painted, use the arrow keys to paint the rest. *This can happen if some rows contain empty cells.*

You: Tap ↩

Result: You have just named your input area INPUT1

Next Step: Until you issue a Data Query command or use a database function, the input and criteria area don't accomplish anything yet.

You are ready to proceed to the next topic—**Database 2—Criteria Area.**

Database 2—Criteria Area

In databases, the criteria area is where you tell 1-2-3 what it is you are searching for. Setting up the criteria area is the second step in setting up a database. Criteria areas are used in / **Data Query** commands and database functions.

OVERVIEW OF STEPS

- Create an input area (see **Database 1**) or use a dBASE database (see **Database 9**).
- Create a criteria area (see examples below).
- To extract data and create an output area, see **Database 3,** then **Databases 5 or 6**.
- To find particular row(s) of data, see **Database 4**.
- To delete particular row(s) of data, see **Database 7.**
- To use database functions, see **Database 8**.

THE CRITERIA AREA

The first row of the criteria area is field names (column names). Copy the field names in the input area to the criteria area. While it is not necessary to copy all the field names, it is a good practice to start with, especially when first using databases. Type your search criteria into the second row of the criteria area. With Release 3 and up, you may now leave blank rows in your criteria.

Related: **Conditions**

Example 1: Set up a criteria area for the following address database:

	A	B	C	D	E	F	G
1			EMPLOYEE DATA BASE				
2							
3	NAME	STREET	CITY	ST	ZIP	PHONE	SALARY
4	Smith, Jane	44 Park	New York	NY	10022	212-222-1234	200.55
5	Rosa, Joe	117 Jay	Brooklyn	NY	11217	718-444-3333	355.85
6	Ward, Sue	21 Main	Stamford	CT	06926	203-555-1234	390.25
7		etc					

You: Refer to instructions in **Database 1** to create the above input area.

Note: Until you issue a Data Query command or use a database function, the input and criteria area don't accomplish anything yet.

You: Highlight cell A3 *the first cell containing your input area field names*

You: Type **/ C** *Copy*

1-2-3:   **Enter range to copy FROM: A:A3..A:A3**

You: Tap the **End** key   *the end key followed with an arrow key allows you to quickly paint a range to its end.*

1-2-3:   **END** appears in the lower-right of the screen.

You: Tap →

1-2-3:   **Enter range to copy FROM: A:A3..A:G3**
          Cells A3 to G3 are highlighted.

You: Tap ←┘
          Position the cursor in cell I3.
          Tap ←┘
          Tap the **F5** key.
          Type **I3** ←┘ *to go to cell I3*

1-2-3:

	I	J	K	L	M	N	O
1							
2							
3	NAME	STREET	CITY	ST	ZIP	PHONE	SALARY

          The field names now appear in columns I3 though O3.

You: If you wish, change the column widths as you did in the input area section.

Result: You are ready to enter selection criteria (conditions) into your criteria area, as shown in the following examples.

Example 2: Using the same input and criteria areas as above, enter the condition for selecting people from the state of CT.

You: Type **/ R E I4..O4** ←┘ *Range Erase*

Note: Be sure all cells are empty. Spaces or stray characters in cells will prevent the criteria area from working.

Highlight cell L4.
Type **CT** ←

1-2-3:

	I	J	K	L	M	N	O
3	NAME	STREET	CITY	ST	ZIP	PHONE	SALARY
4				CT			

You: Save your worksheet.

Example 3: Using the same input and criteria areas as above, enter the condition for choosing all employees earning over $250.

You: Type **/ R E I4..O4** ←   *Range Erase—be sure to type the letter O*
Highlight cell O4.
Type **>250** ←

Note: The symbol ">" means "greater than." We are looking for salaries greater than 250. Alternatively, you could have typed **+SALARY>250** ←   The word **ERR** would have appeared in the cell, but that would be all right.

1-2-3:

	I	J	K	L	M	N	O
3	NAME	STREET	CITY	ST	ZIP	PHONE	SALARY
4							>250

Example 4: This example uses an **AND** condition. Using the same input and criteria areas as above, enter the conditions needed to select people from the state of CT *and* whose salaries are greater than $250. A person must be both from CT *and* make over $250 to be selected.

You: Type **/ R E I4..O4** ←   *Range Erase—be sure to type the letter O*

You: Highlight cell L4.
Type **CT** ←
Highlight cell O4.
Type **>250** ←

1-2-3:

	I	J	K	L	M	N	O
3	NAME	STREET	CITY	ST	ZIP	PHONE	SALARY
4				CT			>250

AND conditions are multiple conditions that are in the same row. All such conditions must be met before an input record is selected.

Example 5:   This example uses an **OR** condition. Using the same input area and criteria area as above, enter the conditions to select employees who are in the state of CT *or* NY.

You: Type **/ R E I4..O5** ←┘ *Range Erase*

Highlight cell L4.
Type **CT** ←┘
Highlight cell L5.
Type **NY** ←┘

1-2-3:

	I	J	K	L	M	N	O
3	NAME	STREET	CITY	ST	ZIP	PHONE	SALARY
4				CT			
5				NY			

Notice that the **OR** condition uses several lines.

Example 6:   Enter conditions to choose employees whose last name is Smith.

You: Type **/ R E I4..O5** ←┘ *Range Erase*

Highlight cell I4.
Type **Smith,∗** ←┘

1-2-3:

	I	J	K	L	M	N	O
3	NAME	STREET	CITY	ST	ZIP	PHONE	SALARY
4	Smith, ∗						

Note: The asterisk (∗) indicates that the field may be longer than shown; that is, the name could be Smith, Mary, or Smith, Tom, or anyone else whose last name is Smith.

Note: Lotus 1-2-3 normally looks for an exact match. Therefore, a condition of Smith would *not* find anyone who also had a first name in the NAME column.

Example 7: This example uses a **NOT** condition. Enter a condition to choose employees who are *not* from NY.

You: Type **/ R E I4..O4** ⟵ *Range Erase*

Highlight cell L4.
Type **~NY**⟵

1-2-3:

	I	J	K	L	M	N	O
3	NAME	STREET	CITY	ST	ZIP	PHONE	SALARY
4				NY			

The tilde (~) in front of NY means *not* NY

Example 8: To make life easier, give your criteria area a range name.

You: Type **/ R N C** *Range Name Create*

Type **CRIT1** ⟵ *name of the range can be any name*

Type **I3..O8** ⟵ *this permits your criteria to expand to five rows (rows 4 through 8, with field names in row 3).*

Result: You have just named your criteria range CRIT1

Next Step: You are ready to proceed to one of the following topics:

Database 3—Output Area
Database 4—Data Query; Find Specified Records
Database 7—Data Query; Delete Specified Records
Database 8—Database Functions

Database 3—Output Area

If you plan to extract data, you need an output area for the extracted data.

The output area is used with the / **Data Query Extract,** / **Data Query Unique,** and / **Data Query Modify** commands. It is where 1-2-3 puts the information that it extracts from the input area.

OVERVIEW OF STEPS

- Create an input area (see **Database 1**) or use a dBASE database (see **Database 9**).
- Create a criteria area (see **Database 2**).
- Create an output area (see examples below).
- Optionally, create a list of the input area (see **Database 5**).
- Optionally, create a list with no duplicate records (see **Database 6**).

The first row of the output area contains the field names copied from the input area. Do not use more than one row for the field names. No two names may be the same. The second row of the output area will contain the first row of your extracted output.

When you specify an output area of just one row, 1-2-3 extends the output area to the bottom row (row 8,192) of the worksheet. Therefore, do not put any information below the output area, because 1-2-3 clears out the entire output area before putting the newly extracted data there.

Example 1: Set up an output area for the following input area (database):

	A	B	C	D	E	F	G
1			EMPLOYEE DATA BASE				
2							
3	NAME	STREET	CITY	ST	ZIP	PHONE	SALARY
4	Smith, Jane	44 Park	New York	NY	10022	212-222-1234	200.55
5	Rosa, Joe	117 Jay	Brooklyn	NY	11217	718-444-3333	355.85
6	Ward, Sue	21 Main	Stamford	CT	06926	203-555-1234	390.25
7		etc					

You: Refer to instructions in **Database 1** to create the above input area.

You: Highlight cell A3 *the beginning of your input area*
Type / **C** *Copy*

Tap the **End** key.

Note: Tapping the End key then an arrow key allows you to paint a range quickly, provided there are no empty cells in the way.

1-2-3:   **END** appears in the lower-right of the screen.

You: Type →

1-2-3:   **Enter range to copy FROM: A:A3..A:G3**   *Cells A3 to G3 are highlighted.*

You: Tap ←⏎
Highlight cell I9.
Tap ←⏎   *The field names are copied*

Tap the **F5** key   *the GoTo key*
Type **I9** ←⏎   *go to the output area*

1-2-3:

	I	J	K	L	M	N	O
9	NAME	STREET	CITY	ST	ZIP	PHONE	SALARY

The field names appear in columns I9 though O9. This is the first row of your output area.

Example 2:   To make life easier, give your criteria area a range name.

You: Type **/ R N C**   *Range Name Create*
Type **OUT1** ←⏎   *the name of the range can be any name*
Type **I9..O9** ←⏎   *the output area*

Result: You have just named your output area OUT1

Example 3:   Given the following input area, set up an output area to hold two columns: employee names and phone numbers.

	A	B	C	D	E	F	G
1			EMPLOYEE DATA BASE				
2							
3	NAME	STREET	CITY	ST	ZIP	PHONE	SALARY
4	Smith, Jane	44 Park	New York	NY	10022	212-222-1234	200.55
5	Rosa, Joe	117 Jay	Brooklyn	NY	11217	718-444-3333	355.85
6	Ward, Sue	21 Main	Stamford	CT	06926	203-555-1234	390.25
7		*etc*					

You: Refer to instructions in **Database 1** to create this input area.

You: Highlight cell A3.
Type / C ↩   *Copy from cell A3*
Highlight cell Q1   *the beginning of the output area*
Tap ↩   *a field name has been copied to the output area*

Highlight cell F3.
Type / C ↩   *Copy*
Highlight cell R1   *the second column of the output area*
Tap ↩   *another field name has been copied to the output area*

Tap the **F5** key   *the GoTo key*
Type **Q1** ↩   *to go to the output area*

Type / **W C S 13** ↩   *Worksheet Column Set-Width to 13*

Tap →   *to highlight cell R1*

Type / **W C S 12** ↩   *Worksheet Column Set-Width to 12*

1-2-3:

	Q	R
1	NAME	PHONE

You: Save your worksheet.

Result: You now have another output area whose range is Q1..R1.

Next Step: You are ready to proceed to one of the following topics:

Database 4—Data Query; Extract Specified Records
Database 7—Data Query; Unique Records Extracted

Database 4—Data Query
Find Specified Records

Command: / **Data Query Find**

Note: / **Data Query Find** provides an interactive way to view specific rows in a database. Use / **Data Query Extract** or **Unique** if you wish to sort or print these records. A quick alternative to Find is described in the section on **Search.**

BEFORE STARTING

- Create an input area (see **Database 1** or **Database 9**).
- Create a criteria area (see **Database 2**).

OVERVIEW OF STEPS

- Start the / **Data Query** command.
- Identify the input and criteria areas.
- Start the **Find** option.
- Find the data, using ↓ and ↑ to highlight records matching your search criteria.
- Tap **F7** to quit and return to **READY** mode.

Example: View the rows for the state of CT in the following input area:

	A	B	C	D	E	F	G
1			EMPLOYEE DATA BASE				
2							
3	NAME	STREET	CITY	ST	ZIP	PHONE	SALARY
4	Smith, Jane	44 Park	New York	NY	10022	212-222-1234	200.55
5	Burns, Jack	3 High	Redding	CT	06896	203-444-9876	800.85
6	Rosa, Joe	117 Jay	Brooklyn	NY	11217	718-444-3333	355.85
7	Ward, Sue	21 Main	Stamford	CT	06926	203-555-1234	390.25
8	Ward, Tom	21 Main	Stamford	CT	06926	203-555-1234	290.95
9	Hankins, Ann	55 First	New York	NY	10003	212-234-8190	650.12
10	etc.						

You: Refer to instructions in **Database 1** to create the above input area.

	I	J	K	L	M	N	O
1							
2							
3	NAME	STREET	CITY	ST		ZIP	PHONE	SALARY
4				CT				

You: Refer to instructions in **Database 2** to create the above criteria area.

Start the Data Query command

You: Type **/ D Q**   *Data Query*

Identify the input and criteria areas (choose one of these three methods)

Tip: 1-2-3 remembers the last specified input, criteria and output areas, so you do not have to identify them again to 1-2-3 unless you want different ones or the **/ Data Query Reset** command was issued.

You: Type **I A3..G9** ↵   *or type* **I INPUT1** ↵ *if you named this range*

Type **C I3..O8** ↵   *or type* **C CRIT1** ↵ *if you named this range*

Or, if you wish to identify these two areas by "painting," do the following instead:

Type **I** *Input*

Tap the **Backspace** key.

Highlight cell A3.

Tap **.**

Tap the **End** key.   Tap →

Tap the **End** key.   Tap ↓ ↵

Type **C** *Criteria*

Tap the **Backspace** key.

Highlight cell I3.

Tap **.**

Tap the **End** key.   Tap → ↓ ↓ ↓ ↓ ↓ ↵

Check that your two areas are correct

>   **You:** Type **I** *Input*
>
>   *1-2-3:* Your input area should appear completely highlighted.
>
>   **You:** Tap the period four times to see all four corners. If the painted range isn't correct, use the arrow keys to correct it.
>
>   Tap ←┘
>
>   Type **C** *for criteria*
>
>   *1-2-3:* Your criteria area appears completely highlighted. If your painted range isn't correct, use the arrow keys to correct it.
>
>   **You:** Tap ←┘

Start find

>   **You:** Type **F** *Find*
>
>   *1-2-3:* **FIND** appears in the upper-right corner.

View each found record

>   **You:** Tap ↓ repeatedly to highlight each found record. To go up, tap ↑
>
>   When there are no more matches, then ↓ or ↑ will cause a beep.
>
>   *1-2-3:* Different rows are highlighted, one at a time, that meet the criteria specifications.
>
>   **You:** If desired, tap → and ← arrows for different columns.
>
>   *1-2-3:* The cursor moves to different fields on the highlighted row.
>
>   **You:** If desired, change the information where the cursor is by typing in new information, or tap the **F2** key to edit the field. When you are finished, tap ←┘ to complete the change.

Quit Find

You: Tap **F7** *to terminate Find*

1-2-3:   **READY** appears in the upper-right corner.

Tips: The next time you do a find, begin with "Start the Data Query command" then continue with the "Check that your two areas are correct" step.

In **READY** mode, you may change the search criteria, then tap the **F7** key to repeat the last / **Data Query** command issued.

Database 5—Data Query
Extract Specified Records

Command: / **Data Query Extract**

Note: **Data Query Extract** is used to copy specified rows from the input to an output area that can then be sorted and printed, and so on.

BEFORE STARTING
- Create an input area (see **Database 1** or **Database 9**).
- Create a criteria area (see **Database 2**).
- Create an output area (see **Database 3**).

OVERVIEW OF STEPS
- Start the / **Data Query** command.
- Identify the input, criteria, and output areas.
- Start the **Extract** option to extract data.
- Look at the output area to see the extracted records.
- Quit to **READY** mode.

Example: Extract the rows for the state of CT from the following:

	A	B	C	D	E	F	G
1			EMPLOYEE DATA BASE				
2							
3	NAME	STREET	CITY	ST	ZIP	PHONE	SALARY
4	Smith, Jane	44 Park	New York	NY	10022	212-222-1234	200.55
5	Burns, Jack	3 High	Redding	CT	06896	203-444-9876	800.85
6	Rosa, Joe	117 Jay	Brooklyn	NY	11217	718-444-3333	355.85
7	Ward, Sue	21 Main	Stamford	CT	06926	203-555-1234	390.25
8	Ward, Tom	21 Main	Stamford	CT	06926	203-555-1234	290.95
9	Hankins, Ann	55 First	New York	NY	10003	212-234-8190	650.12
10	etc.						

You: Refer to instructions in **Database 1** to create the above input area.

	I	J	K	L	M	N	O
1							
2							
3	NAME	STREET	CITY	ST	ZIP	PHONE	SALARY
4				CT			

You: Refer to instructions in **Database 2** to create the above criteria area.

	I	J	K	L	M	N	O
9	NAME	STREET	CITY	ST	ZIP	PHONE	SALARY

You: Refer to instructions in **Database 3** to create the above output area.

Start the Data Query command

> **You:**   Type **/ D Q**   *Data Query*

Identify the input, criteria, and output areas

> **You:**   Type   **I A3..G9** ←┘   *or type* **I INPUT1** ←┘ *if*
> *you named this range*

> Type   **C I3..O4** ←┘   *or type* **C CRIT1** ←┘ *if*
> *you named this range*

> Type   **O I9..O9** ←┘   *or type* **O OUT1** ←┘ *if*
> *you named this range*

> *Or, if you wish to identify these three areas by painting them, do the following instead:*

> Type **I** *Input*
> Tap the **Backspace** key.
> Highlight cell A3.
> Tap **.**
> Tap the **End** key.   Tap →
> Tap the **End** key.   Tap ↓ ←┘

> Type **C** *criteria*
> Tap the **Backspace** key.
> Highlight cell I3.
> Tap **.**
> Tap the **End** key.   Tap → ↓ ←┘

> Type **O** *Output*
> Tap the **Backspace** key.

Highlight cell I9.

Tap .

Tap the **End** key.   Tap → ←⏎

Check that your three areas are correct

You: Type **I** *Input*

1-2-3: Your input area should appear completely highlighted.

You: Tap the period four times to see all four corners. If the painted range isn't correct, use the arrow keys to correct it.

Tap ←⏎

Type **C**   *criteria*

1-2-3: Your criteria area appears completely highlighted. Use the arrow keys to correct the range, if necessary.

You: Tap ←⏎

Type **O** *Output*

1-2-3: Your output area appears completely highlighted. Only one row should be highlighted. If not, use the arrow keys to paint the correct range.

You: Tap ←⏎

Extract desired rows and quit the Data command

You: Type **E Q** *Extract Quit*

1-2-3: **READY** appears in the upper-right corner.

Look at the output area

You: Tap the **F5** key *the GoTo key*

You: Type **O9** ←⏎ *that is, letter O, number 9*

1-2-3: Your output area appears with the extracted records. You may wish to format the values and widen the columns then sort and print these records.

Tips: The next time you want to extract data, start with "Start the Data Query command" then continue with the "Check that your three areas are correct" step.

Use the **F7** key to repeat the last / **Data Query** command that was issued.

Database 6—Data Query
Unique Records Extracted

Command: / **Data Query Unique**

Note: **Data Query Unique** is used to extract nonduplicate rows from a database. **Data Query Unique** is the same as **Data Query Extract**, except that **Data Query Unique** does not extract any completely duplicated rows (i.e., rows in which every field in the output area is identical to those fields in another output row).

BEFORE STARTING

- Create an input area (see **Database 1** or **Database 9**).
- Create a criteria area (see **Database 2**).
- Create an output area (see **Database 3**).

OVERVIEW OF STEPS

- Start the / **Data Query** command.
- Identify the input, criteria, and output areas.
- Start the **Unique** option to uniquely extract data.
- Look at the output area to see the extracted records.
- Quit to **READY** mode.

Example: Make a list of all the states in the following database without having any state appear twice in the list.

	A	B	C	D	E	F	G
1			EMPLOYEE DATA BASE				
2							
3	NAME	STREET	CITY	ST	ZIP	PHONE	SALARY
4	Smith, Jane	44 Park	New York	NY	10022	212-222-1234	200.55
5	Burns, Jack	3 High	Redding	CT	06896	203-444-9876	800.85
6	Rosa, Joe	117 Jay	Brooklyn	NY	11217	718-444-3333	355.85
7	Ward, Sue	21 Main	Stamford	CT	06926	203-555-1234	390.25
8	Ward, Tom	21 Main	Stamford	CT	06926	203-555-1234	290.95
9	Hankins, Ann	55 First	New York	NY	10003	212-234-8190	650.12
10	etc.						

You: Refer to instructions in **Database 1** to create the above input area.

Create the criteria area

Note: This is a special criteria area because it has *no* criteria. This is intentional, so that 1-2-3 will select all the records in the input area.

You: Type   / C A3..G3 ↵   *to copy the input field names*

Type   I3..O3 ↵   *to select the criteria area*

Type   / R E I4..O8 ↵   *Range Erase rows 4 through 8*

Tap the **F5** key.   Type **I3** ↵ *to go to cell I3*

1-2-3:

	I	J	K	L	M	N	O
3	NAME	STREET	CITY	ST	ZIP	PHONE	SALARY
4							
5							
6							
7							
8							

Create the output area

Note: This is a special output area because it has only one column. This is intentional, so that 1-2-3 will only extract state names, and no other information.

You: Type / C D3 ↵ L9 ↵ *to copy the word ST to the output area*

Tap the **F5** key   *the GoTo key*
Type **L9** ↵ *to go to cell L9*

1-2-3:

	L
9	ST

We only want one column—states—in the output area.

Start the Data Query command

You: Type / **D Q** *Data Query*

Identify the input, criteria, and output areas

You: Type **I A3..G9** ↵   *or* Type **I INPUT1** ↵
if you named this range

Type **C   I3..O4** ↵

Type **O   L9..L9** ↵

Check that your three areas are correct

You: Type **I** *for Input*

1-2-3: Your input area should appear completely highlighted.

You: Tap the period four times to see all four corners. If the painted range isn't correct, use the arrow keys to correct it.

Tap ↵

Type **C** *Criteria*

1-2-3: Your criteria area appears, totally highlighted. Use the arrow keys to correct the range, if necessary.

You: Tap ↵

Type **O** *Output*

1-2-3: Only cell L9 should be highlighted.

You: Tap ↵

Extract unique rows of data and quit

You: Type **U Q** *Unique Quit*

1-2-3: **READY** appears in the upper-right corner.

Look at the output area

> **You:**   Tap the **F5** key   *the GoTo key*
>
> Type **L9** ↵   *to go to cell L9*

Result:

	L
9	ST
10	NY
11	CT

a list of nonduplicated states.

You may sort and print these records or use them with Database functions.

Database 7—Data Query
Delete Specified Records

Command: **/ Data Query Delete**

Note: **Data Query Delete** is used to delete specified rows of data from an existing database. Because you are deleting rows that you don't even see on the screen, we recommend taking the following two precautions to prevent any problems.

1. Save your worksheet.
2. Use **/ Data Query Find** to see which rows will be deleted.

BEFORE STARTING

- Create an input area (see **Database 1**).
- Create a criteria area (see **Database 2**).
- Save your worksheet.

OVERVIEW OF STEPS

- Start the **/ Data Query** command.
- Identify the input and criteria areas.
- Issue **Find** command to check the criteria.
- Tap ↓ and ↑ to highlight the found rows in the input area.
- Issue the Delete command.
- Quit to **READY** mode.

Related: **Delete a Row**

Example: Delete the rows for the state of CT from the following input:

	A	B	C	D	E	F	G
1			EMPLOYEE DATA BASE				
2							
3	NAME	STREET	CITY	ST	ZIP	PHONE	SALARY
4	Smith, Jane	44 Park	New York	NY	10022	212-222-1234	200.55
5	Burns, Jack	3 High	Redding	CT	06896	203-444-9876	800.85
6	Rosa, Joe	117 Jay	Brooklyn	NY	11217	718-444-3333	355.85
7	Ward, Sue	21 Main	Stamford	CT	06926	203-555-1234	390.25
8	Ward, Tom	21 Main	Stamford	CT	06926	203-555-1234	290.95
9	Hankins, Ann	55 First	New York	NY	10003	212-234-8190	650.12
10	etc.						

You: Refer to instructions in **Database 1** to create the above input area.

	I	J	K	L	M	N	O
3	NAME	STREET	CITY	ST	ZIP	PHONE	SALARY
4				CT			

You: Refer to instructions in **Database 2** to create the above criteria area.

Remember to put **CT** in L4.

Save your worksheet

You: Type   **/ F S XXXXXXX** ←┘   *File Save*
This change XXXXX to your desired file name.

If **Cancel Replace Backup** appears, tap **R** to replace the file on disk. If you don't want to replace it, tap **C** *Cancel* or **B** *Backup*.

Start the Data Query command

You: Type   **/ D Q**   *Data Query*

Identify the input and Criteria areas

You: Type   **I A3..G9** ←┘   *or*   Type   **I INPUT1** ←┘
                                                    if you named this range

Type   **C I3..O4** ←┘   *or*   Type   **C CRIT1** ←┘
                                                if you named this range

Or, if you wish to identify these two areas by painting them, do the following instead:

Type **I** *Input*
Tap the **Backspace** key.
Highlight cell A3.
Tap .
Tap the **End** key.   Tap →
Tap the **End** key.   Tap ↓ ←┘

Type **C** *criteria*
Tap the **Backspace** key.
Highlight cell I3.
Tap .
Tap the **End** key.   Tap → ↓ ←┘

Check that your two areas are correct

You: Type **I** *Input*

1-2-3:   Your input area should appear completely highlighted.

You: Tap the period four times to see all four corners. If the painted range isn't correct, use the arrow keys to correct it.

Tap ←┘

Type **C** *Criteria*

1-2-3:   Your criteria area appears completely highlighted. Use the arrow keys to correct the range, if necessary.

You: Tap ←┘

Use find to view what you intend to delete

You: Type **F** *Find*

1-2-3:   **FIND** appears in the upper-right corner.

You: Tap ↓ repeatedly to highlight each found record.

> To go up, tap ↑

1-2-3:   The CT rows are highlighted one at a time.

You: If any other rows are highlighted, tap **Esc** until **READY** appears and then fix your criteria area.

Warning: Every row you can highlight will be deleted in the next step. If this isn't what you want, tap **Esc** until **READY** appears and *do not continue.*

You: Tap ←┘ *to terminate Find*

1-2-3:   **MENU** appears in the upper-right corner.

Delete the records you found

You: Tap **D** *Delete*

1-2-3:   **Cancel   Delete**

Warning: Are you sure? If so, continue.

You: Tap **D** *Delete again*

1-2-3:

	A	B	C	D	E	F	G
1			EMPLOYEE DATA BASE				
2							
3	NAME	STREET	CITY	ST	ZIP	PHONE	SALARY
4	Smith, Jane	44 Park	New York	NY	10022	212-222-1234	200.55
5	Rosa, Joe	117 Jay	Brooklyn	NY	11217	718-444-3333	355.85
6	Hankins, Ann	55 First	New York	NY	10003	212-234-8190	650.12
7		etc.					

The CT records are deleted, and the input area is consolidated. Of the original six records, only these three non-CT records remain.

Quit the data query mode

You: Tap **Q** *Quit*

Database 8—Database Functions

@Functions:
@DAVG(*input,offset,criteria*)	calculate averages
@DCOUNT(*input,offset,criteria*)	counts nonblank cells
@DSUM(*input,offset,criteria*)	calculates totals
@DMAX(*input,offset,criteria*)	finds the largest value
@DMIN(*input,offset,criteria*)	finds the smallest value
@DVAR(*input,offset,criteria*)	population variance
@DSTD(*input,offset,criteria*)	standard deviation

Note: Database functions are very useful when you need statistics about your database. They answer questions such as "How many clients live in NYC?" or "What is the average salary of the employees in the Marketing Division?"

BEFORE STARTING

- Create an input area (see **Database 1** or **Database 9**).
- Create a criteria area (see **Database 2**).

Example: Calculate total and average salary for each state in the following database.

	A	B	C	D
1	INPUT AREA			
2				
3		NAME	STATE	SALARY
4		Zak, Jane	NY	$60,000
5		Smith, Tom	AL	$20,000
6		Watson, Ed	NY	$85,000
7		Harris, Sue	AL	$40,000
8		Hankins, Pat	NY	$90,000

Create an input area for your database

You: Type in the above database into an empty worksheet. Use the following hints:

Set the column widths

You: Highlight cell A1 and type / W C S 5 ↵ *to set the column width to 5*
Highlight cell B1 and type / W C S 15 ↵
Highlight cell C1 and type / W C S 6 ↵
Highlight cell D1 and type / W C S 12 ↵
Highlight cell E1 and type / W C S 2 ↵

Center the states

You: Highlight cell C3.
Type / R L C ↓↓↓↓↓ ↵   *to center states in column C using Range Label Center*

Format the salary

You: Highlight cell D4.
Type / R F C Ø ↵ ↓↓↓↓ ↵   *to format salaries as currency with no decimal places, using Range Format Currency*

Create a criteria area for your database

You: Type the following into rows 10 through 13:

	A	B	C	D
10	CRITERION AREA			
11				
12		STATE		STATE
13		NY		AL

Note: These are the two criteria areas—**B12..B13** and **C12..C13**—that we will use to select people from NY or AL.

Center the states

You: Highlight cell B12.
Type / R L C ↓ → ↵ *to center the information in B12 ..C13*

Create an area for your database functions

Set the column widths

You: Highlight cell F3   *or any cell in column F*
Type **/ W C S 14** ← *to widen column F to 14*

Enter column and row headings

You: Highlight cell G3.   Type **^NY** ← *The ^ means center*
Highlight cell H3.   Type **^AL** ←
Highlight cell F5.   Type **Average salary** ←
Highlight cell F7.   Type **Total salary** ←

1-2-3:

	F	G	H
3		NY	AL
4			
5	Average salary		
6			
7	Total Salary		

Format the cells for the average and total salaries

You: Highlight cell G5.
Type **/ R F C Ø** ←↓↓→ ← *Range Format Currency Ø decimals*

Enter your formulas

You: Highlight cell G5.
Type **@DAVG(B3..D8,"SALARY",B12..B13)** ←

Note: This function calculates the average salary for all the people in NY state. The result—$78,333—is the average of $60,000, $85,000, and $90,000.

This function has three items within the parentheses, separated by commas. Items in a function are called *arguments*.

The **first argument, B3..D8,** is our input area, including the column headings (field names).

The **second argument, "SALARY",** is the column we want to average.

The **third argument, B12..B13,** is our criteria area, including the column headings. It means we will search for people in NY.

1-2-3:

	F	G	H
3		NY	AL
4			
5	Average salary	$78,333	
6			
7	Total Salary		

You: Highlight cell H5.
Type **@DAVG(B3..D8,"SALARY",C12..C13)** ↵

Note: This formula calculates average salary for people in the state AL because our third argument, **C12..C13**, specifies the state of AL.

1-2-3:

	F	G	H
3		NY	AL
4			
5	Average salary	$78,333	$30,000
6			
7	Total Salary		

$30,000 is the average of $20,000 and $40,000—the salaries for the two people in the state of AL.

You: Highlight cell G7.
Type **@DSUM($B$3..$D$8,"SALARY",B12..B13)** ↵

Note: The $ in front of the column letter and row number specify absolute cell addresses. To be able to copy this formula, we specify absolute cell addresses for the input area—**B3..D8**. If the input area was not an absolute cell reference, it would change to **C3..E8** when the formula was copied to cell H7. To prevent the input area range from changing when we copy it, we made it absolute.

1-2-3:

	F	G	H
3		NY	AL
4			
5	Average salary	$78,333	$30,000
6			
7	Total Salary	$235,000	

You: Type **/ C** ↵ → ↵ *to copy the formula to cell H7*
Tap **Home**

1-2-3:

	A	B	C	D	E	F	G	H
1	INPUT AREA							
2								
3		NAME	STATE	SALARY			NY	AL
4		Zak, Jane	NY	$60,000				
5		Smith, Tom	AL	$20,000		Average salary	$78,333	$30,000
6		Watson, Ed	NY	$85,000				
7		Harris, Sue	AL	$40,000		Total Salary	$235,000	$60,000
8		Hankins, Pat	NY	$90,000				
9								
10	CRITERION AREA							
11								
12		STATE		STATE				
13		NY		AL				

Result: The average and total salaries have been calculated for the people in NY and AL states.

Database 9—dBASE Input

In 1-2-3 Release 3, when you are extracting data, you may use a dBASE III or III Plus database as your database, instead of the input area described in **Database 1**. In this section, we will create a simple dBASE database, extract rows of data from it, and put the extracted rows into an output area.

OVERVIEW OF STEPS

- Create a dBASE database.
- Create a criteria area (see **Database 2**).
- Create an output area (see **Database 3**).
- Establish an external connection to your dBASE file.
- Identify your input, criteria, and output areas.
- Extract (or Uniquely extract) data.

DATABASE SIZE

While 1-2-3 databases can theoretically be as large as 8,192 rows and 256 columns, the RAM size of your computer is usually the limiting factor for your actual database size. If your disk were large enough, dBASE databases could contain several billion characters (a 120 megabyte disk only holds 120 million characters).

Example: Create a dBASE database with Name, Salary, and Dept columns, then, using Data Extract, copy records from the MT department into our current worksheet.

You: Save your current worksheet. Reminder: **/ F S** *File Save etc.*

Type **/ Q Y** *Quit Yes to quit to the operating system*

1-2-3: The operating system prompt or a menu should appear.

Create a small dBASE database

You: Start dBASE as usual. One way may be the following:

Type **CD \DBASE** ↵ *to move to the dBASE directory*
Type **DBASE** ↵

Tap **Esc** several times until the dBASE prompt (a small dot) appears in the lower-left corner.

Type **SET CONFIRM ON** ←⏎ *this makes life easier*

Type **SET BELL OFF** ←⏎ *so that other people won't think you are constantly making mistakes*

Type **CREATE EMPLOYEE** ←⏎ *to create a database*

dBASE: A menu appears.

You: Type **NAME** ←⏎ **C 22** ←⏎ *these are the field names*
Type **SALARY** ←⏎ **N 6** ←⏎ **2** ←⏎
Type **DEPT** ←⏎ **C 2** ←⏎

Hold **Ctrl** and tap the **End** key

dBASE: **Do you want to input data (Y or N)**

You: Type **Y**   *do not tap Enter*

Type **SMITH** ←⏎ **300** ←⏎ **MX** ←⏎ *these are data records*
Type **JONES** ←⏎ **200** ←⏎ **QQ** ←⏎
Type **ADAMS** ←⏎ **400** ←⏎ **MT** ←⏎
Type **MEYERS** ←⏎ **100** ←⏎ **AB** ←⏎
Type **DAVIS** ←⏎ **400** ←⏎ **MT** ←⏎

Hold **Ctrl** and tap the **End** key   *to end the append mode*

Type **LIST** ←⏎ *to list your records*

dBASE:

NAME	SALARY	DEPT
SMITH	300.00	MX
JONES	200.00	QQ
ADAMS	400.00	MT
MEYERS	100.00	AB
DAVIS	300.00	MT

You: Type **QUIT** ←⏎ *to quit dBASE*

You: Start 1-2-3 as you usually do.

Establish an external connection to your dBASE database

You: Type **/ D E U**   *Data External Use*

1-2-3:   A list of database drivers appears, including **SAMPLE**

You: Highlight the word **SAMPLE** (or other driver name, if the person who installed your 1-2-3 suggests another driver name).

Tap ↵

1-2-3:   **Enter name of table to use: Sample**

You: Type **C:\DBASE** ↵   *or type the appropriate drive and directory where the dBASE databases are located. You may need to ask the person who installed dBASE.*

Tap the **F3** key   *the name key*

1-2-3:   A list of database files appears, including **EMPLOYEE**

You: Highlight the word **EMPLOYEE**
Tap ↵
Type **Q**   *to quit the Data command*

1-2-3:   **READY** appears in the upper-right corner.

List the fields in your database

You: Highlight cell B1 on your empty worksheet
Type **/ D E L F**   *Data External List Fields*
Highlight the word **EMPLOYEE**
Tap ↵ ↵   *yes, twice—I don't know why*
Type **Q**   *to quit the Data command*

1-2-3:

	A	B	C	D	E	F	G
1		NAME	Character	22	NA	NA	NA
2		SALARY	Numeric	6.2	NA	NA	NA
3		DEPT	Character	2	NA	NA	NA
4							

Column B shows the field names. Column C shows the field types in dBASE. Character means Label (or Text) in 1-2-3. Column D shows the widths and will be useful for setting column widths later on. The **6.2** means that SALARY is 6 positions wide, with 2 of those positions used for decimal places, and one for the decimal point. The largest number, therefore, is 999.99. Ignore all the NAs. You may erase them if you wish.

Create the criteria and output areas

You: Highlight cell B1.

Type **/ R T ↓ ↓ ←⏎ A5 ←⏎**   *Range Trans to copy the vertical list of field names to row 5, rotating the names horizontally*

1-2-3:

	A	B	C	D
1		NAME	Character	22
2		SALARY	Numeric	6.2
3		DEPT	Character	2
4				
5	NAME	SALARY	DEPT	

You: Highlight cell C6.

Type **MT ←⏎**   *This is our criteria condition for selection. Leave this cell blank to bring the entire dBASE database into 1-2-3.*

Type **/ R T B1..B3 ←⏎ A10 ←⏎**   *Range Trans*

1-2-3:

	A	B	C	D
1		NAME	Character	22
2		SALARY	Numeric	6.2
3		DEPT	Character	2
4				
5	NAME	SALARY	DEPT	
6			MT	
7				
8				
9				
10	NAME	SALARY	DEPT	

Extract MT department records from dBASE into 1-2-3

You: Type **/ D O I**   *Data Query Input*
Tap the **F3** key   *the name key*
Highlight the word **EMPLOYEE**   *this is our external input area*
Tap ←┘
Type **C A5..C8** ←┘   *this is our criteria area*
Type **O A10..C10** ←┘   *this is the first line of our output area*
Type **E Q**   *Extract Quit*

1-2-3:

	A	B	C	D
1		NAME	Character	22
2		SALARY	Numeric	6.2
3		DEPT	Character	2
4				
5	NAME	SALARY	DEPT	
6			MT	
7				
8				
9				
10	NAME	SALARY	DEPT	
11	ADAMS	400	MT	
12	DAVIS	400	MT	
13				

Result: 1-2-3 has extracted the MT records from our dBASE database and placed them in row 11 and down.

If nothing appears in row 11 and down, highlight cell C6, type **/ R E** ←┘ to erase that cell, and repeat the instructions from the "Extract MT department records from dBASE into 1-2-3" step.

Data Fill

Command: **/ Data Fill**

Note: **Data Fill** provides a quick way to enter a long series of values into a worksheet—values such as 1, 2, 3, 4, 5, 6, or 1990, 1991, 1992, 1993, and so on. See **Problems and Solutions** in Chapter 3 if you have any difficulty with this command.

Example 1: Number the following list of names:

	A	B
1	Number	Names
2		
3		Burns
4		Edwards
5		Hankins
6		Rosa
7		Smith

You: Create the above worksheet.

Highlight cell A3   *where the numbering is to begin*

Type **/ D F**   *Data Fill*

1-2-3: **Enter Fill range:**   *some cell or range appears*

You: Tap the **Backspace** key

Type **.**   *period*

Tap ↓ ↓ ↓ ↓ until you reach row 7, which has the last name

Tap ↵

1-2-3: **Start:** *some number appears*

You: Type **1** ↵

1-2-3: **Step:** *some number appears*

You: Type **1** ↵

1-2-3:   **Stop:** *some number appears*

You: Type **9999** ←⏎

Result: The following appears:

	A	B
1	Number	Names
2		
3	1	Burns
4	2	Edwards
5	3	Hankins
6	4	Rosa
7	5	Smith

Example 2:   Enter a series of dates across row 10 of a worksheet.

You: Highlight cell A10   *where the date series is to begin*

Type **/ D F**   *Data Fill*

Tap the **Backspace** key.
Type **.**   *period*
Tap → → → → → → → → → → →   *11 times or more*
Tap ←⏎

Type **1/31/91** ←⏎   *this is the beginning date. Alternatively,
you could have typed* **1-JAN-91**

Type **1M** ←⏎   *means one month intervals*

Note: Alternative entries are: 1D for one-day intervals, 2W for two-week intervals, 1Q for quarterly intervals, 1Y for yearly intervals, 5Y for five-year intervals, and so on.

You: Type **12/31/91** ←⏎   *this is the ending date*

1-2-3:   A bunch of funny numbers may appear. Don't worry—be happy.

You: Type **/ W C C A1..L1** ←⏎ **10** ←⏎   *to set column width to 10*
Type **/ R F D 1 A10..L10** ←⏎   *to format a range as a date*

Result: The following appears:

	A	B	C	D	E	F
10	31-Jan-91	28-Feb-91	31-Mar-91	30-Apr-91	31-May-91	30-Jun-91

	G	H	I	J	K	L
10	31-Jul-91	31-Aug-91	30-Sep-91	31-Oct-91	30-Nov-91	31-Dec-91

You now have a series of dates showing the last day of each month, sometimes called month ending dates.

Example 3:   Enter a series of times down column A of a worksheet.

You: Highlight cell A3   *where the time series is to begin*

You: Type **/ D F**   *Data Fill*

Tap the **Backspace** key
Type **.**   *period*
Tap **PgDn**   *highlights the range A3..A23*
Tap ←⏎

Type **8:00** ←⏎   *this is the beginning time*

Type **30MIN** ←⏎ *this means thirty-minute intervals*

Note: Alternative entries are: 1MIN for one-minute intervals, 1S for one-second intervals, 20S for twenty-second intervals, 1H for hourly intervals, and so on.

You: Type **18:00** ←⏎ *this is the ending time of 6 PM in international time*

Type **/ W C S 9** ←⏎ *to set column width to 9*

Type **/ R F D T 2 A3..A23** ←⏎ *to format range as a time*

Result: The following appears:

	A	B
1		
2		
3	8:00 AM	
4	8:30 AM	
5	9:00 AM	
6	9:30 AM	
7	10:00 AM	
8	10:30 AM	
9	11:00 AM	
10	11:30 AM	
11	12:00 PM	
12	12:30 PM	
13	13:00 PM	
14	1:30 PM	
15	2:00 PM	
16	2:30 PM	
17	3:00 PM	
18	3:30 PM	
19	4:00 PM	
20	4:30 PM	
21	5:00 PM	
22	5:30 PM	
23	6:00 PM	

You now have a series of times showing each half hour of a typical working day (consultants do not know of such days).

Print this worksheet and use it as an hourly schedule of events.

Dates

@Functions: **@NOW, @TODAY, @DATE, @YEAR, @MONTH, @DAY, @DATEVALUE, @D360**

Note: In the following examples, you will create a series of dates, calculate the number of days between two dates, display the date that is 30 days beyond another date, and so on.

Most dates are stored as values (numbers). These numbers (called *date numbers*) represent the number of days since the turn of the century, so that **1** represents **January 1, 1900**, *the first day past the turn of the century*, **2** represents **January 2, 1900**, *the second day past the turn of the century*, and so on. The number **32021** represents **September 1, 1987**, *the 32,021st day past the turn of the century*. The highest date number is 73050, corresponding to December 31, 2099.

Don't bother remembering these numbers. Just remember that dates are numbers. Only after formatting does a number look like a date.

A date can be stored as a label (text beginning with a label prefix character), but then you can't do any arithmetic with it. However, dates prior to the Twentieth century must be entered as labels.

Release 3 and up have simplified the entering of dates. If what you type looks like a date (for example, 5/7/91 or 30-NOV-92), 1-2-3 assumes it is a date and converts it to its corresponding date number. But, you still have to format it to look like a date.

See Example 1 to correct the date and time in your computer.

Related: **Clock**
Data Fill
Formatting Numbers

OVERVIEW OF THE STEPS

- Enter a date function or value. A date number appears, not a date.
- Format the number as a date using / **Range Format Date**
- If you see asterisks in the cell—*************—widen the column using / **Worksheet Column Set-Width**

SOME COMMON DATE FUNCTIONS

@NOW   Gives today's date and time as a value.

Time is the fraction of the day since midnight and is represented as the decimal part of the **@NOW** value.

On September 1, 1987, at 6 A.M., **@NOW** gave the value 32021.250. 32021 is the number of days since the turn of the century. The decimal .250 represents 6 A.M., or one-quarter of a 24-hour day starting at midnight.

@TODAY   Different releases of 1-2-3 treat this function differently. In Release 3, **@TODAY** gives today's date with no time, so on June 7, 1991, **@TODAY** appears as 33396 before formatting.

@DATE(*yy,mm,dd*) Computes the number of days since the turn of the century for the specified date. **@DATE(91,6,7)** produces the value 33396 .

@YEAR(*number*) This function computes the year, where *number* is the number of days since the turn of the century. **@YEAR(33396)** produces the value 91, representing the year 1991. If today were July 4, 1995, then **@YEAR(@TODAY)** would produce the value 95.

@MONTH(*number*) This function computes the month, where *number* is the number of days since the turn of the century. **@MONTH(33396)** produces the value 6 *for June.* If today were July 4, 1995, then **@MONTH(@TODAY)** would produce the value 7.

@DAY(*number*)   This function computes the day as a value, where *number* is the number of days since the turn of the century. **@DAY(33396)**

computes the value 7 *for the seventh day of the month.* If today were July 4, then **@DAY(@TODAY)** would produce the value 4.

Example 1: Correct the internal date in your computer if it is incorrect.

You: Type **/ S** *System*

Type **DATE**   **7/4/91** ←┘   *to change the date to today's date, assuming it is July 4, 1991*

Type **TIME**   **14:22** ←┘   *to change the time to the current hour:minutes. In this example, 14 : 22 is 2 : 22 P.M.*

Type **EXIT** ←┘ *to return to 1-2-3*

Example 2: Enter the date May 3, 1955 into a worksheet.

You: Highlight cell A2.

Type **5/3/55** ←┘   *format is month/day/year*

Or, type **3-MAY-55** ←┘

Or, type **@DATE(55,5,3)** ←┘   *note that the year is first*

Note: You may type month-slash-day-slash-year, assuming the date is set to this form. Use **/ Worksheet Global Default Other Date** to set the date format to another form.

1-2-3:

	A	B	C
1			
2	20212		

You: Type **/ R F D 1** ←┘   *command Range Format Date 1, where 1 is the first of five choices of date formats*

1-2-3:

	A	B	C
1			
2	* * * * * * *		

You: Type / W C S **10** ↵   *to widen the column to 10*

Result: The following appears:

	A	B	C
1			
2	03-May-55		

Example 3: Enter today's date into a worksheet in such a way that it will change to tomorrow's date tomorrow, and so on.

You: Highlight cell C1.

Type **@TODAY** ↵
or, type **@NOW** ↵

1-2-3:   *line 1:*   **@TODAY** *or* **@NOW**

	A	B	C
1			33396

The number will be different, depending on today's date. **@TODAY** will have no fractional portion in the cell.

You: Type / R F D **1** ↵   *Range Format Date 1st choice*

1-2-3:

	A	B	C
1			* * * * * * *

You: Type / W C S **10** ↵   *to widen the column to 10*

Result: The following appears (assuming today is June 7, 1991:

	A	B	C
1			07-Jun-91

This date only changes when the worksheet is recalculated.

Example 4: Enter today's date into a worksheet in such a way that it will *not* change to tomorrow's date tomorrow.

You: Highlight cell C1.

Type **@TODAY**   *do not tap ←┘ yet*
Tap the **F9** key   *the **Calc** key, converts a formula to a value*
Tap ←┘

1-2-3:   The cell contains just a number, not a formula, look at the upper-left corner of the screen.

line 1:   **A:C1:   33396**

	A	B	C
1			33396

@TODAY produces the current date. This assumes today is June 7, 1991. The actual number shown will depend on today's date.

You: Type **/ R F D 1** ←┘ *Range Format Date 1st choice*

Type **/ W C S 10** ←┘ *to widen the column to 10*

Result: The following appears:

	A	B	C
1			07-Jun-91

Example 5:   Create a series of date headers for a voucher or similar spreadsheet, starting with September 1, 1991.

You: Highlight cell B2.
Type **9/1/91** ←┘

1-2-3:

	A	B	C	D	E	F
1						
2		33482				

You: Tap →   *to highlight cell C1*
Type **+B2+1** ←┘   *this adds one to the 9/1/91 date*

1-2-3:

	A	B	C	D	E	F
1						
2		33482	33483			

You: Type   / C ↵ . → → → ↵   *to copy the formula across*

1-2-3:

	A	B	C	D	E	F
1						
2		33482	33483	33484	33485	33486

You: Highlight cell B2.

Type   **/ R F D 2** → → →   → ↵   *Range Format Date 2nd choice*

Result: The following appears:

	A	B	C	D	E	F
1						
2		01-Sep	02-Sep	03-Sep	04-Sep	05-Sep

Example 6:   Show the day of the week in the cell next to the date.

You: Enter the following lookup table in the designated cells:

	A	B
2 5	0	Saturday
2 6	1	Sunday
2 7	2	Monday
2 8	3	Tuesday
2 9	4	Wednesday
3 0	5	Thrusday
3 1	6	Friday

You: Highlight cell A2.   *or desired cell*

Type   **5/3/55** ↵

1-2-3:

	A	B	C
1			
2	20212		

You: Type   **/ R F D 1** ↵   *Range Format Date*

Type   **/ W C S 10** ↵   *to widen column to remove asterisks*

1-2-3:

	A	B	C
1			
2	03-May-55		

You: Tap →   *to highlight cell B2*

Type the following:

@VLOOKUP(@INT(@MOD(A2,7)),A25..B31,1) ←⏎

Result: The following appears:

	A	B	C
1			
2	03-May-55	Tuesday	

If the computer beeps and goes into **EDIT** mode, make sure the formula is exactly like the one shown here. That is, no spaces anywhere, not even at the beginning or the end. Be sure there are two close parentheses after the number 7.

Example 7:   Calculate a past due date that is 60 days after the invoice date.

You: Create the following worksheet:

	A	B	C	D
1		INV DATE	DUE DATE	MESSAGE

You: Highlight cell B2   and type   **3/15/91** ←⏎
Highlight cell B3   and type   **6/15/91** ←⏎

1-2-3:

	A	B	C	D
1		INV DATE	DUE DATE	MESSAGE
2		33312		
3		33404		

You: Highlight cell C2.

Type **+B2+60** ←⏎   *to add 60 days to the invoice date to calculate the due date*

Type **/ C** ←⏎ **. ↓** ←⏎   *to copy down the column*

1-2-3:

	A	B	C	D
1		INV DATE	DUE DATE	MESSAGE
2		33312	33372	
3		33404	33464	

You: Type   **/ W C C S B1..C1** ←⏎ **10** ←⏎   *Worksheet Column Column-Rnnge Set to 10*

Type   **/ R F D 1 B2..C3** ←⏎   *Range Format Date 1*

Note: There are five different ways dates can be formatted. If these choices are not sufficient, try / **Worksheet Global Default Other International Date** for others.

1-2-3:

	A	B	C	D
1		INV DATE	DUE DATE	MESSAGE
2		15-Mar-91	14-May-91	
3		15-Jun-91	14-Aug-91	

You: Highlight cell D2.

Type **@IF(@NOW<C2,"","**PAST DUE**")** ↵

Helpful hint: After C2: comma, quote, quote, comma, quote, asterisk, asterisk, PAST DUE, asterisk, asterisk, quote, close parenthesis.

Note: Read this formulas as follows: If today is less than (before) the due date, the person still has time to pay, so nothing is displayed (indicated by two quote marks with nothing in between). Otherwise, display the message ****PAST DUE****.

You: Type **/ C** ↵ **.↓** ↵   *to copy formula down the column*

Result: The following appears, assuming today is June 7, 1991:

	A	B	C	D
1		INV DATE	DUE DATE	MESSAGE
2		15-Mar-91	14-May-91	
3		15-Jun-91	14-Aug-91	**PAST DUE **

Since today isn't June 7, 1991, enter some other dates in cells B2 and B3 that will cause the **PAST DUE** message to appear.

If you got the **PAST DUE** message for dates that should be okay, check that the date at the bottom of the screen is today.

Delete a Column

Command: / **Worksheet Delete Column**

Note: When a column is deleted from the worksheet, it is deleted across all 8,192 rows. Any unseen information anywhere in that column is deleted without warning. It is prudent to save your worksheet first.

See **Multiple Sheets** for suggestions on separating information across several sheets. If **GROUP** mode is disabled, then deleting a column only deletes it in the one sheet. If **GROUP** is enabled, deleting a column causes that column to be deleted in all sheets.

Related: **Erase**
Printing—Nonadjacent Columns
Move
Multiple Sheets

Example: Delete column D containing DEPEND.

	A	B	C	D	E
1	ID	NAME	STATE	DEPEND	SALARY
2	1	SMITH	NY	3	200
3	2	JONES	AL	5	300
4	3	ADAMS	CA	4	100

You: Save your current worksheet. Reminder: **/ F S** *File Save* etc.
Create a worksheet similar to the one above.

Highlight any cell in column D
Type **/ W D C** ↵ *Worksheet Delete Column*

Result:

	A	B	C	D
1	ID	NAME	STATE	SALARY
2	1	SMITH	NY	200
3	2	JONES	AL	300
4	3	ADAMS	CA	100

The salary column moved over.

Delete a Row

Command: /   Worksheet Delete Row

Note: When a row is deleted from the worksheet, it is deleted across all 256 columns. Any unseen information anywhere in that row is deleted without warning. It is prudent to save your worksheet first.

See **Multiple Sheets** for suggestions on separating information across several sheets. If **GROUP** mode is disabled, then deleting a row only deletes it in the one sheet. If **GROUP** is enabled, deleting a row causes that row to be deleted in all sheets.

Related: **Erase**
Move
Multiple Sheets

Example 1: Delete row 4, which contains information on ADAMS.

	A	B	C	D	E
1	ID	NAME	STATE	DEPEND	SALARY
2	22	SMITH	NY	3	200
3	45	JONES	AL	5	300
4	88	ADAMS	CA	4	100
5	12	WATSON	NJ	2	200
6	33	HARRIS	CT	1	100

You: Save your current worksheet. Reminder: / F S *File Save* etc.
Create a worksheet similar to the one above.

Delete one row

Highlight any cell in row 4
Type / **W D R** ↵ *Worksheet Delete Row*

Result:

	A	B	C	D	E
1	ID	NAME	STATE	DEPEND	SALARY
2	22	SMITH	NY	3	200
3	45	JONES	AL	5	300
4	12	WATSON	NJ	2	200
5	33	HARRIS	CT	1	100

Notice the other rows moved up and closed the gap.

Example 2: Delete rows 3 through 5 (containing JONES, ADAMS, and WATSON).

	A	B	C	D	E
1	ID	NAME	STATE	DEPEND	SALARY
2	22	SMITH	NY	3	200
3	45	JONES	AL	5	300
4	88	ADAMS	CA	4	100
5	12	WATSON	NJ	2	200
6	33	HARRIS	CT	1	100

You: Save your current worksheet as usual.
Reminder: **/ F S** *File Save* etc. See **Save** in Chapter 2 for details.

Create a worksheet similar to the one above.

Delete multiple rows

You: Highlight any cell in row 3
Type **/ W D R↓ ↓** ↵ *Worksheet Delete Row*

Result:

	A	B	C	D	E
1	ID	NAME	STATE	DEPEND	SALARY
2	22	SMITH	NY	3	200
3	33	HARRIS	CT	1	100

Designing Spreadsheets

Note: Examples are given for different types of spreadsheets that are typically used. These are:

1. Allocation of funds
2. Budgets
3. Balance brought forward, using multiple files
4. Projection
5. Voucher

Here are some design hints:

- Sketch out and plan your worksheet on paper before you enter it into the computer.

- Try to duplicate the format of any familiar spreadsheets, such as your existing voucher sheets, account payables, receivables of budgets.

- Test out your worksheets. Use a calculator to check calculations. Try different values.

- Annotate complex formulas.

- Document your worksheet. Use meaningful labels.

- Use range names for commonly used ranges.

There are many worksheet examples throughout this book. Specifically, refer to the **Database, Sort, Function, Formulas, Multiple Sheets, Multiple (Linked) Files, Copy, Relative and Absolute, Printing—Cell Formulas, Macro, Data Fill,** and **Date** sections for a variety of examples.

Allocation of Funds

Note: Allocation of funds involves percentages. Some organizations, especially nonprofit ones, allocate a percentage of the available funds to each department, where the percentage is known before the dollar amount of available funds.

Two spreadsheets are involved. The first shows the percent allocation and, later, it is modified to become the second spreadsheet, showing actual dollar amounts.

Example 1: Create a spreadsheet that allocates funds by percentage. You will use this spreadsheet to be sure that exactly 100 percent of the funds are allocated.

	A	B	C
1		ALLOCATION OF FUNDS	
2			
3	DEPARTMENT	% of FUNDS	AMOUNT
4	outreach	30%	
5	welfare	35%	
6	fund raising	25%	
7	research	10%	
8			
9	TOTAL	100%	

@SUM(B4..B7)

Enter information

You: Highlight cell B4 .   Type **.3** *or* **30%**   Tap ↓
Highlight cell B5.   Type **.35** *or* **35%**   Tap ↓
Highlight cell B6.   Type **.25** *or* **25%**   Tap ↓
Highlight cell B7.   Type **.1** *or* **10%**   Tap ↵

Type the remaining numbers, labels, and formula into this worksheet.

Format cells

You: Highlight cell B4.   Type   **/ R F P Ø** ⟵ ↓ ↓ ↓ ↓ ↓ ⟵
to format with percent signs and no decimal places

Enter formula in cell B9

You: Highlight cell B9.   Type **@SUM(B4..B7)** ⟵

Set column widths

You: Highlight cell A1.   Type   **/ W C S 20** ⟵ *to set width to 20*

Highlight cell B1.   Type   **/ W C S 10** ⟵ *to set width to 10*

Possible modifications

You: Enter dates, the name of the preparer, and so on.

Example 2: $200,000 is available to this organization. Divide up the funds to each department according to the indicated percentage.

In this example, you will type the $200,000 into cell C9. If the funding changes, you will type in the new amount. The department dollar amounts will automatically change.

	A	B	C	
1		ALLOCATION OF FUNDS		
2				
3	DEPARTMENT	% of FUNDS	AMOUNT	
4	outreach	30%	60,000	← +B4*$C$9
5	welfare	35%	70,000	← +B5*$C$9
6	fund raising	25%	50,000	← +B6*$C$9
7	research	10%	20,000	← +B7*$C$9
8				
9	TOTAL	100%	200,000	

@SUM(B4..B7)   just a number—your total funds

Enter TOTAL funds in cell C9

You: Highlight cell C9.   Type **200000** ⟵

Enter formula in cell C4

> **You:** Highlight cell C4.   Type **+B4*$C$9** ←┘
>
> *The dollar signs in the formula +B4*$C$9 make the cell address for the total amount absolute. This prevents that cell address from being changed during the following copy.*

Copy formula in cell C4

> **You:** Highlight cell C4.
>
> Type **/ C** ←┘ **. ↓ ↓ ↓** ←┘ *to copy C4 down to C5..C7*

Set column widths

> **You:** Highlight cell C1.
>
> Type **/ W C S 10** ←┘   *or other width of your choice*

Format cells

> **You:** Highlight cell C4.
>
> Type **/ R F , Ø** ←┘ **↓ ↓ ↓** ←┘ *to format with comma and no $ sign or Ø decimals*
>
> Highlight cell C9.
>
> Type **/ R F C Ø** ←┘ ←┘ *to format with $ sign and Ø decimals*

Funds change

> **You:** If the total funding changes, type the new figure in cell C9. All other allocated amounts will automatically change.

Budget

Budget spreadsheets essentially show totals and subtotals. Here is a brief example, with pointers indicating the formulas.

Example: Create a budget spreadsheet.

You: Enter the text, values, and formulas shown below:

	A	B
1		B U D G E T
2		
3	INCOME	
4	sales	50,000
5	rentals	2,000
6	dues	500
7	contributions	1,111
8	interest	78
9	===============	=========
10	TOTAL INCOME	$53,689	◄── @SUM(B4..B8)
11		
12	EXPENSE	
13	rent	6,000
14	salary	22,000
15	travel	400
16	equipment	15,000
17	utilities	900
18	miscellaneous	200
19	===============	=========
20	TOTAL EXPENSE	$44,500	◄── @SUM(B13..B18)
21		
22		
23	NET PROFIT	$9,189	◄── +B10-B20

Set column widths

You: Highlight cell A1. Type **/ W C S 20** ↵ *or width of your choice*
         Highlight cell B1. Type **/ W C S 10** ↵ *or width of your choice*

Format cells

You: Type / **W G F , Ø** ⮠   *to set global format to comma*

Highlight cell B1.

Type / **R F C Ø** ⮠ ⮠   *Range Format Currency zero decimal places, to format with dollar signs*

Highlight cell B20. Type / **R F C Ø** ⮠ ⮠

Highlight cell B23. Type / **R F C Ø** ⮠ ⮠

Possible modifications

You: Enter the date prepared, the dates of application, the name of the preparer, and so on. Expenses are sometimes divided between fixed and variable costs.

Balance Brought Forward (YTD)

Note: Balance brought forward processing permits monthly expenses to be
in separate files. Another file contains year-to-date (YTD) figures,
which are the sums of the monthly figures on the other files. In this
example, the **File Combine** command is used to add the monthly
figures together. Alternatively, multiple sheets or multiple (linked)
files can be used.

File Combine is useful when the files are very large and are supplied
from different computers. Multiple sheets are useful when all the
information is entered into the same computer and will fit in memory
simultaneously. Multiple (linked) files are good in either case. See
Multiple Sheets and **Multiple (Linked) Files**.

Since repeating any command 12 times can become tedious, the
following example uses a simple balance brought forward macro,
which is placed on a separate sheet of the worksheet. Macros are
precoded instructions. See **Macros** for details.

OVERVIEW OF STEPS

- Zero out the YTD column.

- Add the January figures from disk using **File Combine Add.**

- Add the February figures from disk using **File Combine Add.**

- Likewise, add March through December figures using **File
Combine Add.**

- If the current month is March, you won't yet have the expenses
for March through December. When our macro attempts to
combine the March figures, it will get an error, because the March
file doesn't exist. In this case, the error is expected and our macro
knows enough to stop combining files because it contains a
special macro command—{ONERROR} (read as *"on error"*)—
that is used to stop the macro in case of error.

Example: Given expense figures in up to 12 separate files, one for each month, use a macro to combine all the figures into a total, year-to-date spreadsheet.

Create the January expense file

You: Create the following expense file for January:

	A	B	C	D
1		1991 EXPENSES for JANUARY		
2				
3		AMOUNT		
4				
5	PHONES	55		
6	RENT	555		
7	TRAVEL	55		
8	MISC.	5		

Did you remember to put an apostrophe in front of **1991 EXPENSES for JANUARY**?

You: Type **/ R N C AMOUNT** ⟵ *Range Name Create—do not type spaces before or after AMOUNT*

Type **B5..B8** ⟵

1-2-3: *It looks like nothing happened, yet 1-2-3 now associates the name **AMOUNT** with the range B5..B8*

You: **/ F S JAN91** ⟵ *save this file with the name JAN91*

If **Cancel Replace Backup** appears, tap **R** to replace the file on disk. If you don't want to replace it, tap **C** *Cancel* or **B** *Backup*.

Create the February expense file

You: Create the following expense file for February:

	A	B	C	D
1		1991 EXPENSES for FEBRUARY		
2				
3		AMOUNT		
4				
5	PHONES	66		
6	RENT	666		
7	TRAVEL	66		
8	MISC.	6		

You: Type **/ R N C AMOUNT** ←┘   *Range Name Create—do not type spaces before or after AMOUNT*

Type **B5..B8** ←┘

1-2-3:   The name **AMOUNT** is now associated with the range **B5..B8**. The same range name may be used in different files with no confusion to 1-2-3.

You: Type   **/ F S FEB91** ←┘   *save this file with the name FEB91*

If **Cancel Replace Backup** appears, tap **R** to replace the file on disk. If you don't want to replace it, tap **C** *Cancel* or **B** *Backup*.

Note: Let's assume that it is March. If it were later in the year, we would continue creating expense files for the other months of the year, using the same layout as for the January expense file. You would call these files MAR91, APR91, MAY91, JUN91, JUL91, AUG91, SEP91, OCT91, NOV91, and DEC91.

Create a YTD (Year-to-Date) file for total expenses

Note: Create a YTD worksheet containing the total year-to-date expenses and a macro to add up the expenses from the existing monthly files.

You: Create the following worksheet:

	A	B	C	D
1		1991 YTD EXPENSES		
2				
3	Expenses to month:			
4				
5	PHONES			
6	RENT			
7	TRAVEL			
8	MISC.			
9				
10	TOTAL	0		

@SUM(B5..B8)

You: Type **/ R N C TOTALS** ←┘ *Range Name Create*

Type **B5..B8** ←┘ *this range has been named TOTALS*

Type **/ R N C MONTH** ←┘ C3 ←┘ *cell C3 is named MONTH*

Type **/ F S YTD91** ←┘ *to save this file with the name YTD91*

If **Cancel Replace Backup** appears, tap **R** to replace the file on disk. If you don't want to replace it, tap **C** *Cancel* or **B** *Backup.*

Insert a second sheet for the macro

You: Type **/ W I S A** ←┘ *Worksheet Insert Sheet After—insert a second sheet where the macro will be typed.*

1-2-3: Don't panic. Your spreadsheet is still there. You are now looking at sheet **B.** Notice the **B** in the upper-left corner of the sheet. Your YTD91 spreadsheet is on sheet **A.** Let's look at it.

You: Type **/ W W P** *Worksheet Windows Perspective, to show three sheets*

Type **/ W W C** *Worksheet Windows Clear—back to one sheet*

TIPS FOR TYPING MACROS

- Save every 15 minutes. Reminder: **/ F S** *File Save* etc.

- For readability, the keywords and commands are in lowercase and the cell addresses, range names, and file names are in uppercase.

- Type an apostrophe before each macro entry.
- Be sure to type a **Backslash**, not a slash in cell A1.
- This sign, ~ , is a tilde located somewhere on your keyboard.
- { } is not ( ). The { } are used extensively in macros and are probably located on your keyboard to the right of the letter **P**.

You: Highlight cell B1 in the B sheet.
Type / **W C S 25** ←⏎ *widen column B to 25*
Enter the following macro, starting in column **A** of sheet **B**:

B	A	B	C
1	\M	{goto}TOTALS~Ø~	init B5 to zero
2		/c~TOTALS~	copy zeros down
3		{onerror STOP}	set up error action
4		/fcanAMOUNT~JAN91~	add jan expense
5		{let MONTH,"January"}	
6		/fcanAMOUNT~FEB91~	add feb expense
7		{let MONTH,"February"}	
8		/fcanAMOUNT~MAR91~	add mar expense
9		{let MONTH,"March"}	
10		/fcanAMOUNT~APR91~	add apr expense
11		{let MONTH,"April"}	
12		/fcanAMOUNT~MAY91~	add may expense
13		{let MONTH,"May"}	
14		/fcanAMOUNT~JUN91~	add Jun expense
15		{let MONTH,"June"}	
16		/fcanAMOUNT~JUL91~	add jul expense
17		{let MONTH,"July"}	
18		/fcanAMOUNT~AUG91~	add aug expense
19		{let MONTH,"August"}	
20		/fcanAMOUNT~SEP91~	add sep expense
21		{let MONTH,"September"}	
22		/fcanAMOUNT~OCT91~	add oct expense
23		{let MONTH,"October"}	
24		/fcanAMOUNT~NOV91~	add nov expense
25		{let MONTH,"November"}	
26		/fcanAMOUNT~DEC91~	add dec expense
27		{let MONTH,"December"}	
28	STOP	{quit}	error branches to here

Name your macro ranges

> **You:** Highlight cell A1.
>
> Type / **R N L R A1..A28** ↵   *Range Name Label Right*
>
> **Note:** The command **Range Name Label Right** uses the names in column A to name cells to their right. STOP is now the name of cell B28 and \M is now the name of cell B1.

Run your macro

> **You:** Hold **Ctrl** and tap **PgDn** *to switch to sheet A*
> Hold the **Alt** key (the **Macro** key) and tap the letter **M**
>
> **Result:** Watch while the expense figures from the monthly files are added into this worksheet. Assuming it is March, 1991, the following appears:

	A	B	C	D
1		1991 YTD EXPENSES		
2				
3	Expenses to month:		February	
4				
5	PHONES	121		
6	RENT	1221		
7	TRAVEL	121		
8	MISC.	11		
9				
10	TOTAL	1474		

Projection

Note: Spreadsheets are often used to project financial growth. While the calculations used for such projections can be complex, often they are just a percentage of the previous year.

Example: Project this year's financial growth based on an estimated five-percent increase in income and a three-percent increase in expenses over last year.

You: Create the following spreadsheet, entering formulas where indicated:

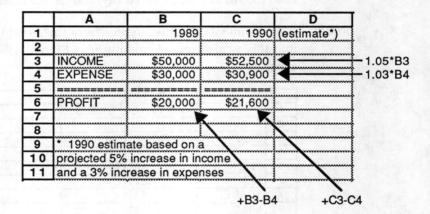

	A	B	C	D
1		1989	1990	(estimate*)
2				
3	INCOME	$50,000	$52,500	◄── 1.05*B3
4	EXPENSE	$30,000	$30,900	◄── 1.03*B4
5	==========	==========	==========	
6	PROFIT	$20,000	$21,600	
7				
8				
9	* 1990 estimate based on a			
10	projected 5% increase in income			
11	and a 3% increase in expenses			

+B3-B4   +C3-C4

Note: The formula 1.05*B3 is the value in B3 plus five percent of that value (.05 times B3). Take your percent (5%), convert it to a decimal (5% becomes .05) and then add 1 (.05 becomes 1.05) to show percent growth.

Set column widths

You: Type / W G C 10 ←⏎   *Worksheet Global Column-Width to 10*

Format cells

You: Type / W G F C Ø ←⏎   *Worksheet Global Format Currency*

Voucher

Note Voucher spreadsheets reflect monies spent by date, by expense item, and the total spent. They may also show the amount of any "advanced" money.

Example: Report travel expenses for a period of one week, indicating the amount of money advanced by the company.

You: Create the following spreadsheet, entering formulas where indicated. Appropriate copy and formatting instructions follow the spreadsheet.

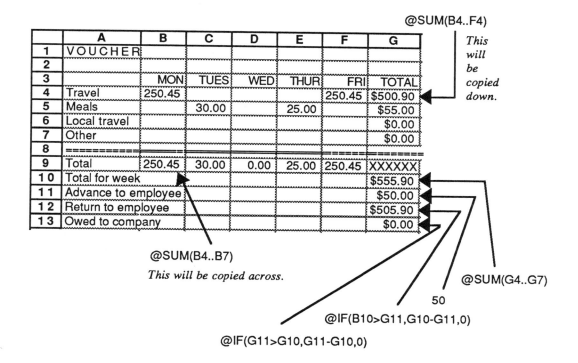

@SUM(B4..F4)

	A	B	C	D	E	F	G
1	VOUCHER						
2							
3		MON	TUES	WED	THUR	FRI	TOTAL
4	Travel	250.45				250.45	$500.90
5	Meals		30.00		25.00		$55.00
6	Local travel						$0.00
7	Other						$0.00
8	==========						========
9	Total	250.45	30.00	0.00	25.00	250.45	XXXXXX
10	Total for week						$555.90
11	Advance to employee						$50.00
12	Return to employee						$505.90
13	Owed to company						$0.00

This will be copied down.

@SUM(B4..B7)
This will be copied across.

@SUM(G4..G7)

50

@IF(B10>G11,G10-G11,0)

@IF(G11>G10,G11-G10,0)

Copy formulas

You: Highlight cell G4.
Type / C ←┘ . ↓ ↓ ↓ ←┘ *to copy the formula down the column*

You: Highlight cell B9.

Type   / C ↵ . → → → → ↵   *to copy the formula across the row*

Set column widths

You: Highlight cell A1.

Type   / W C S 20 ↵   *to set width of column A to 20*

Type   / W G C 10 ↵   *to set column width to 10, except for A*

Format cells

You: Type   / W G F , 2 ↵   *Worksheet Global Format comma*

Highlight cell G4.
Type   / R F C ↵ ↓ ↓ ↓ ↵   *to format G4 as currency*

Highlight cell G10.
Type   / R F C ↵ ↓ ↓ ↓ ↵   *to format G10 as currency*

Right-align text

You: Highlight cell B3.
Type   / R L R → → → → → ↵   *Range Label Right*

Other modifications

You: Enter dates, name of person, place for signature, and so on.

Directories

Command: **/ File Dir**
                / Worksheet Global   Default   Dir
                / System

Note: Disks are divided into one or more directories. When you put a file on disk, you are also putting it into a directory on that disk. You can organize your files (worksheets) by putting similar files into each directory. Therefore, directories permit you to organize your files. Every disk has a directory called the *root directory*. Hard disks usually have other directories as well. When you install 1-2-3 on a hard disk, it is usually put into a directory called 123R3. When you save or retrieve a file, 1-2-3 will use either 123R3 or another directory that you indicate.

Each directory is like a folder in a file cabinet. Just as you would probably put 1990 financial documents in a separate folder from 1991 documents, you would probably put 1990 worksheet files in a separate directory from 1991 worksheet files. For this example, the two directories could be called YEAR1990 and YEAR1991. Think of the directory name as the name you write on the manila paper folder, and files as the pieces of paper that you put into that folder.

When 1-2-3 looks for a file, it does not search the entire disk. It only searches in one directory, which you can specify. You may temporarily or permanently change the search directory. A temporary change means that 1-2-3 will only look at your specified directory until you Quit 1-2-3. 1-2-3 will use a permanent change until you make another permanent change.

The directory you specify must exist on disk before you issue the 1-2-3 command. The DOS **MD** (make directory) command is used to make a new directory.

Example: Change the directory that 1-2-3 uses to a directory named **C:\123TEST** on your C disk drive.

Create a new subdirectory, using the MD system command

> **You:** Type **/ S** *System*
>
> *1-2-3:* This message appears:
> **(Type EXIT and press [ENTER] to return to 1-2-3)**
>
> **You:** Type **C:** ↵
> Type **MD \123TEST** ↵
>
> Note: If DOS responds
> **Unable to create directory**
> it is probably because the directory already exists.
>
> **You:** Type **EXIT** ↵ *to return to 1-2-3 and your worksheet*

Permanently change the search directory

> **You:** Type **/ W G D D** *Worksheet Global Default Directory*
>
> *1-2-3:* **Default directory: C:\123R3**   If the startup directory has already been changed, you will see a different drive and/or directory instead of **C:\123R3**
>
> **You:** **Write down the name** of the directory that appears here. We will need this name later on.
>
> Tap the **Esc** key once
> Type **C:\123TEST** ↵ *you can use upper- or lowercase letters*
> Type **U Q** *Update Quit*
>
> Result: 1-2-3 will save and retrieve all files from the 123TEST directory, even after you quit and start 1-2-3 again.
>
> **You:** To change this default directory back to the original, repeat this step, using the name you wrote down instead of 123TEST.

Temporarily change the directory until you quit 1-2-3

> **You:** Type   **/ F D C:\123TEST** ↵ *File Directory*
>
> Result: Until you quit and start 1-2-3, it will use the 123TEST directory.
>
> **You:** To change your directory back to the original, repeat this step using the name you wrote down instead of 123TEST.

Editing Cell Contents

Note: When editing text, use the Wysiwyg Edit in the next section. For numbers and formulas, use the edit described here.

Use the **Edit (F2)** key to modify the existing contents of a cell. Alternatively, you can replace the contents of a cell if you highlight it and type in new information.

Related: **Editing with Wysiwyg**

Example: Modify the contents of a cell.

Highlight desired cell

You: Highlight the cell containing information you wish to modify.

1-2-3: The cell contents appear on line 1 of the control panel.

You: Tap the **F2** key *the Edit key*

1-2-3: **EDIT** appears in the upper-right corner. The cell contents appear on line 2 as well as on line 1.

Edit cell contents

You: Move the cursor on line 2 of the control panel to desired position for the change, using one of the following keystrokes:

Tap → *or* ← *or* the **Home** key *or* the **End** key
or hold the **Ctrl** key and tap → *or* ←

You: Make changes using one or more of the following:

Tap the **Del** key to delete the underlined character (cursor location).

Or tap the **Backspace** key to remove character to the left of the cursor.

Or type any character(s) you want inserted.

Or tap the **Ins** key (the insert key) and type any character(s) that are to overlay existing character(s).

1-2-3: All your changes are still on line 2 at the top of the screen. Now you have a choice: whether or not to replace the cell contents with your changes.

To replace the cell contents with the changes on line 2

You: Tap ←┘ *or* ↑ *or* ↓ *or* **PgUp** *or* **PgDn** keys

1-2-3: Cell contents are replaced.

READY appears in the upper-right corner.

To exit without changing the cell contents (if you really messed up)

You: Tap the **Esc** key **twice**

1-2-3: **READY** appears in the upper-right corner.

Cell contents are not changed.

Editing with Wysiwyg

Note: When editing text, use this Wysiwyg Edit. For numbers and formulas, use the edit described in the previous section.

Example: Modify text in several cells.

You: Create the following worksheet:

	A	B	C
1	Budget		
2			
3	Rent		
4	Travel		

You: Type : T E A1 . . C4 ↵

1-2-3: **A:A1 row: 1 col: 0 Left-Aligned** appears in the upper-left

You: Type **1991**

Tap the space bar.

Use the arrow keys to position the cursor to the right of **Rent**

Type **–for Corporate Office**

Tap Esc (or tap the right mouse button) *to end Wysiwyg edit*

1-2-3:

	A	B	C
1	1991 Budget		
2			
3	Rent-for Corporate Office		
4	Travel		

Note: Use the arrow keys to position the cursor for editing. The mouse doesn't work here. Even though we specified three columns for edit, everything you type is really going into column A. Only the overflow appears in columns B and C.

Erase

Command: **/ Range Erase**

Note: This command removes the contents of a cell, but does not alter any formatting or reset column widths.

Warning: There is a major difference between empty (or blank) cells and cells with spaces. When you tap the space bar, you get a space. Cells with spaces have something in them—the space character. Some functions treat such cells as if they had the value zero while other functions produce the **ERR** message. If cells in your range have spaces, you may get incorrect answers when calculating averages and counts. Therefore, use the **Range Erase** command to remove the contents of a cell. Do not type spaces to make a cell appear empty. **Edit (F2)** cannot make a cell empty.

If you highlight a cell containing a space, you will see an apostrophe in the first line of the panel, as follows:

A:A24:   **READY**

	A	B	C	D
2 3				
2 4				

In this example, cell A24 *looks* empty, but in fact it is not; the top line shows an apostrophe.

Related: **Erase Worksheet**
Delete a Column
Delete a Row

Example 1: Remove the contents of a single cell.

First, let's put something in a cell, so that it can be erased

You: Highlight cell A24 .   Tap the space bar.   Tap ⏎

Erase the cell contents

You: Highlight cell A24.

1-2-3:   **A:A24:**   **READY**

	A	B	C	D
2 3				
2 4	██████████			

Notice the apostrophe in cell A:A24.

You: Tap / **R E** ↵   *Range Erase*

1-2-3:   **A:A24:**   **READY**

	A	B	C	D
2 3				
2 4	██████████			

The apostrophe has disappeared, and cell A24 is now empty.

Example 2:   Remove the contents of the range **D3..D5**.

You: Create a worksheet similar to the one below:

	A	B	C	D
1	Item	Cost	Location	Comments
2				
3	Rug	500	NYC	Cheap
4	Table	250	CHI	Funny color
5	Chair	85	NYC	No padding

You: Highlight cell D3.

Tap / **R E** ↓ ↓   *Range Erase—don't tap* ↵ *yet*

1-2-3:

	A	B	C	D
1	Item	Cost	Location	Comments
2				
3	Rug	500	NYC	**Cheap**
4	Table	250	CHI	**Funny color**
5	Chair	85	NYC	**No padding**

The range D3..D5 is highlighted.

You: Tap ↵

Result: The following appears:

	A	B	C	D
1	Item	Cost	Location	Comments
2				
3	Rug	500	NYC	
4	Table	250	CHI	
5	Chair	85	NYC	

The contents of cells D3..D5 are removed.

Erase a File on Disk

Command: **/ File Erase**

Note: This command removes a file from disk, but it does not affect the
worksheet you are currently viewing. If you erase a file for security
reasons, remember that the actual information remains on the disk
for a while. It remains until you save another file that reuses that
disk space. Until then, someone with The Norton Utilities or a
similar package could find your information on the disk by
"unerasing" the file.

Related: **Erase**
Erase Worksheet

Example: Erase a file.

You: Type **/ F E W**   *File Erase Worksheet*
Tap the **F3** key   *the Name key*

1-2-3: A screen full of file names appears.

You: Highlight the name of the file to be erased
Tap ↵

1-2-3: **No   Yes**

You: Tap **Y** *Yes, to confirm the delete*
If you do not want to erase this file, type **N** *No*

Note: You cannot erase a file if you are currently viewing it.

1-2-3: **READY** appears in the upper-right corner.

Result: Your screen will appear the same as before. However the file has
been removed from your disk. To prove it, try to retrieve it (**/ F R**
and tap **F3**). The name won't be there.

Erase Worksheet

Command: **/ Worksheet Erase**

Warning: **SAVE FIRST**, or you may lose the entire worksheet you are currently working on, including any changes since the last time you saved. 1-2-3 does warn you first if you haven't saved your changes.

Note: This command returns your worksheet to its initial settings: empty cells, column width of 9, cell format of General, and label alignment of left.

Warning: If you have multiple sheets, this command erases all the sheets. If you have multiple files open, this command erases all the open worksheets.

This command does not affect files on disk.

Related: **Erase**
File Erase
New Worksheet

Example: Erase the current worksheet(s) in order to start a new worksheet.

You: Save your current worksheet, by typing **/ F S** type the file name if it isn't already displayed, then tap ←⏎

If **Cancel Replace Backup** appears, tap **R** to replace the file on disk. If you don't want to replace it, tap **C** *Cancel* or **B** *Backup*.

You: Type **/ W E Y** *Worksheet Erase Yes*

If **No Yes** appears on the screen, it means you haven't saved all the changes to your current worksheet(s). Type **N** to cancel this command. Type **Y** to proceed with removing all open worksheets.

Result: An empty worksheet appears.

Export Data to Word Processing

Command: / **Print File**

Note: Use the **Print File** command to create a plain text file that can be imported into most word processors, especially WordPerfect, Microsoft Word, WordStar, and MultiMate.

This plain text file is also called an ASCII file. It is a standard for transporting data between different software packages. In case you're interested, ASCII stands for American Standard Code for Information Interchange. See **File Choices** for more comments on ASCII.

Example 1: Create a file that can be imported, or directly used, by a word processor.

You: Create or retrieve the worksheet you wish to put into a word processing document.

You: Type / **P F REPORT.DOC** ↩ *Print File*

If **Cancel Replace Backup** appears, tap **R** to replace the file on disk. If you don't want to replace it, tap **C** *Cancel* or **B** *Backup*.

1-2-3: **Range Line Page Options Clear Align Go Image Sample Hold Quit**
This is the print menu

You: Type **R** *Range*

1-2-3: **Enter Print range:** *some range appears*

Note: Don't worry—you won't be printing. This command will write to disk data in a form sometimes called *print format*.

You: Type the range you want to transport to your word processor.

Tap ↩

Type **O O U**   *Options Other Unformatted*

Type **M L Ø ←┘ Q**   *Margin Left Ø Quit*

Type **G**   *Go*

Type **O O F Q Q**   *Options Other Formatted Quit Quit*

1-2-3:   **WAIT** then **READY** appear in the upper-right corner.

Result: You now have a file on disk called REPORT.DOC, which you can use in your word processor.

Example 2:   Import REPORT.DOC into your word processor. The following examples assume that REPORT.DOC is in the same directory or subdirectory as the word processors described.

Into WordPerfect

You: Start WordPerfect as usual (one way is to type **WP** at the DOS prompt).

Tap the **F5** key *the ASCII text key*

Highlight REPORT.DOC (you may need to make WordPerfect refer to your 123R3 directory).

Tap **5** *text in*

Result: Your worksheet is loaded into WordPerfect.

Into Microsoft Word

You: Start Word as usual (one way is to type **WORD** at the DOS prompt).

Tap the **Esc** key   *this brings up the commands in Word*

Type **T L** *Transfer Load*

Type **REPORT ←┘**

Note: You may need to type **C:\123R3\REPORT.DOC** ↵ to refer to the 123R3 directory.

Result: Your worksheet is loaded into WORD.

Into WordStar

You: Start WordStar as usual (one way is to type **WS** at the DOS prompt).

Type **N** *Non-document mode*

Type **REPORT** ↵

Note: You may need to type **C:\123R3\REPORT.DOC** ↵ to refer to the 123R3 directory.

Result: Your worksheet is loaded into WordStar.

Into MultiMate Advantage II

You: Start MultiMate as usual (one way is to type **MM** at the DOS prompt).

Type **3** *MultiMate Advanced Utilities and Conversions option*

Type ↓↓ *highlight the File Conversion line*

Tap the **F10** key *to choose the highlighted option*

If you see the message **CANNOT FIND UTILITY SYSTEM FILE**, tap the **F10** key again *to create this file*

MM: Convert Document(s) *is highlighted*

You: Tap the **F10** key *to choose the highlighted option*

MM: The menu: **Convert A Document** appears.

You: Under Source: type **REPORT** ↵ **DOC** ↵ **ASCII** ↵

Type the appropriate path or directory, such as **123R3** ↵

Under Destination: type **REPORTMM** ↵ **DOC** ↵ **MM** ↵

Type the appropriate path or directory, such as **MM** ↵

Tap the **F10** key   *to start the conversion*

When finished, tap the **Esc** key three times to back out to the original MultiMate Advantage menu.

Type **1** ↵   *to choose MultiMate Professional Word Processor*

Type **1** ↵   *to choose Edit an Old Document*

Type **REPORTMM**

Tap the **F10** key   *indicates that the document name has been entered*

Tap the **F10** key *to pass by the screen titled: DOCUMENT SUMMARY SCREEN*

Result: Your worksheet is converted and loaded into MultiMate.

Export Data to dBASE

Command: **Translate** in the 1-2-3 Access Menu

Note: Translate on the Access Menu is used to transfer data between dBASE II, dBASE III and III Plus, DIF, Symphony, and different releases of 1-2-3. Choose dBASE III to convert to either dBASE III or III Plus databases. dBASE III and III Plus databases can be directly used by dBASE IV, although the reverse is not true.

Prepare your 1-2-3 worksheet as follows:

- Enter your 1-2-3 database (see **Database 1**).

- You may have a maximum of 128 columns (fields).

- The first row of the database consists of field names. These field names conform to dBASE's rules for field names, which start with a letter of the alphabet and may consist of letters, numbers, and the underscore. These field names may not contain spaces.

- The second row of the database contains the first data record. Each cell in this row must contain data or be formatted. Do not leave any blank fields in the second row.

- Format the database so that the desired number of decimal places appear and dates look like dates. Avoid Scientific format, because dBASE has no equivalent.

- Widen columns so that all information appears; otherwise, some data will be truncated. The column widths should accommodate the data, not the field names, which will not be truncated if the column is too narrow. Numeric columns should not be wider than 19.

- Name the range of the 1-2-3 database.

- Save the worksheet.

The command / **Data External** is an alternate method.

If you wish to bring dBASE data into 1-2-3, refer to **Database** then to **Database 9—dBASE Input** to import some or all of your dBASE database into a 1-2-3 worksheet.

Related: **File Choices** (a list of cross-references)

Example: Export a 1-2-3 database to dBASE III, III Plus, or IV using Translate.

Prepare your 1-2-3 database

You: Create the following worksheet, using the hints below:

	A	B	C
1		EMPLOYEES	
2			
3	NAME	SALARY	DATE
4	Davis	500	18-Feb-91
5	Jones	2500	12-Oct-67
6	Morrisson	1500	11-Dec-77
7	Hobbs	550	15-Jun-91

You: Type the text into colunm A and into Rows 1 and 3.

Type numbers in cells B4 through B8.

Highlight cell C4

Type **18-Feb-91** ↵ Enter similar dates into cells C5 through C8. These dates will appear as numbers until formatted as dates.

Type **/ R F D 1** ↵ C4..C8 *to format date cells as dates*

Highlight cell A1. Type **/ W C S 20** ↵ *to set width to 20*

Highlight cell B1. Type **/ W C S 10** ↵ *to set width to 10*

Highlight cell C1. Type **/ W C S 10** ↵ *to set width to 10*

Name the database range

You: Type **/ R N C DATABASE** ↵ **A3..C8** ↵ *to name the range of the database; do not type a space in front of DATABASE*

Save the worksheet

> **You:** Type **/ F S 123DB** ↩   *to save with the file name 123DB*
>
> If **Cancel Replace Backup** appears, tap **R** to replace the file on disk. If you don't want to replace it, tap **C** *Cancel* or **B** *Backup.*

Quit 1-2-3

> **You:** Type **/ Q Y**   *Quit Yes*
>
> If the 1-2-3 Access Menu does not appear, restart Lotus by typing **LOTUS** instead of typing **123**
>
> *1-2-3:* **1-2-3 Translate Install View Exit** *this is the Access Menu*

Translate from 1-2-3 to dBASE III or dBASE III Plus

> **You:** Type **T** *Translate*
>
> *1-2-3:*
>
> | FROM |
> | --- |
> | 1-2-3 release 1A |
> | 1-2-3 release 2 |
> | 1-2-3 release 3 |
> | dBASE II |
> | dBASE III and III + |
> | DIF |
> | Multiplan |
> | SYMPHONY 1 and 1.01 |
> | SYMPHONY 1.1, 1.2 and 2 |
> | Move the menu pointer to your selection and press ENTER. |
> | Press ESC to leave the Translate Utility. |
> | Press F1 for more information. |

> **You:** Tap ↓ ↓   to highlight **1-2-3 release 3**
>
> Tap ↩

1-2-3:

```
                         TO
           1-2-3 release 1A
           1-2-3 release 2
           dBASE II
           dBASE III and III +
           DIF
           Multiplan
           SYMPHONY 1 and 1.01
           SYMPHONY 1.1, 1.2 and 2
Move the menu pointer to your selection and press  ENTER.
         Press  ESC to leave the Translate Utility.
               Press F1 for more information.
```

You: Tap ↓ ↓ ↓ to highlight **dBASE III and III +**

Tap ←⟋

1-2-3: Two pages of rules appear.

You: Tap ←⟋←⟋

You: Tap the **Esc** key.

1-2-3:

```
Translate FROM: 1-2-3  release 3            Translate TO:  dBASE  III and ...
   Source File: drive: \ path \ *.WK1
        filename   WK3   date and time last modified      size in bytes



            list of filenames

Move the menu pointer to the file you want to translate and press  ENTER.
          Press  ESC to edit the source file path or name.
               Press F1  for more information.
```

You: Tap ↓ until **123DB   WK3,** the file to be translated, is highlighted.

Tap ←⟋

1-2-3:

> Translate FROM: 1-2-3 2.01   Translate TO: dBASE III
> Source File: *drive:* \ *path* \ 123DB.WK1
> Destination File: *drive:* \ *path* \ 123DB.DBF
>   *filename*   WK1   *date and time last modified*   *size in bytes*
>
>
>   *list of filenames*
>
> Edit the destination file path or name if necessary and press ENTER.
>   Press ESC to select a different source file.
>   Press F1 for more information.

You: If your dBASE file is to go on a different disk drive or path than the one specified, tap the **Esc** key, make the changes, and tap ←┘

You: Tap ←┘ *to confirm that the displayed information is correct*

If the following appears:

> **The the target file already exists. Should it be overwritten? Yes No**

Type **N** or **Y** as appropriate.

1-2-3:

> Translate entire file
> File   Named range

You: Tap **N** *Named range*

1-2-3:

> Enter range name:

You: Type **DATABASE** ←┘   *this is the range name of your 1-2-3 database—cell addresses won't work*

Note: If you had entered **F** for File in answer to the previous question, the following would have appeared instead of athe range name question:

> Translate all worksheets in the file
> All worksheets   One worksheet

In this case, you would have typed **A**   *All worksheets*

1-2-3:

```
Proceed with translation
 Yes  No  Quit
```

You: Tap **Y** *Yes*

Error messages may appear here. If so, read them carefully, then fix the worksheet and restart the translation process.

1-2-3:

```
Translation in progress
```

1-2-3:

```
Translation  Successful
```

You: Tap the **Esc** key until 1-2-3 beeps at you.

1-2-3:

```
Do you want to leave Translate?
   No  Yes
```

You: Tap **Y** *Yes*

123 responds: **1-2-3 Translate Install View Exit**   *the Access Menu*

Result: You now have a dBASE database file containing the data from the 1-2-3 worksheet. Start dBASE. At the dBASE dot prompt, type **USE 123DB** ←┘ **LIST** ←┘ to see your data in dBASE.

eXtract Data to 1-2-3 Files

Command: / **File Xtract**

Note: This command allows you to create another worksheet file that contains information from the current worksheet. Use it to divide up a large worksheet. Also, use it for certain types of year-to-date processing.

Related: **Designing Spreadsheets—Balance Brought Forward**
File Choices (a list of cross-references)

Example: Calculate year-to-date (YTD) sales amounts using a typical balance brought forward process. We will enter current monthly sales figures into column **C** of our worksheet, eXtract these figures to a file on disk, then, using **File Combine**, add them from disk to the **YTD SALES** column.

Enter the first month's sales in the current sales column

You: Create the following worksheet with the current month's sales in column C:

	A	B	C
1	ITEMS	YTD SALES	CURRENT SALES
2			
3	WIDGETS	0	45.66
4	TOYS	0	800.25
5	KITS	0	12.34
6	THINGS	0	5.67

Extract the first month's sales

You: Highlight cell C3
Type / **F X V CSALES** ←┘↓ ↓ ↓ ←┘ *File eXtract Values*

If **Cancel Replace Backup** appears, tap **R** to replace the file on disk. If you don't want to replace it, tap **C** *Cancel* or **B** *Backup*.

1-2-3: **WAIT** then **READY** appear in the upper-right corner. The file CSALES now contains the first month's sales.

Add the first month's sales to the YTD column

You: Highlight cell B3.
Type **/ F C A E CSALES** ⏎ *File Combine Add Entire*

1-2-3:

	A	B	C
1	ITEMS	YTD SALES	CURRENT SALES
2			
3	WIDGETS	45.66	45.66
4	TOYS	800.25	800.25
5	KITS	12.34	12.34
6	THINGS	5.67	5.67

You: Highlight cell C3.
Type **Ø** ⏎ *zero*
Type **/ C** ⏎ **. ↓ ↓ ↓** ⏎ *to copy zero down the column*

1-2-3:

	A	B	C
1	ITEMS	YTD SALES	CURRENT SALES
2			
3	WIDGETS	45.66	0
4	TOYS	800.25	0
5	KITS	12.34	0
6	THINGS	5.67	0

Enter the second month's sales figures under CURRENT SALES

You: Highlight cell C3.

Type 10 ↓   *these are the second month's sales*
Type 20 ↓
Type 30 ↓
Type 40 ⏎

1-2-3:

	A	B	C
1	ITEMS	YTD SALES	CURRENT SALES
2			
3	WIDGETS	45.66	10
4	TOYS	800.25	20
5	KITS	12.34	30
6	THINGS	5.67	40

You: Highlight cell C3.

Type / **F X V CSALES** ←↵ ↓ ↓ ↓ ←↵ **R** *File eXtract Values —
to extract values into CSALES and Replace the file on disk*

1-2-3:   **WAIT** then **READY** appear. The file CSALES now contains the
second month's sales.

Add the second month's sales to the YTD column

You: Highlight cell B3.
Type / **F C A E CSALES** ←↵ *File Combine Add Entire*

Result: The following appears:

	A	B	C
1	ITEMS	YTD SALES	CURRENT SALES
2			
3	WIDGETS	55.66	10
4	TOYS	820.25	20
5	KITS	32.34	30
6	THINGS	45.67	40

Next month, you are ready to put zeroes in column C again, and
then enter the third month's sales figures. This process is called
balance brought forward.

You: Type / **F S BBF** ←↵ *File Save— to save the main worksheet*

If **Cancel Replace Backup** appears, tap **R** to replace the file on
disk. If you don't want to replace it, tap **C** *Cancel* or **B** *Backup.*

File Choices

Files exist on disk and contain your stored worksheets and other saved information. When you **retrieve** a file using / **File Retrieve**, you are copying the disk information into your working area (whose technical name is memory or RAM).

Opening a file, using / **File Open**, also copies a file from disk to your working area. It is used with multiple file linking (see **Multiple (Linked) Files**).

Importing a file also copies a disk file into your working area, but importing is used when the disk file is not in the format 1-2-3 uses. For example, you *import* a text file into your work area, but you do not *retrieve* it because text files are not in 1-2-3 format. When a file is imported from disk, 1-2-3 goes through a conversion process to put the data into 1-2-3 format.

When you **save** a file using / **File Save**, you are copying a worksheet from your working area to disk.

Exporting a file also copies a worksheet to disk but *exporting* is used only when the disk file will not be in the format 1-2-3 uses. For example, you *export* a worksheet to disk where it would be in the format useable by WordPerfect. When a file is exported to disk, 1-2-3 goes through a conversion process to put the data into a different format. 1-2-3 uses the terms Translate and External to describe the exporting process.

Combining 1-2-3 files copies (or arithmetically adds or subtracts) information from disk into your current worksheet. In this case, the files on disk are already in 1-2-3 format.

eXtracting data to disk means writing some of the information in your current worksheet to disk. This new file on disk is written in 1-2-3 format.

The following topics are all involved with files on disk.

Combining 1-2-3 Files	**Import Data into 1-2-3**
Database 9—dBASE Input	**List File Names**
Directories	**Loading Data**
Erase a File on Disk	**Multiple (Linked) Files**
Export Data to Word Processing	**Retrieve a File**
Export Data to dBASE Files	**Save a File**
eXtract Data to 1-2-3 Files	**Translate Data**

Formatting Diskettes

Command: / System

Note: Floppy diskettes must be formatted before they can be used by the computer.

Think of formatting a diskette as setting up a table in a restaurant. Some restaurants use forks, others use chopsticks. Just as different restaurants need different table settings, different computers need different disk formats. Therefore, diskette manufacturers don't format diskettes for you, since the same diskette could be used on a number of different types of computers. In other words, you end up doing your own diskette formatting.

Formatting a disk wipes off any information that you may have saved on it. Do not format your hard disk, or you may lose all the information on it. Software packages such as Norton Utilities can sometimes retrieve information lost when a hard disk is formatted. The DOS FORMAT command permanently wipes information off of a floppy diskette, but Norton provides an alternate "safe format" that gives you a chance to retrieve lost information, if you're quick.

Example: Format a diskette while you are still in Lotus 1-2-3.

You: Type / S *System—to get to DOS*

1-2-3: **(Type EXIT and press [ENTER] to return to 1-2-3)** appears followed by other system and copyright messages and the system prompt. You are now in the DOS system.

You: Type **FORMAT**

Tap the space bar

Type A: ↵

DOS: (Messages vary, depending on the release of your system.)
Insert new diskette for A:
and strike ENTER when ready

You: Insert your new diskette in drive A.
Tap ⟵

DOS: (Messages vary, depending on the release of your system.)
Formatting ...

then, after about a minute
Formatting ... Format complete
bytes total disk space
bytes available on disk
Format another (Y or N)?

You: Type N ⟵ *No. Or type Y and format the entire box of diskettes*

DOS: **C>** *messages vary, depending on how your system is customized*

You: Type **EXIT** ⟵ *to return to 1-2-3*

Result: Your worksheet appears, and your disk is formatted.

Formatting Numbers

Command: / **Range Format**
/ **Worksheet Global Format**

Note: Use format commands to control the number of decimal places and to add commas, dollar signs, and percent signs to numbers. Numbers are always right aligned in the cell. Only labels (text) can be centered or left aligned.

Use the **Worksheet Global Format** command to format all the numbers on the worksheet. It is common to leave the global format as General, or change it to comma.

Use the **Range Format** command to format individual cells and ranges. Ranges formatted with **Range Format** are not affected by the **Worksheet Global Format** command.

Use **Automatic** formatting to cause 1-2-3 to format your numbers as you enter them and not in a separate step. Be careful, 1-2-3 may not format your numbers as you intend. See the second example.

Frequently, you need to widen columns after formatting, especially if cells fill up with asterisks ************.

To make negative numbers appear red, see the last example.

When you format a cell, you are telling 1-2-3 that any number you already have there, or any number you put there in the future, is to be formatted in a certain way. Even when you erase that cell, the formatting instructions remain. If you never format anything, then the formatting instructions are the initial ones that 1-2-3 starts with, usually General.

Related: **Column Width**
Numeric Entries
Dates

Example 1:   Format the following numbers appropriately with comma, dollar, and percent signs.

You: Create a worksheet like the following:

	A	B	C	D
1	DEPARTMENT	AMOUNT	PERCENT of TOTAL	
2	Personnel	40000	0.158103	
3	Accounting	8000	0.031621	
4	Production	5000	0.019763	
5	Sales	200000	0.790514	
6				
7	TOTAL	253000		

You: Type   **/ W G F , Ø ↵**   *Worksheet Global Format "," (comma)*
zero-decimal-places

1-2-3:

	A	B	C	D
1	DEPARTMENT	AMOUNT	PERCENT of TOTAL	
2	Personnel	40,000	0	
3	Accounting	8,000	0	
4	Production	5,000	0	
5	Sales	200,000	1	
6				
7	TOTAL	253,000		

All the numbers on the worksheet are globally formatted as "comma" with zero decimal places.

Some numbers should be formatted differently, such as **B7** (**TOTAL**) and **C2..C5** (**PERCENT of TOTAL**). For these, we use the **Range Format** command.

You: Highlight cell B7.
Type   **/ R F C Ø ↵ ↵**   *Range Format Currency zero-decimals*

1-2-3:

	A	B	C	D
1	DEPARTMENT	AMOUNT	PERCENT	of TOTAL
2	Personnel	40,000	0	
3	Accounting	8,000	0	
4	Production	5,000	0	
5	Sales	200,000	1	
6				
7	TOTAL	$253,000		

Now cell B7 now has a dollar sign.

You: Highlight cell C2.

Type / **R F P 1** ↵ ↓ ↓ ↓ ↵ *Range Format Percent one—to give percentages one decimal place*

Result: The following appears:

	A	B	C	D
1	DEPARTMENT	AMOUNT	PERCENT of TOTAL	
2	Personnel	40,000	15.8%	
3	Accounting	8,000	3.2%	
4	Production	5,000	2.0%	
5	Sales	200,000	79.1%	
6				
7	TOTAL	$253,000		

Now the numbers in column C show percentages.

Example 2: Create a worksheet using automatic formatting.

You: Save your current worksheet. Reminder: / **F S** *File Save* etc.

Start with a new worksheet (type / **W E Y** *Worksheet Erase Yes*)

Turn on automatic formatting

You: Type / **W G F O A** *Worksheet Global Format Other Automatic— to turn on automatic formatting*

You: Highlight cell B5.

Type **14%** ↵

1-2-3: Cell appearance: **14%**

Upper-left corner: **A:B5 (PØ) .14** *PØ means percent, zero decimal places*

You: Highlight cell B6.

Type **1,222.35** ↵

1-2-3: Cell appearance: **1,222.35**

Upper-left corner: **A:B6 (,2) 1222.35** *,2 means comma, two decimal places*

You: Highlight cell B7.
Type **$35** ↵

1-2-3:   Cell appearance: **$35**
Upper-left corner: **A:B6 (CØ) 35**   *CØ means currency,*
zero decimal places

Result: With automatic formatting, you type a number into a cell, and 1-2-3 automatically does a **Range Format** to match the format of the value you entered into the cell.

Warning: If you type a number that does not match one of 1-2-3's number formats, you get the **L** (Label) format. In this case, the number looks like a value, but it is really a label, with a value of zero. Here is an example:

You: Highlight cell B8.
Type **12,45** ↵   *here is our "accidental" error*

1-2-3:   Cell appearance: **12,45**
Upper-left corner: **A:B6 (L) 12,45**   *L means label*

Tip: If you see a number with (L) in the upper-left corner that should be a value, use **/ Range Format Reset** to remove the (L). Then type the number in again, correctly.

You: Highlight cell B8.
Type **/ R F R** ↵   *Range Format Reset*
Type **1,245** ↵   *this time the number is entered correctly.*

1-2-3:   Cell appearance: **1,245**
Upper-left corner: **A:B6 (CØ) 1245**   *CØ means currency,*
zero decimal places

Example 3:   Display negative numbers in color (usually red) on a color monitor.

You: Enter some negative numbers (such as **-22**) on your worksheet.

Type **/ W G F O C N**   *Worksheet Global Format Other*
Color Negative

1-2-3: All negative numbers appear in red.

Note: If your cell has **(L)** then the number is treated as a label and won't turn red.   Either remove the label option, or type your negative numbers into a different cell.

Reset color back to white

You: Type **/ W G F O C R**   *Worksheet Global Format Other*
Color Reset

1-2-3: All negative numbers again appear in the same color as positive numbers.

Formulas

Note: Creating the right formulas is the most important part of your worksheet preparation. Formulas are your way of telling 1-2-3 how to process the information in your worksheet.

There are two ways to enter a formula:

1. The typing method—you type the entire formula.
2. The pointing method—you highlight (point to) each cell involved in the calculation.

Both methods are shown for each example. While the second method may seem to take longer to enter, it is usually more accurate, and is therefore faster because in the long run you won't have so many mistakes.

There are three types of formulas: numeric, string, and logical. Numeric formulas are the most common in spreadsheets.

Numeric formulas start with one of the following characters:
+ - . (@ # 0 1 2 3 4 5 6 7 8 9 *or* $
(assuming $ is the default currency symbol).

In numeric formulas, the mathematical operators are (in the order they are performed):

exponentiation	^	caret
multiplication	*	asterisk
division	/	slash
addition	+	plus sign
subtraction	-	minus sign (hyphen)

Examples of formulas:

+C3-D3	Subtract the number in D3 from the number in C3.
+C3*5	Multiply the number in C3 by 5.
+C3/5	Divide the number in C3 by 5.
+5^3	Multiply 5 times itself three times (5*5*5 = 125).

If **CALC** appears at the bottom of the screen, tap the **F9** key to recalculate your formulas.

Warning: If your formula looks like a date, for example 12/5/21, 1-2-3 will replace it with its date number instead of doing the division.

Warning: If **CIRC** appears at the bottom of the screen you probably have an error, usually disastrous, in some formula in your worksheet. **CIRC** stands for *circular reference*, and in rare situations is intentional. When you fix the error, the **CIRC** message goes away. Here is an example of a bad formula causing **CIRC** to appear:

	A	B
1	EXPENSES	
2	Phone	25
3	Travel	400
4	Supplies	55
5	Salary	400
6	Misc	25
7	========	========
8	TOTAL	905

This formula should be **@SUM(B2..B6)**.
It actually is **@SUM(B2..B8)** which is wrong, because it includes itself (**B8**).

In this example, the value appearing in cell B8 will get bigger and bigger because 905 will be added to its current contents every time the worksheet is recalculated.

Related: **Numeric Entries**
Dates
Functions
Recalculation and the Calc Key
Relative and Absolute Cell References
Designing Spreadsheets

Example 1:   Calculate the sum of the following list of numbers:

	A	B
1	Phone	50
2	Rent	800
3	Utilities	95
4	Miscellaneous	22
5	- - - - - - - - -	- - - - - - - - -
6	TOTAL	

You: Create a spreadsheet that looks like the one above.

Method one

You: Highlight cell B6   *where the formula goes*

Type   **@SUM(B1..B4)** ←┘   *to add together the numbers in cells B1 through B4*

Method two

You: Highlight cell B6   *where the formula goes*

Type **@SUM(↑↑.↑↑↑)**   *to sum the range B1..B4*

or type **@SUM(↑↑↑↑↑.↓↓↓)**

1-2-3:   While you were using the arrows, **POINT** appeared in the upper-right corner. Now **VALUE** appears.

You: Tap ←┘

Result: With either method, the following appears:

	A	B
1	Phone	50
2	Rent	800
3	Utilities	95
4	Miscellaneous	22
5	- - - - - - - - -	- - - - - - - - -
6	TOTAL	967

Example 2: Calculate the net gain in the following spreadsheet:

	A	B
1	Income	5000
2	Expense	3500
3	========	========
4	Net Gain	

You: Create a spreadsheet that looks like the one above.

Method one

You: Highlight cell B4 *where the formula goes*

Type **+B1-B2** ↵

Method two

You: Highlight cell B4 *where the formula goes*

Type **+ ↑ ↑ ↑ - ↑ ↑** ↵ *remember the plus and minus signs*

Result: With either method, the following appears:

	A	B
1	Income	5000
2	Expense	3500
3	========	========
4	Net Gain	1500

Function Keys

Note: On IBM computers, compatibles, and many other keyboards there are 10 function keys with specific predefined meanings. If your keyboard does not have **F1** through **F10** keys, refer to your Lotus 1-2-3 manual for the keys that correspond to these functions.

Key	Function	Meaning
F1	Help	Displays a help screen. Tap the **Esc** key to return to your worksheet.
F2	Edit	In **READY** mode, tap to enter **EDIT** mode.
F3	Name	In **POINT** mode, displays a list of range names. During some **File** commands, displays a list of file names.
		After the **F5** key, displays list of range names.
		After typing **@**, displays a list of @ functions.
		After typing **{**, displays a list of advanced macro commands.
F4	Absolute	In **POINT** mode, makes a cell or range address absolute (adds dollar signs to the address: **$C$5**).
F5	GoTo	In **READY** mode, moves the cell pointer to a specified cell.
F6	Window	In split-screen mode, moves the cell pointer to the other window.
F7	Query	In **READY** mode, repeats the most recent **Data Query** operation. Useful when you are changing search criteria.
F8	Table	In **READY** mode, repeats the most recent **Data Table** operation.
F9	Calc	In **READY** mode, causes the formulas that may have changed as a result of changes to the worksheet (except for Data Tables) to be recalculated.
		In **EDIT** or **VALUE** mode, causes a formula to be replaced with its numeric value.
F10	Graph	In **READY** mode, causes a graph to be drawn according to the most recent specifications. If no graph is currently specified, creates and displays a graph using data in the worksheet range where the cell pointer is located.
Alt-F1	Compose	To create characters not on your keyboard.

Alt-F2	Record	For macros. To copy recorded keystrokes to cells on your worksheet, or to playback (do over) keystrokes you have already typed. When testing macros, turns Step mode on and off.
Alt-F3	Run	To select a macro to run.
Alt-F4	Undo	When the undo feature is on, use this to cancel your last action Useful for cancelling a variety of mistakes.
Alt-F6	Zoom	Enlarges current window to full size or shrinks it to original size.

Note: This book refers specifically to keys found on IBM computers and compatibles. If your computer does not have function keys (**F1** through **F10**) and an **Alt** key, refer to your 1-2-3 documentation for the keys to tap for these functions—**Help, Edit, Name, Absolute, GoTo, Window, Query, Table, Calc, Graph,** and **Macro.**

Related:
F1,	see	**Help**
F2,		**Editing Cell Contents**
F3,		**Highlight a Cell, Retrieve a File, Ranges**
F4,		**Relative and Absolute Cell Reference**
F5,		**Highlight a Cell, GoTo**
F6,		**Windows**
F7,		**Database—5, 6, 7, and 8**
F9,		**Recalculation Modes and Calc**
F10,		**Graphs**
Alt-F2,		**Macros**
Alt-F3,		**Macros**
Alt-F4,		**Undo**
Alt-F6,		**Windows**

Functions

Note: Functions are built-in formulas that perform specialized and often difficult calculations. Most work with numbers; some work with text (called labels or strings).

All functions start with @. Most have parentheses ( ). You put cell references or information within the ( ). Anything within the ( ) is called an argument or parameter. Multiple arguments are separated by commas.

Examples of arguments in functions:

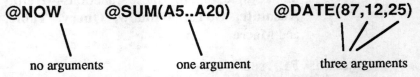

@NOW	**@SUM(A5..A20)**	**@DATE(87,12,25)**
no arguments	one argument	three arguments

Arguments can be of these types (depending on the function):

values	**@DATE(87,12,28)**
cell addresses	**@DATE(B5,C5,D5)**
range names	**@DATE(YEAR,MONTH,DAY)**
functions	**@INT(@NOW)**
calculations	**@DATE(B5+3,C5-1,D5+1)**
strings (in quotes)	**@IF(A5=12,"GOOD JOB"," ")**
conditions (A5=12)	**@IF(A5=12,"GOOD JOB"," ")**

Just like values and formulas, functions have *no spaces*, except in strings enclosed in quotes; for example:

@IF(A5=12,"GOOD   JOB"," ")

"GOOD JOB" is a string in quotes. **" "** is a string of spaces.

The following chart shows different categories of functions. Examples are given for the most commonly used functions, shown in boldface type. The Lotus 1-2-3 documentation includes many pages on functions where you can refer for information not included here.

Type of Functions	Uses and Examples
Statistical	**SUM, AVG, COUNT, MAX**, min, variance, standard deviation
Logical	**IF**, others mainly for advanced spreadsheets
Special	**CHOOSE, VLOOKUP**, others
Mathematical	**INT, ROUND, MOD** (remainder), Trig functions (sine, cosine), log, pi
String	**PROPER**, string manipulation
Date & Time	*see* **Dates**
Financial	**PMT**, loans, annuities, cash flows
Database statistical	*see* **Database 8—Database Functions**

Related: **Dates**
Database 8—Database Functions
Designing Spreadsheets
Formulas

Example 1: Use **@SUM**, **@AVG**, **@COUNT**, and **@MAX** in a sales report.

You: Create the following spreadsheet:

	A	B	C	D	E	F	G	H	I	J
1	Sales	Mon	Tues	Wed	Thur	Fri		Total	Avg	Sales
2	Person	Sales	Sales	Sales	Sales	Sales		Sales	Sales	Count
3	------	-----	-----	-----	-----	-----	—	-----	-----	-----
4	Jones	200	500		300					
5	Smith	800	900	850	900	800				
6	Adams	50		50						
7										
8	Highest									

Format all the cells as fixed with zero decimal places

You: Type **/ W G F , Ø ←**   *to format the worksheet as Fixed,*
no decimals

Use @SUM to find the total sales for each person

You: Highlight cell H4.
Type **@SUM(← ← . ← ← ← ←) ←**

Note: The arrow keys paint the range B4..F4

1-2-3:   **@SUM(B4..F4)** *in upper-left corner of screen*

You: Type **/ C ← . ↓ ↓ ←**   *to copy the formula down*

1-2-3:

	A	B	C	D	E	F	G	H	I	J
1	Sales	Mon	Tues	Wed	Thur	Fri		Total	Avg	Sales
2	Person	Sales	Sales	Sales	Sales	Sales		Sales	Sales	Count
3	--------	-------	-------	-------	-------	--------		-------	-------	-------
4	Jones	200	500		300			1000		
5	Smith	800	900	850	900	800		4250		
6	Adams	50		50				100		
7										
8	Highest									

Use @AVG to find the average sales

You: Highlight cell I4.
Type **@AVG(← ← ← . ← ← ← ←) ←**

Note: The arrow keys paint the range B4..F4

1-2-3:   **@AVG(B4..F4)** *in upper-left corner of screen*

You: Type **/ C ← . ↓ ↓ ←**   *to copy the formula down*

1-2-3:

	A	B	C	D	E	F	G	H	I	J
1	Sales	Mon	Tues	Wed	Thur	Fri		Total	Avg	Sales
2	Person	Sales	Sales	Sales	Sales	Sales		Sales	Sales	Count
3	--------	-------	-------	-------	-------	--------		-------	-------	-------
4	Jones	200	500		300			1000	333	
5	Smith	800	900	850	900	800		4250	850	
6	Adams	50		50				100	50	
7										
8	Highest									

Use @COUNT to count the numbers of sales days

You: Highlight cell J4.

Type @COUNT(← ← ← ← . ← ← ← ←) ↵

Note: the arrow keys paint the range B4..F4

1-2-3:   **@COUNT(B4..F4)** *in upper-left corner of screen*

You: Type / C ↵ . ↓ ↓ ↵   *to copy the formula down*

1-2-3:

	A	B	C	D	E	F	G	H	I	J
1	Sales	Mon	Tues	Wed	Thur	Fri		Total	Avg	Sales
2	Person	Sales	Sales	Sales	Sales	Sales		Sales	Sales	Count
3	---------	-------	-------	-------	-------	-------	--	-------	-------	-------
4	Jones	200	500		300			1000	333	3
5	Smith	800	900	850	900	800		4250	850	5
6	Adams	50		50				100	50	2
7										
8	Highest									

Use @MAX to determine the highest sales on each day

You: Highlight cell B8.

Type **@MAX(↑ ↑ . ↑ ↑)** ↵

Note: The arrow keys paint the range B4..B6

1-2-3:   **@MAX(B4..B6)** *in upper-left corner of screen*

You: Type / C ↵ . → → → → ↵   *to copy the formula across*

1-2-3:

	A	B	C	D	E	F	G	H	I	J
1	Sales	Mon	Tues	Wed	Thur	Fri		Total	Avg	Sales
2	Person	Sales	Sales	Sales	Sales	Sales		Sales	Sales	Count
3	---------	-------	-------	-------	-------	-------	--	-------	-------	-------
4	Jones	200	500		300			1000	333	3
5	Smith	800	900	850	900	800		4250	850	5
6	Adams	50		50				100	50	2
7										
8	Highest	800	900	850	900	800				

Example 2:   Use **@IF** in an hours-worked report.

You: Create the following spreadsheet:

	A	B	C	D	E	F
1	pay	total hours		straight time	overtime	worked
2	rate	worked		hours	hours	overtime
3	$5	40				
4	$4	30				
5	$15	55				

You: Highlight cell D3.
       Type   **@IF(B3>40,40,B3)** ⏎

Note: If the person works more than 40 hours, display 40 in cell D3.
       Otherwise, display the value of B3 in cell D3.

You: Highlight cell E3.
       Type **@IF(B3>40,B3-40,Ø)** ⏎

Note: If the person worked more than 40 hours, subtract 40 from the
       hours worked, and show the result in E3. Otherwise, show a zero
       for no overtime.

You: Highlight cell F3.
       Type **@IF(E3>0,"YES","   ")**

Note: If the person worked overtime, show the word YES in cell F3.
       Otherwise, show spaces.

1-2-3:

	A	B	C	D	E	F
1	pay	total hours		straight time	overtime	worked
2	rate	worked		hours	hours	overtime
3	$5	40		40	0	
4	$4	30				
5	$15	55				

You: Highlight cell D3.
       Type **/ C → → ⏎ . ↓ ↓ ⏎**

Note: Copy to copy the formulas from row 3 to rows 4 and 5.

1-2-3:

	A	B	C	D	E	F
1	pay	total hours		straight time	overtime	worked
2	rate	worked		hours	hours	overtime
3	$5	40		40	0	
4	$4	30		30	0	
5	$15	55		40	15	YES

Example 3: @CHOOSE allows you to pick choices from a list where the choices are numbered 0, 1, 2, 3, etc. Here is an example reporting how a person heard of a job opening. By assigning a code to each source for new employment, you save time typing when entering new employees.

Here are the source codes for the sources of new employees:

choice 0	Advertising
choice 1	Friend
choice 2	Relative
choice 3	Agency
choice 4	Other

You: Create the following spreadsheet:

	A	B	C
1	Employee name	Source #	Source
2	Smith	3	
3	Jones	0	
4	Adams	2	

You: Highlight cell C2.

Type **@CHOOSE(B2,"advertising","friend","relative", "agency","other")** ←┘

Note: The first argument (B2) has values 0, 1, 2, 3, or 4. If it is 0, then advertising is chosen, If it is a 1, then friend is chosen.

1-2-3:

	A	B	C
1	Employee name	Source #	Source
2	Smith	3	agency
3	Jones	0	
4	Adams	2	

You: Type / C ↵ . ↓ ↓ ↵   *to copy down the column*

1-2-3:

	A	B	C
1	Employee name	Source #	Source
2	Smith	3	agency
3	Jones	0	advertising
4	Adams	2	relative

Example 4:   @IF gives you two choices to put into a cell. @VLOOKUP gives many choices, but it needs a separate table showing those choices. In this example, different discount rates are given to employees based on their number of years with the firm.

You: Create the following spreadsheet:

	A	B	C	D	E	F
1	Name	Years with company	Discount		Discount table	
2	Smith	10			2	0%
3	Jones	3			5	3%
4	Adams	30			10	7%
5					15	15%
6					25	24%

Note: The discount table in E2..F6. The lookup function uses this table.

You: Highlight cell C2.
       Type   @VLOOKUP(B2,$E$2..$F$6,1) ↵

Note: The value of the first argument, B2, is looked up in the left-most column of the table, E2..F6.   The dollar signs "$" make the table address absolute, for copying purposes. The value in the table's second column (column F) appears in the cell where the function is located (column C).   The third argument, 1, means the second column of the table.

You: Type / C ↵ . ↓ ↓ ↵   *Copy*

1-2-3:

	A	B	C	D	E	F
1	Name	Years with company	Discount		Discount table	
2	Smith	10	0.07		2	0%
3	Jones	3	0.01		5	3%
4	Adams	30	0.24		10	7%
5					15	15%
6					25	24%

You: Type **/ R F P Ø** ←⏎↓↓←⏎   *Range Format Percent Zero*

1-2-3:

	A	B	C	D	E	F
1	Name	Years with company	Discount		Discount table	
2	Smith	10	7%		2	0%
3	Jones	3	1%		5	3%
4	Adams	30	24%		10	7%
5					15	15%
6					25	24%

Example 5: When you format a number such as 5.43 to show Ø decimal places, it will appear as 5, but calculations using this cell will use the actual value of 5.43. Therefore, formatting a number to show Ø decimal places when the actual number has decimal data can result in the appearance of errors. The following illustrates this dilemma.

Use **@INT** or **@ROUND** to make the answers look correct. This is a problem not just with computer spreadsheets, but with manual spreadsheets, also.

You: Create the following spreadsheet:

	A	B	C	D	E
1		General	Comma Ø	Round	Truncate
2	number 1	55.7	55.7		
3	number 2	2.1	2.1		
4	number 3	6.6	6.6		
5					
6	total				

You: Highlight cell B6.
Type **@SUM(B2..B4)** ←⏎ *to add the numbers in column B*
Type **/ C** ←⏎ **.** → → → ←⏎ *Copy*

1-2-3:

	A	B	C	D	E
1		General	Comma Ø	Round	Truncate
2	number 1	55.7	55.7		
3	number 2	2.1	2.1		
4	number 3	6.6	6.6		
5					
6	total	64.4	64.4	0	0

Notice that the sum is 64.4. This is correct.

You: Highlight cell C2.

Type **/ R F, Ø** ↵ ↓ ↓ ↓ ↓ ↵ *Range Format with zero decimals*

1-2-3:

	A	B	C	D	E
1		General	Comma Ø	Round	Truncate
2	number 1	55.7	56		
3	number 2	2.1	2		
4	number 3	6.6	7		
5					
6	total	64.4	64	0	0

The total in column C looks **wrong!**

In column C the numbers appear as rounded numbers: 55.7 appears as 56 and 6.6 appears as 7, but the actual contents of column C are the same as in column B.   The numbers used in the addition were the actual contents in the cells of column C, not the rounded numbers that appear there. The answer is right, it just *looks* wrong.

There are two methods we can use to correct this apparent error: either round the numbers up, or truncate all the decimal places. In either case, we will make the actual numbers the same as the numbers that appear to be in the cells.

A rounding solution using @ROUND

You: Highlight cell D1.

Type **"Round** ↵

Tap ↓

Type **@ROUND(B2,Ø)** ↵   *to round to zero decimal places*

Type **/ C** ↵ **. ↓ ↓** ↵   *Copy*

1-2-3:		A	B	C	D	E
	1		General	Comma Ø	Round	Truncate
	2	number 1	55.7	56	56	
	3	number 2	2.1	2	2	
	4	number 3	6.6	7	7	
	5					
	6	total	64.4	64	65	0

The total—65—looks correct for the numbers in column D.

A truncation solution using @INT

You: Highlight cell E1.

Type **"Truncate ←⅃**

Tap ↓

Type **@INT(B2) ←⅃**   *to drop the decimal places without rounding*

Type   **/ C ←⅃ . ↓ ↓ ←⅃**   *Copy*

1-2-3:		A	B	C	D	E
	1		General	Comma Ø	Round	Truncate
	2	number 1	55.7	56	56	55
	3	number 2	2.1	2	2	2
	4	number 3	6.6	7	7	6
	5					
	6	total	64.4	64	65	63

The total—63—looks correct for the numbers in column E.

Result: Remember, 64 is the closest integer answer for the sum of these numbers. Our formatting with zero decimal places in column C showed an apparently wrong answer. Rounding (column D) shows 65, while truncation (column E) shows 63 as the correct answer. Most applications round, but you can take your choice. Depending on the data, either rounding or truncation could be more accurate. Column C has the right answer, but it will look wrong to anyone reviewing your spreadsheet.

Example 6:   Sometimes you want the remainder, not the quotient, from a division. The function that provides the remainder is **@MOD**. A good example is in the **Dates** section.

Example 7:   @PROPER is used to convert lower- or uppercase data to a proper form, where only the first character of each word is capitalized. This is especially useful for mailing labels or other situations where names and addresses are incorrectly entered.

You: Create the following spreadsheet, entering upper- and lowercase as shown:

	A	B	C
1	JANE EVANS		
2	JIM MAC INTIRE		
3	john smith		

You: Highlight cell C1.

Type @PROPER(A1) ↵

Type / C ↵ . ↓ ↓ ↵   *Copy*

Result: The following appears:

	A	B	C
1	JANE EVANS		Jane Evans
2	JIM MAC INTIRE		Jim Mac Intire
3	john smith		John Smith

Example 8:   Calculate monthly payments, given principle, interest, and term of loan, using @PMT.

You: Create the following spreadsheet:

	A	B	C
1	Principal		50000
2	Yearly interest rate		7%
3	Term in years		15
4			
5	Monthly payments		

You: Highlight cell C5.
Type @PMT(C1,C2/12,C3*12) ↵

Note: The *first argument,* **C1,** is the principal, or loan amount. The *second argument,* **C2/12** is the monthly interest rate. Because **C2** is an annual rate, we divide by 12. The *third argument,* **C3*12** is the number of months the money is borrowed. Because **C3** is in years, we multiply by 12.

1-2-3:

	A	B	C
1	Principal		50000
2	Yearly interest rate		7%
3	Term in years		15
4			
5	Monthly payments		449.4141

You: Type **/ R F C ←┘←┘** *Range Format Currency*

1-2-3:

	A	B	C
1	Principal		50000
2	Yearly interest rate		7%
3	Term in years		15
4			
5	Monthly payments		$449.41

Now you can calculate how much the bank will charge for your latest loan.

GoTo

Note: The **GoTo** key, **F5**, is used to highlight a specified cell, especially one far from the currently highlighted cell. Here are two ways to use this key:

1. Tap **F5**   *the GoTo key*
    Type in desired cell address, sheet letter, or opened file name.
    Tap ←┘

2. Tap **F5**   *the GoTo key*
    Tap **F3** twice   *the Name key*
    Highlight desired range or file name.
    Tap ←┘

Examples of addresses you can go to:

AB100	Go to this cell address on the current sheet.
C:	Go to sheet C in a multiple sheet file.
C:A1	Go to A1 on sheet C of a multiple sheet file.
<<COST>>A100	Go to A100 on the COST file. The COST file must be open, in addition to the worksheet that this formula is in.

Related: **Highlight a Cell**
Multiple Sheets
Multiple (Linked) Files

Example: To highlight cell W200.

You: Tap the **F5** key.
Type **W2ØØ** ←┘

Result:

	W	X	Y	Z	AA	AB
200	██					
201						
202						

Cell W200 will be in the upper-left corner if it was not already on the screen before you tapped the GoTo key.

Graphing with Wysiwyg

Command: / **Graph**
/ **Worksheet Windows Graph**

Note: Graphs visually illustrate your data and are a powerful means of communication. You can view graphs on most computers. (Your monitor must have graphics capabilities. Many IBM computers with monochrome monitors do not support graphics.)

You can print graphs on dot matrix printers (including those with multiple colored ribbons), laser printers, ink jet printers, and plotters. Most letter-quality daisy wheel or thimble printers do not support graphics.

Worksheet Windows Graph splits your screen so you can view your spreadsheet in the left half and your graph in the right half.

OVERVIEW OF STEPS

- Decide what you want graphed (like sales versus dates).
- Create and save your worksheet.
- Start the **Graph** command.
- Choose the data ranges to graph.
- Choose the type of graph (line, pie, bar, stacked bar, etc.).
- View the graph (to check it).
- Set options—titles, legends, and so on.
- View the graph.
- **Quit** the graph command.
- **SAVE** your worksheet.
- **Print** the graph.

PLANNING: Determining what to graph against the X- and Y-axes requires planning. The rest is like filling in the blanks.

AXES: Normally, the axes are X and Y, as follows:

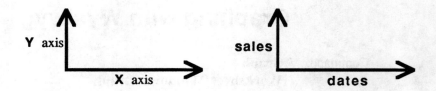

One could graph dates on the X-axis and sales on the Y-axis.

Lotus 1-2-3 permits you to graph up to six separate data ranges on the same graph, so it has renamed the Y-axis with six names, the A-axis, the B-axis, and so on, through F.

The data ranges you graph should be parallel to each other in the worksheet. For example, if you graph sale amounts on the Y-axis and dates on the X-axis, then sale amounts and dates should both be rows of data (or they should both be columns of data).

MENUS: The **Graph Menu** appears after you type / G. It is:

**Type X A B C D E F Reset View Save Options
Name   Group Quit**

The **Options Submenu** is seen by choosing Options in the Graph Menu. It says:

**Legend   Format   Titles   Grid   Scale   Color   B&W
Data-Labels Advanced   Quit**

There are many submenus. To get out of a submenu, choose **Q** for **Quit,** or tap the **Esc** key. This returns you to the previous Menu.

Here is a chart showing how to move between menus.

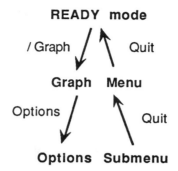

READY mode

/ Graph   Quit

Graph Menu

Options   Quit

Options Submenu

Tip: Be careful not to choose Quit from the main 1-2-3 menu, because you will quit 1-2-3 and lose all your graph settings. If you see the message **No Yes**, tap **Esc** twice to get out of this situation, or type **N**.

Example 1: Plot sales against dates for each city in this spreadsheet:

A	A	B	C	D	E
1			SALES		
2					
3		1984	1985	1986	1987
4	Akron	200	220	250	190
5	Boston	500	700	300	400
6	Chicago	600	700	800	750

Create and save your worksheet

You: Create the above spreadsheet.

Notice all the ranges are rows:

the X range is row 3—dates
the A range is row 4—sales for Akron
the B range is row 5—sales for Boston
the C range is row 6—sales for Chicago

If we were plotting sales versus cities, each range would be a column. That is:

the X range would be column A—names of the cities
the A range would be column B—year 1984
the B range would be column C—year 1985
the C range would be column D—year 1986
the D range would be column E—year 1987

You: Type / F S SALES1 ↵   *File Save*

If **Cancel Replace Backup** appears, tap **R** to replace the file on disk. If you don't want to replace it, tap **C** *Cancel* or **B** *Backup*.

Start the Graph command

You: Type / G *Graph*

Type **R G** *Reset Graph—to remove settings from any prior graphs*

1-2-3: **Type X A B C D E F Reset View Save Options Name   Group   Quit**
the Graph Menu

Choose the data ranges to graph

You: Type G B3..E6 ↵   *Group, where B3 to E6 contains the X, A, B and C ranges*

You: Type **R** *Rowwise*

Note: If your X range is a row, choose **Rowwise**. In our example, X is the row of dates in row 3, so you specified **Rowwise**. If the X range were a column (the column of cities in column A) you would choose **Columnwise**.

The **Group** option permits us to select all our ranges at once. Otherwise, we would need to specify each range, X, A, B, and C separately.

Choose the type of graph

You: Type **T B** *Type Bar*

Note: Bar charts tend to look more spectacular than line graphs. Stacked bar charts show totals while revealing the component parts, so stacked bar is also appropriate here. Don't include a "totals" row when graphing stacked bar charts because the height of the stacked bar is the total. XY charts require that the X range also contain numbers. Pie charts and HLCO (high-low-close-open) are special and are illustrated in examples following this one.

View the graph (to check it)

You: Tap **F10** *to view current graph*

1-2-3:

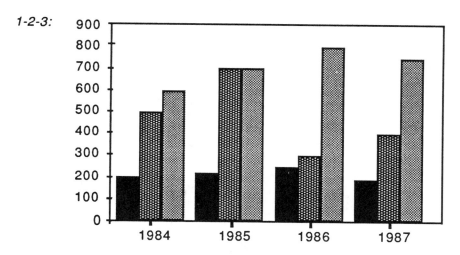

If you have a color monitor, this will automatically be in color. If your printer is black and white, 1-2-3 will automatically convert the colors to cross-hatching.

You: Tap ← *or any key, to get back to the menus and worksheet.*

1-2-3: **Type X A B C D E F Reset View Save Options Name Group Quit**
the Graph Menu

Set options—like titles, legends, and so on

You: Type **O** *Options*

1-2-3: **Legend Format Titles Grid Scale Color B&W Data-Labels Advanced Quit** *the Options Submenu*

You: Type **L R A4..A6** ⏎   *Legend Range, the range contains the names of the three cities*

Type **T F WIDGET** ⏎   *Titles First. Your main title.*

Type **T S SALES HISTORY** ⏎ *Titles Second*

Type **Q**   *Quit—to quit the Options submenu and get back to the Graph menu*

View the graph

You: Tap **F10** *to view current graph*

1-2-3:

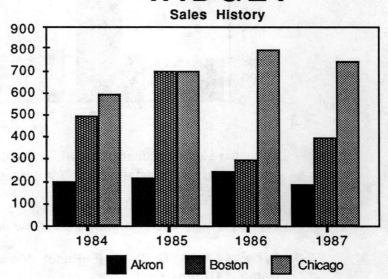

You: Tap ⏎ *to return to the Graph menu*

1-2-3: **Type X A B C D E F Reset View Save Options Name Group Quit** *the Graph Menu*

Quit the Graph menu

>**You:** Type **Q** *Quit—to quit the Graph menu*

>*1-2-3:* **READY**

Save your worksheet

>**You:** Type / **F S SALES1** ↵ *File Save—to save your worksheet and graph settings*

>If **Cancel Replace Backup** appears, tap **R** to replace the file on disk. If you don't want to replace it, tap **C** *Cancel* or **B** *Backup*.

Print the graph

>**You:** Turn on the printer or plotter. Adjust paper to the top of the perforation if it is continuous feed. Be sure the printer is in ready mode (on-line).

>**You:** Type / **P P I C A G P Q** *Print Printer Image Current Align Go Page Quit*

>With continuous feed paper, type this instead: / **P P I C A G P P Q** *Print Printer Image Current Align Go Page Page Quit*

>**Wait.** Printing, even on laser printers, can take several minutes or more. But, since 1-2-3 prints in the background, you can continue working.

View your graph in split screen

>**You:** Move the cell pointer until it is in a cell approximately in the middle of the screen.

>Type / **W W G** *Worksheet Windows Graph*

>*1-2-3:* Both your spreadsheet and graph appear on the screen.

>**Note:** Any changes you now make to your spreadsheet data will be instantly reflected in your graph.

Remove split screen

You: Type **/ W W C** *Worksheet Windows Clear*

Example 2: Print a pie chart of the total sales (row 8) by year (row 3) using the following spreadsheet:

	A	B	C	D	E
1			SALES		
2					
3		1984	1985	1986	1987
4	Akron	200	220	250	190
5	Boston	500	700	300	400
6	Chicago	600	700	800	750
7					
8	Total	1300	1620	1350	1340
9					
10	color	1	11	7	108
11	indicators				

Create and save your worksheet

You: Create the above spreadsheet. For row 8, follow these instructions:

Highlight cell B8.
Type   **@SUM(B4..B6)** ←┘
Type   **/ C B8** ←┘ **C8..E8** ←┘   *to copy the formula across*

You: Type   **/ F S SALES2** ←┘   *File Save*

If **Cancel Replace Backup** appears, tap **R** to replace the file on disk. If you don't want to replace it, tap **C** *Cancel* or **B** *Backup*.

Start the Graph command

You: Type **/ G** *Graph*

Type **R G** *Reset Graph—to remove settings from any prior graphs*

Choose the data ranges to graph

Pie charts can only graph an A range. The B range is used for color and separated slice indication. Because the ranges are not in adjacent rows, we do not use the Group option.

You: Type **X B3..E3** ↵   *X range is the dates*

             Type **A B8..E8** ↵   *A range is the total sales*

             Type **B B10..E10** ↵   *B range is color and separated slices*

The numbers in row 10 are color indicator numbers. Use numbers 1 through 14 for different colors. Use 101 through 114 for separated slices (where the slice is slightly separated from the pie).

Choose the type of graph (line, pie, bar, stacked bar, etc.)

       You: Type **T P** *Type Pie*

View the graph (to check it)

       You: Tap **F10** *to view current graph*

             Tap ↵ *to return to the Graph menu*

Set options, like titles and color (you automatically get a legend)

       You: Type **O** *Options*

             Type **T F SALES** ↵ *Titles First—for first line of title*

             Type **T S PROJECTION** ↵   *Titles Second—for second line of title*

             Type **Q** *Quit*

    1-2-3:   **Type X A B C D E F Reset View Save Options Name Group Quit**
               the Graph Menu

View the graph

       You: Tap the **F10** key *to view the graph*

1-2-3:

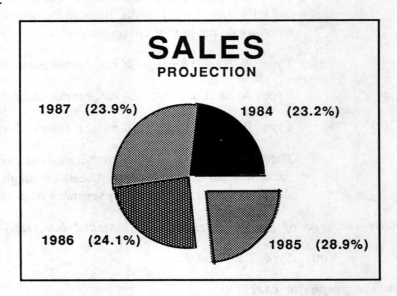

You: Tap ⟵ *or any key, to get back to the menus and worksheet*

Quit the Graph menu

You: Type **Q** *Quit—to quit the Graph menu*

1-2-3: READY

Save your worksheet

You: Type **/ F S SALES2** ⟵ *to save your worksheet*

If **Cancel Replace Backup** appears, tap **R** to replace the file on disk. If you don't want to replace it, tap **C** *Cancel* or **B** *Backup*.

Print the graph

You: Turn on the printer or plotter. Adjust paper. Be sure printer is ready (on-line).

Type **/ P P I C A G P Q** *Print Printer Image Current Align Go Page Quit.*

Example 3: Print an HLCO (high-low-close-open) chart for the stock prices shown on the following spreadsheet:

	A	B	C	D	E
1			WIDGETS COMPANY		
2					
3		day 1	day 2	day 3	day 4
4	high	150	150	156	157
5	low	130	130	135	136
6	close	132	135	144	146
7	open	144	144	144	144

Create and save your worksheet

You: Create the above spreadsheet.

Type **/ F S STOCK1** ← *File Save*

If **Cancel Replace Backup** appears, tap **R** to replace the file on disk. If you don't want to replace it, tap **C** *Cancel* or **B** *Backup*.

Start the Graph command

You: Type **/ G** *Graph*

Type **R G** *Reset Graph—to remove settings from any prior graphs*

Choose the data ranges to graph

You: Type **G B3..E7** ← *Group where B3 to E7 contains the date (X range), high, low, close, and open ranges*

You: Type **R** *Rowwise*

Choose the type of graph (line, pie, bar, stacked bar, etc.)

You: Type **T H** *Type HLCO*

View the graph (to check it)

You: Tap the **F10** key *to view the graph*
Tap ← *to return to the Graph menu*

Set options, like titles and color

You: Type **O** *Options*

Type **T F \C1** ← *Titles First—use contents of C1 as the title*

Type **T S STOCK PRICES** ← *Titles Second—for second line of title*

Type **Q** *Quit*

1-2-3: **Type X A B C D E F Reset View Save Options Name   Group   Quit**
the Graph Menu

View the graph

You: Tap the **F10** key *to view the graph*

1-2-3:

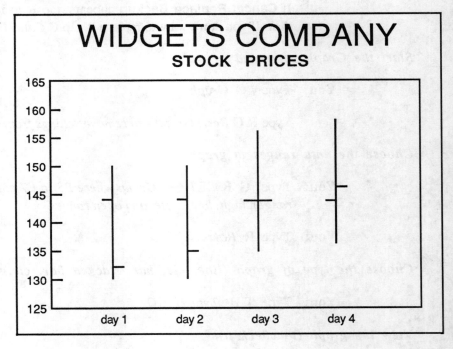

You: Tap ← *or any key, to get back to the menus and worksheet*

Quit the graph menu

> **You:** Type **Q** ~~*Quit*~~—*to quit the Graph menu.*

Save your worksheet

> **You:** Type **/ F S STOCK1** ←┘ *to save your worksheet and graph settings*
>
> If **Cancel Replace Backup** appears, tap **R** to replace the file on disk. If you don't want to replace it, tap **C** *Cancel* or **B** *Backup.*

Print the graph

> **You:** Turn on the printer or plotter. Adjust paper. Be sure printer is ready (on-line).
>
> Type **/ P P I C A G P Q** *Print Printer Image Current Align Go Page Quit.*

HELP

Note: You may request **Help** at any time, even in the middle of a command, by tapping **F1** (the **Help** key). Various items for selection will appear on the screen. Highlight a selection then tap ↵   The Help Index is a useful choice; selecting it produces an index of all the available topics.

Help is content sensitive, which means that 1-2-3 tries to figure out what you are in the middle of doing, and displays the appropriate help screen.

To get out of **Help** mode, tap the **Esc** key.

Example: Get some help.

You: Tap the **F1** key   *the help key*

1-2-3:   Your worksheet is replaced with a help screen.

You: Tap an arrow key to highlight any selection you wish.

Tap ↵

1-2-3:   Another help screen appears.

You: Choose other selections.

When finished, tap the **Esc** key.

1-2-3:   You are back to your worksheet.

Hiding Cell Contents

Command: / **Range Format Hidden**

Note: Occasionally you may wish to enter comments on your worksheet
that will not be printed, such as the name of the file or the
completion date. If you format a cell as Hidden, it will display and
print as if it were empty. The only way to see the contents of a
hidden cell is to highlight the cell and look at the upper-left corner of
the screen.

Related: **Annotating Numbers with Hidden Comments**
Formatting Numbers

Example: Hide the file name in cell A1.

You: Highlight cell A1.

Type **XXXXX** ←⏎   *Enter the real file name instead of XXXXX*

1-2-3:   **A:A1: 'XXXXX**   **READY**

A	A	B	C	D
1	XXXXX			

You: Type / **R F H** ←⏎ *Range Format Hidden*

Result: **A:A1: (H) 'XXXXX**   **READY**

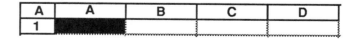

A	A	B	C	D
1				

Because cell A1 is highlighted, you can see its contents at the
upper-left. However, the cell itself appears empty.

Hiding Columns

Command: **/ Worksheet Column Hide**
/ Worksheet Column Display

Related: **Titles   Printing—Borders**
Windows   Printing—Nonadjacent Columns

Example: Hide the appearance of columns B through I in this worksheet:

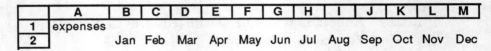

Hide columns

You: Type **/ W C H B1..I1 ←** *Worksheet Column Hide*

1-2-3:

	A	J	K	L	M
1	expenses				
2		Sep	Oct	Nov	Dec

Columns B through I have disappeared from the screen.

To redisplay the hidden columns

You: Type **/ W C D** *Worksheet Column Display*

1-2-3: The hidden columns are temporarily displayed with asterisks:

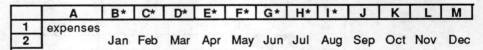

You: Type **B1..I1 ←**   *or highlight cells in desired columns*

1-2-3: The hidden columns have reappeared:

	A	B	C	D	E	F	G	H	I	J	K	L	M
1	expenses												
2		Jan	Feb	Mar	Apr	May	Jun	Jul	Aug	Sep	Oct	Nov	Dec

Highlight a Cell

Note: Highlighting one or more cells selects them for an intended action. The highlight may appear on the screen as reverse video, a different color, or a box around the cell(s).

Highlight the desired cell before entering information. Highlight the desired cell before starting commands to format or copy, and so on. During many commands you can highlight a range of cells. This is called painting.

Here are keyboard techniques to highlight one or more cells:

Tap ↑ ↓ → ←	Move to the next cell.
Tap **PgUp PgDn**	Move up or down one screen.
Tap ⇆ (**Tab**)	Move right one screen.
Hold **Ctrl** and tap →	Move right one screen.
Hold **Shift** and tap ⇆	Move left one screen.
Hold **Ctrl** and tap ←	Move left one screen.
Tap **Home**	Move to cell A1 unless titles is on.
Tap **End**, then tap **Home**	Move to lower-right of worksheet; this is a good way to see the size of the worksheet.
Tap **End**, then tap an arrow	If current cell is empty, move to the next cell that contains data. If current cell contains data, then move to the last contiguous cell containing data. Good for painting ranges.
Tap the **F5** key, (the **GoTo** key)	You are prompted for a cell address. See **GoTo**.

Tip: Use the **F5** (**GoTo**) key to navigate large distances.

Use **PgUp PgDn** and ⇆ to navigate intermediate distances.

Use ↑ ↓ → ← to navigate on the same screen.

Better yet, use the mouse, if you have one.

Related: **GoTo**
           Mouse Basics

Example: Use the **End** key to highlight a range during a command. This only works if there are no empty cells along the edges of the range you are painting. In this case, notice that B3..B8 and B8..D8 have no empty cells, so we are okay.

You: Create the following worksheet:

	A	B	C	D	E
1					
2					
3		XXXXX	XXXXX	XXXXX	
4		XXXXX	XXXXX	XXXXX	
5		XXXXX	XXXXX	XXXXX	
6		XXXXX	XXXXX	XXXXX	
7		XXXXX	XXXXX	XXXXX	
8					
9					

Use any data you wish in place of the XXXXXs.

Try a command that uses a range

You: Highlight cell B3.

           Type **/ P P R**   *Print Printer Range*

1-2-3: **Enter Print range:**

You: Tap the **Backspace** key   *to change the range reference to B3*
           Tap **.**   *tapping a period to changes B3 into the range B3..B3*
           Tap the **End** key.

1-2-3: **END** appears in the lower-left corner of the screen.

You: Tap ↓

1-2-3:   **Enter Print range: B3..B7**

	A	B	C	D	E
1					
2					
3		XXXXX	XXXXX	XXXXX	
4		XXXXX	XXXXX	XXXXX	
5		XXXXX	XXXXX	XXXXX	
6		XXXXX	XXXXX	XXXXX	
7		XXXXX	XXXXX	XXXXX	
8					
9					

You: Tap the **End** key.

1-2-3:   **END** appears in the lower-left corner of the screen.

You: Tap →

1-2-3:   **Enter Print range: B3..D7**

	A	B	C	D	E
1					
2					
3		XXXXX	XXXXX	XXXXX	
4		XXXXX	XXXXX	XXXXX	
5		XXXXX	XXXXX	XXXXX	
6		XXXXX	XXXXX	XXXXX	
7		XXXXX	XXXXX	XXXXX	
8					
9					

Import Data into 1-2-3

Command: / **File Import**
          / **Data Parse**

Note: Use the / **File Import** command to load information from ASCII files.

What is an ASCII file? You don't need to know what ASCII stands for, but to impress people at parties, tell them it means American Standard Code for Information Interchange. And be sure you pronounce it correctly—say *ASS KEY*.

So what is an ASCII file? Your word processor may call such a file a *text, non-binary, ASCII,* or *unformatted* file. 1-2-3 calls them *print* files. dBASE refers to them as *SDF* or *DELIMITED* files. Your mainframe computer may download such files to you. Essentially, ASCII files are files with no special control (or binary) characters—just plain old data.

If you have an ASCII file, you may use **File Import** to copy that file into a 1-2-3 worksheet. While 1-2-3 assumes the file extension is .PRN, it can be anything else.

To use **File Import** effectively, the file looks like this, with quotes around the character strings and information lined up in columns:

```
"JONES"    53.25    400.90
"SMITH"    90.80    876.65
"ZAK"     100.55    600.55
```

File Import has two versions:

1. **Numbers**—Each column of information is put into a separate column. Nonnumeric information must be enclosed in quotes or it is ignored (example "SALES").

2. **Text**—All information goes into one column. This requires the use of an additional command / **Data Parse** to separate the

data into separate columns. Choosing text is probably not what you want to do, even if you are entering text.

dBASE documentation provides additional techniques for transporting data to 1-2-3 from dBASE. In dBASE, you may create files to import into 1-2-3, using either of the dBASE commands that follow:

1. LIST *memo-field* TO MEMO1.PRN
   creates a text file for Memo fields

2. COPY TO *filename*.PRN FIELDS DELIMITED
   creates an ASCII file with quotes around each character field

Related: **File Choices** (a list of cross-references)

Example: Import an ASCII text file into 1-2-3. This file could have been created and downloaded from your mainframe computer, or it could have been created in dBASE, or in any other software package that creates ASCII files.

Create an ASCII file

You: If you don't have an ASCII file available, type the following to create one called JUNKXX:

/ S *System—you are now in DOS. Just keep typing.*
COPY *tap a space* CON *tap a space* JUNKXX.PRN ←┘
"JONES"   53.25   400.90 ←┘
"SMITH"   90.80   876.65 ←┘
"ZAK"   100.55   600.55 ←┘

Tap the **F6** key *to indicate the end of file in DOS*
Tap ←┘
Type **EXIT** ←┘   *Exit takes you back to your spreadsheet.*

1-2-3:   Your worksheet reappears.

Import an ASCII file

You: Highlight the cell where importing is to start. The cells below and to the right will receive the imported data. If these cells already contain data, existing data will be replaced by the new data.

Type **/ F I N** *File Import Number*
Type **JUNKXX.PRN** ⟵ *this is the name of our ASCII file*
Save as usual. Reminder: **/ F S** *File Save* etc.

Notes: If 1-2-3 can't find your ASCII file, you may need to type the drive and directory in front of the file name, for example you might have typed **C:\DBASE\EMPLOYEE.TXT** ⟵ if such a file existed in your \DBASE directory.

If **/ File Import Numbers** does not work, erase those cells and try **/ File Import Text,** followed by **/ Data Parse** to spread the data in the first column across the adjacent columns.

Insert a Column

Command: / **Worksheet Insert Column**

Note: When a column is inserted in the worksheet it is inserted across all 8,192 rows, producing one or more blank columns. It can separate unseen information on your worksheet that should not be separated.

See **Multiple Sheets** for suggestions on separating information across several sheets. If **GROUP** mode is disabled, then inserting a column only inserts it in the sheet you are working on. If **GROUP** is enabled, inserting a column causes that column to be inserted in all the sheets of your worksheet.

Related: **Move**
Multiple Sheets

Example: Insert three columns between columns B and C.

	A	B	C	D	E	F
1	Code	Name	Salary			
2						
3	HIP	Zak	600			
4	FUN	Smith	900			
5	JAZ	Watson	450			

You: Highlight any cell in column C.

Type / **W I C** *Worksheet Insert Column*

Tap → → ↵ *cells in three columns become highlighted*

1-2-3:

three new columns

	A	B	C	D	E	F
1	Code	Name				Salary
2						
3	HIP	Zak				600
4	FUN	Smith				900
5	JAZ	Watson				450

Insert a Row

Command: / **Worksheet Insert Row**

Note: When a row is inserted in the worksheet it is inserted across all 256 columns, producing one or more blank rows. It can separate unseen information on your worksheet that should not be separated.

See **Multiple Sheets** for suggestions on separating information across several sheets. If **GROUP** mode is disabled, then inserting a row only inserts it in the one sheet you are working on. If **GROUP** is enabled, inserting a row causes that row to be inserted in all the sheets of your worksheet.

Related: **Move**
Multiple Sheets

Example: Insert one row between rows 3 and 4.

	A	B	C
1	Code	Name	Salary
2			
3	HIP	Zak	600
4	FUN	Smith	900
5	JAZ	Watson	450

You: Highlight any cell in row 4.
Type   / **W I R** *Worksheet Insert Row*

Note: To insert more than one row, tap ↓ for each additional row.

You: Tap ↵

1-2-3:

	A	B	C
1	Code	Name	Salary
2			
3	HIP	Zak	600	← new row
4			
5	FUN	Smith	900
6	JAZ	Watson	450

Label (Text) Entries

You can enter two types of information into a cell: label information (text) and value information (numbers and formulas). Labels are textual information, like names and addresses, titles, and so on, as well as any information *not* used in computations, like ZIP codes and phone numbers.

Labels may begin with a special character called a label prefix.

- If your label starts with Ø 1 2 3 4 5 6 7 8 9 + - . (@ # / < *or* $ you need to type one of the label prefix characters first or format the cell as a label.
- The apostrophe label prefix (') provides left alignment. Use the apostrophe if you can't decide.
- The quote label prefix (") provides right alignment.
- The caret label prefix (^) centers your label.
- The Backslash label prefix (\) repeats your label within the cell.
- The broken bar label prefix (¦) prevents your label from being printed.
- If a cell is formatted as label **(L)** using / **Worksheet Global Format Other Label** or / **Range Format Other Label**, then you only need a label prefix for entries that begin with / or < . See the example in **Formatting Numbers**.

Related: **Aligning Labels**
                    Formatting Numbers

Example 1: Enter a ZIP code, left aligned.

     You: Highlight the cell where a ZIP code is to be entered.

              Type an apostrophe followed by the ZIP code.

              For example, type **'00622** ←⏎

Example 2: Enter a street address, left aligned.

     You: Highlight the cell where the street address is to be entered.

              Type an apostrophe followed by the street address.

              For example, type **'35 HIGH STREET** ←⏎

Example 3:   Enter the following underlining characters in row 5:

	A	B
1	23	44
2	42	55
3	52	7
4	12	22
5	=====	------

You: Highlight cell A5.

Type   \ = ←⏎   *be sure to tap the Backslash key*

Highlight cell C5.

Type   \ - ←⏎   *this is the minus or hyphen key*

Example 4:   Enter the following right aligned label in cell C1:

	A	B	C	D	E	F
1			AMT			

You: Highlight cell C1.

You: Type **"AMT** ←⏎   *be sure you type the quote at the beginning*

Example 5:   To enter a long label, like PITTSBURGH, PENNSYLVANIA, in cell C1:

	A	B	C	D	E	F
1			PITTSBURGH PENNSYLVANIA			

You: Highlight cell C1.

Type **PITTSBURGH, PENNSYLVANIA** ←⏎

Result: This long label overlaps (spreads) into column D and beyond. Despite appearances however, this label is entirely in cell C1.

If this label does not overlap, it is because already there is something in cells D1 and E1, and it has squatters' rights. Highlight cell D1. If you don't see anything there, you may have spaces (instead of nothing) in cells D1 and E1. In this case use the **Range   Erase** command to erase D1..F1   (/ **R E D1..F1** ←⏎).

Large Worksheets

Large worksheets may present problems because of their bulkiness and the longer time it takes to recalculate formulas. Here are some hints.

- Make backup copies of your work. Keep one copy off-site. That means keep one copy at home if your working copy is at work, or vice versa.

- Once you know a formula is correct, protect it. That way, you won't accidentally destroy it (see **Protecting Cells**).

- Test your spreadsheet in pieces; small pieces are easier to troubleshoot than large pieces.

- Avoid scattering your data across the two billion cells. Cluster your data towards the left columns and top rows. Tap **End** then **Home** periodically to see where the lower-right corner of the worksheet is.

- If possible, use multiple sheets or multiple (linked) files to divide up your information into more manageable chunks.

- If your data is diverse or has recognizable separate pieces, consider putting each piece in its own sheet or file (see **Multiple Sheets** and **Multiple (Linked) Files**).

- If you use macros, put them into a separate sheet or file (see **Macros, Multiple Sheets,** and **Multiple (Linked) Files**).

- You can split the worksheet into multiple files using **File eXtract.** Use **File Combine** or multiple file linking to compute totals as needed (see **File eXtract, Multiple (Linked) Files, File Combine,** and **Designing Spreadsheets—Balance Brought Forward**).

- Consider buying a Math coprocessor chip (hardware) if data entry is too slow for your taste.

- Consider buying memory expansion boards if your worksheet doesn't fit in memory (see the error message **Memory Full**).

List File Names

Command: / **File List**

Note: Use the / **File List** command to list your worksheets, print files, graph files, and so on.

Related: **Directories**
File Choices (this contains a cross-reference)

Example: List your worksheet files.

You: Type / **F L W**   *File List Worksheets*

1-2-3: A screen full of files appears.

You: ← *to end this list mode*

1-2-3: Your worksheet reappears.

Loading Data

Command: / **File Retrieve**
/ **File Combine**
/ **File Import**
/ **File Open**
/ **Data External**

Note: To load a 1-2-3 file from disk, use / **File Retrieve**.

To load part of a 1-2-3 file from disk, use / **File Combine**.

To load an ASCII (text) file with no special control characters, use / **File Import**.

To retrieve multiple files, use / **File Open**.

Related: **Combining 1-2-3 Files**
Database 9—dBASE Input
File Choices (this contains a cross-reference)
Import Data into 1-2-3
Retrieve a File

Macros 1—Creating and Running Macros

A Macro performs a task for you. But first, you create the macro by typing the macro instructions for this task into a worksheet.

Consider these tasks: typing the same thing again and again, or doing the same 1-2-3 command again and again. A macro could help. For instance, it would be nice to format a cell as currency with just two keystrokes, instead of at least six. Especially if you have a lot of separate cells to format!

You *do not need* macros to use your worksheet. Macros can sometimes make your work faster, but they take time to write. In fact, most users don't use macros at all—unless someone else wrote the macros.

Macros can be more than just saved keystrokes. They can be sophisticated programs. Writing such macros is not fast. It can take weeks. Hire an expert to write complex macros if you don't have a strong programming and logic background.

We will limit ourselves to the easier macros—those that consist mainly of commands such as formatting or printing.

OVERVIEW OF STEPS

1. **Write** down (on paper) all the keystrokes you usually use for the commands you plan to put into the macro.

2. **Type** these keystrokes into your worksheet using macro format.

3. **Name** the macro with a **Backslash** and a single letter (for example: \ S). In Release 3, you may use any range name and run the macro with the **Alt-F3** key (the **Run** key).

4. **Save** the worksheet. If your macro has errors, it can mess up the worksheet when you run the macro.

5. **Run** the macro—hold the **Alt** key (the **Macro** key) and tap the single letter which is its name.

The standard in writing macros is to type commands and keywords in lowercase and named ranges and cell addresses in uppercase, or vice versa, to provide a contrast. It is recommended that macros avoid referring to cells and ranges by address and use range names instead. This provides flexibility for future modifications of the worksheet.

Related: **Designing Spreadsheets—Balance Brought Forward**

Example: Write two macros to format a cell as currency or comma.

You: Create the following worksheet:

A	A	B	C
1	Phones	1234.56	
2	Rent	5555	
3	Travel	234.5	
4			
5	TOTAL	7024.06	

1. Write down the keystrokes of the macro

You: Try formatting any cell as currency with zero decimal places. Write down all the keystrokes (including the ↵). One set of keystrokes is / **R F C Ø** ↵ ↵   You may have written a slightly different set involving arrow keys.

2. Type the macro

Let's type it into a separate sheet of a multiple sheet worksheet.

You: Type / **W I S A** ↵ *Worksheet Insert Sheet After-1 sheet*

1-2-3:

B	A	B	C	D	E
1					
2					

This is sheet B of a multiple sheet worksheet.

You: Type / **W W P**   *Worksheet Windows Perspective—to see both sheets*

Note: Now we convert the keystrokes that we wrote down into macro language. For instance, a ↵ becomes a ~ (tilde). Use the following macro conversion table:

Use This	For This	Use This	For This
~	↵	{edit}	F2 key, the Edit key
{up}	up arrow	{name}	F3 key, the Name key
{down}	down arrow	{abs}	F4 key, the Abs key
{right}	right arrow	{goto}	F5 key, the GoTo key
{left}	left arrow	{window}	F6 key, the Window key
{end}	end key	{query}	F7 key, the Query key
{home}	Home key	{table}	F8 key, the Table key
{pgdn}	PgDn key	{calc}	F9 key, the Calc key
{pgup}	PgUp key	{graph}	F10 key, the Graph key
{bs}	Backspace key	{esc}	Esc key

When typing your macro, use this table to convert your keystrokes into macro keystrokes. For example → becomes **{right}** and you must use the correct brackets **{ }**. Parentheses will not work!

Do *not* type spaces into a macro. In the instructions below there may appear to be spaces between keystrokes, but that is only for readability.

You: Highlight cell B1   *you should still be in sheet B*

Type   **' / r f c Ø ~ ~ ↵**   *don't forget the apostrophe*

1-2-3:

B	A	B	C	D
1		/rfcØ~~		

Note: You now have a small macro in cell B:B1 that formats a highlighted cell as **currency** with **zero** decimal places.

The keystrokes ~ ~ in the macro replace the ↵ ↵ that you tap when doing this command.

The apostrophe does not appear in the cell because it is a label prefix character.

Note: When typing a macro, start each cell with an apostrophe. When you type keystrokes of a 1-2-3 command into a cell, you can type as many or as few keystrokes as you wish into each cell. When you run a macro, the stored keystrokes in the first cell of the macro are performed, then the keystrokes in the next cell down. The macro stops running the keystrokes when it finds an empty cell (or one with a value instead of a label).

Let's enter the second macro.

You: Highlight cell B4.

Type **' / r f , Ø ~ ~ ←**   *don't forget a comma after the f*

1-2-3:

B	A	B	C	D
1		/rfcØ~~		
2				
3				
4		/rf,Ø~~		

You now have a small macro in cell B4 that formats a highlighted cell as **comma** with **zero** decimal places.

Let's type commentary in the cells beside the macro statements.

You: Highlight cell C1.

Type **Format - currency, zero decimal places** ←

You: Highlight cell C4.

Type **Format - comma, zero decimal places** ←

Type **/ W C S 40** ← *widen column C to 40 characters*

1-2-3:

B	A	B	C
1		/rfcØ~~	Format - currency, zero decimal places
2			
3			
4		/rf,Ø~~	Format - comma, zero decimal places

3. Name the macro

You: Highlight cell A1.

Type **' \ D** ← *this Backslash letter represents the macro name*

Type **/ R N L R** ↩ *Range Name Label Right—names the macro*

Highlight cell A4.

Type **' \ C** ↩ *this represents the macro name*

Type **/ R N L R** ↩   *Range Name Label Right—to name the macro*

1-2-3:

B	A	B	C
1	\D	/rfcØ~~	Format - currency, zero decimal places
2			
3			
4	\C	/rf,Ø~~	Format - comma, zero decimal places

The Range Name command actually names the macro. The names entered on the worksheet only remind us of the names we gave the macros.

4. Save the worksheet

You: Type **/ F S COST3** ↩

If **Cancel Replace Backup** appears, tap **R** to replace the file on disk. If you don't want to replace it, tap **C** *Cancel* or **B** *Backup*.

5. Run the macro

You: Hold **Ctrl** and tap **PgDn** *to switch to sheet A*

Highlight cell B1 in sheet **A**.

Hold the **Alt** key (the **Macro** key) and tap the letter **C**

1-2-3:

A	A	B	C
1	Phones	1,235	
2	Rent	5555	
3	Travel	234.5	
4			
5	TOTAL	7024.06	

The number in cell B1 now has a comma and no decimals.

You: Highlight cell B5.

Hold the **Alt** key (the **Macro** key) and tap the letter **D**

1-2-3:

A	A	B	C
1	Phones	1,235	
2	Rent	5555	
3	Travel	234.5	
4			
5	TOTAL	$7,024	

The number in cell B5 now has a $, comma, and no decimals.

For practice: Try writing a simple macro to widen a column to 15, right align a label, or save or print a worksheet.

A macro enhancement

Replace the macro in cell B:B1 with the following:

' / r f c Ø ~{END}{DOWN}~ ←⏎

Try out your new macro by highlighting cell B1 in sheet A, then hold the **Alt** key and tap **D**. The **{end}{down}** paints a range of numbers for formatting.

Macros 2—Prompts and Input

Example: Write a macro to put a title, invoice number, and date into cells C1, B3, and D3 of any sheet in a multiple sheet worksheet.

You: Save your current worksheet. Reminder: **/ F S** *File Save* etc.
Type **/ W E Y** *Worksheet Erase Yes*
Type **/ W I S A** ← *Worksheet Insert Sheet After*
Type **/ W W P** *Worksheet Windows Perspective*

1-2-3: You are now in sheet **B** of a two sheet worksheet.

You: Highlight cell A1.
Type   **' \ M** ←
Highlight cell B1.

Note: When typing the following macro, where there is an obvious space, tap the space bar *once*, otherwise, do *not* type any spaces.

You: Type the following:

'{getlabel "Enter a title ",C1}↓

'{let A3,"INVOICE#"}↓

'{getlabel "Enter Invoice Number ",B3}↓

'{getnumber "Enter date in the form mm/dd/yy ",D3}↓

'{goto}D3~↓

'/wcs10~↓

'/rfd1~←

1-2-3:

B	A	B	C	D	E
1	\M	{getlabel "Enter a title ",C1}			
2		{let A3,"INVOICE#"}			
3		{getlabel "Enter Invoice Number ",B3}			
4		{getnumber "Enter date in the form mm/dd/yy ",D3}			
5		{goto}D3~			
6		/wcs10~			
7		/rfd1~			

Note: When this macro runs, the first **getlabel** instruction displays the message **Enter a title** and waits for you to type something, in this case, the title for the worksheet. 1-2-3 puts your answer in cell C1.

The **let** instruction puts the text **INVOICE#** in cell A3.

The second **getlabel** instruction also displays a message at the top of the screen and waits for you to type in an invoice number, which 1-2-3 puts in cell B3.

The **getnumber** instruction gets a date, which is a number, and puts it in cell D3.

The last three instructions in the macro widen column D to 10 and format the date number in cell D3 to look like a date.

Name the macro

You: Highlight cell A1   *where the macro's name is represented*

Type   **/ R N L R** ↵   *Range Name Label Right*

Save the macro

You: Type / **F S MACRO2** ↵

If **Cancel Replace Backup** appears, tap **R** to replace the file on disk. If you don't want to replace it, tap **C** *Cancel* or **B** *Backup*.

Run the macro

You: Hold the **Ctrl** key and tap **PgDn**   *to switch to sheet A*

Hold the **Alt** key, and tap the letter **M**   *to run the macro*

Various messages appear at the top of the screen. First, you type a title, such as **WIDGETS** ↵   then an invoice number, such as 4455 ↵   then a date, such as 5/21/89 ↵   Your result is a worksheet with a title, invoice number, and date.

Macros 3—Automatic Running

Command: **/ Worksheet Global Default Automatic**

Note: Macros can be set to automatically run when you **/ File Retrieve** your worksheet. Many automatically run macros are complex macros written by programmers. However, the balance brought forward macro in the **Designing Spreadsheets** section is a typical macro for automatic running.

OVERVIEW OF STEPS

- **Run the macro** to be sure it works.

- **Give it a second name—\Ø** *Backslash zero*. Highlight the first cell of the macro and type **/ R N C \ Ø** ←┘ ←┘

- **Save** the worksheet. Reminder: **/ F S** *File Save* etc.

- **Retrieve** the worksheet. The macro will automatically run (type **/ F R** etc.).

Note: To automate the running of 1-2-3, use DOS BAT files. To automate the loading of a specific worksheet, save that worksheet using **/ File Save AUTO123** ←┘   To automate the running of a macro when a file is retrieved, name the macro **\Ø** , For examples, see the section **Automatically Loading 1-2-3 Worksheets.**

You can also control whether 1-2-3 runs the **\Ø** macro by using the command **/ Worksheet Global Default Autoexec Yes** *or* **No.** If you choose **No,** then a **\Ø** macro will not run when you load a file containing one.

Related: **Automatically Loading 1-2-3 Worksheets**

Mouse Basics

Note: A mouse is a small handheld piece of hardware. As you move it around on the desktop, a small marker moves around on the screen. You don't need a mouse, but it is often a convenient alternative to your keyboard.

You need to load the Wysiwyg add-in before the mouse works. Move the mouse around. If you see an arrow moving, then the mouse is working. To start Wysiwyg, see **Wysiwyg**, Example 1.

To use a mouse, you need an associated mouse driver, a graphics display unit, and an associated graphics adaptor board. Usually the person who installs your DOS or 1-2-3 software also sets this up. If you need to set up your mouse driver, see **CONFIG.SYS**.

On the right side of the screen, there is an icon panel, which looks like this:

	A	B	C	D	E	F	G	H
1								
2								
3								
4								
5								
6								
7								
8								
9								

◀ ▶ ▲ ▼ ↑ ↓ ?

If you move the mouse to the right of the spreadsheet over the icon panel, you can select one of these icons.

If you move the mouse above the spreadsheet, a menu appears.

Example 1: Select a cell and enter information.

You: Be sure Wysiwyg is started.

Move the mouse pointer to the desired cell.

Click the left mouse button.

1-2-3:   That cell is highlighted.

Example 2:   Select a cell.

You: If the screen isn't white, start Wysiwyg as usual.

Move the mouse pointer to the desired cell.

Click the left mouse button.

1-2-3:   That cell is highlighted.

Example 3:   Select or preselect a range.

You: If the screen isn't white, start Wysiwyg as usual.

Move the mouse pointer to a corner of the desired range (rectangle of cells). Make sure the mouse pointer is in the white area, and not on a border of the spreadsheet.

On the keyboard, press and hold the **Ctrl** key.

Press and hold the left mouse button as you drag the mouse to the opposite corner of the range.

Release the mouse button and the **Ctrl** key.

1-2-3:   That range is highlighted.

Example 4:   Cancel a selected range.

You: If a range isn't selected, select one as in Example 3.

Click the right mouse button to deselect the selected range.

Alternatively, tap Esc to deselect the range.

Example 5:   Select or preselect a three-dimensional range.

You: If the screen isn't white, start Wysiwyg as usual.

Move the mouse pointer to a corner of the desired range.

Press and hold the left mouse button as you drag the mouse to the opposite corner of the range.

Release the button.

Click on the ↑ or ↓ icons (upper-right side of sheet) to move forward or backward to another sheet.

Click the left button again.

1-2-3:   That range is highlighted.

Example 6:   Highlight a range before selecting the command.

You: If the screen isn't white, start Wysiwyg as usual.

Move the mouse pointer to a corner of the desired range.

Hold down **Ctrl**. Press and hold the left mouse button, as you drag the mouse to the opposite corner of the range. Release **Ctrl**.

Release the button. Do *not* press ←⏎

(With keyboard strokes, you would tap F4 and use pointer-movement keys.)

Click on desired command.

1-2-3:   That range is highlighted

Example 7:   Select multiple ranges, for use with : Format, : Named-Style, and : Print commands.

You: If the screen isn't white, start Wysiwyg as usual.

Type a comma or semicolon between each range address.

Move

Command: / Move

Note: **Move** is used to transfer information or formulas from one cell to another cell or from one range to another range

Be attentive using this command because it has two parts:

1.   First you specify the "FROM" cell(s) (a single cell or a range; each cell in this range contains information).
Tap ↵

2.   Then specify the "TO" cell(s) (usually a single cell).
Tap ↵

If you move a named or unnamed range that is referenced in Data Input, Data Criterion, Data Output, Print Ranges, and so on, the command range is changed appropriately. The command range is also changed if you move any of the edges of the range. For example, say the Print Range specifies A1..C5 and you move the fifth row down to the seventh row. The Print Range will now specify A1..C7.

Related: **Insert a Row**
Insert a Column
Copy
Relative and Absolute Cell References

Example 1:   Move data and formulas down three rows.

You: Create the following worksheet:

	A	B
1	Phones	55
2	Rent	555
3	Travel	5
4	Misc	5
5		
6	Total	

You: Highlight cell B6.

Type **@SUM(B1..B4)** ↵

1-2-3:

	A	B
1	Phones	55
2	Rent	555
3	Travel	5
4	Misc	5
5		
6	Total	620

Move this spreadsheet down three rows to make room for a title

You: Tap the **Home** key.

Type **/ M A1..B6** ↵ **A4** ↵ *Move*

1-2-3:

	A	B
1		
2		
3		
4	Phones	55
5	Rent	555
6	Travel	5
7	Misc	5
8		
9	Total	620

You: Highlight cell B9.

Notice the formula has changed to **@SUM(B4..B7)**

Example 2: Move data and formulas up three rows and remove blank lines.

You: Create the following worksheet:

	A	B
1		
2		
3		
4	Phones	55
5	Rent	555
6	Travel	5
7	Misc	5
8		
9	Total	620

Move this spreadsheet up three rows to remove blank lines

You: Type   / M A4..B9 ⟵ A1 ⟵   *to move range A4..B9 up to cell A1*

1-2-3:

	A	B
1	Phones	55
2	Rent	555
3	Travel	5
4	Misc	5
5		
6	Total	620

Multiple (Linked) Files

Commands: / **File Open**
/ **Worksheet Window Perspective**
/ **File New**

Note: You may have multiple files active using / **File Open** instead of / **File Retrieve**. Use the **F6** (GoTo) key or hold **Ctrl** and tap **PgUp** or **PgDn** to switch between open files.

Your worksheet formulas may refer to cells in other files. Worksheets with such formulas are called **linked files**.

Here is an example of a formula linked to another file:

+<<EAST>>C6+<<WEST>>G80

The formula is linked to the files **EAST** and **WEST**. This formula takes values in cell **C6** in the **EAST** file and in cell **G80** in the **WEST** file and adds those values together.

You can open (view simultaneously) several files, even if they are not linked, to compare the contents or to use a macro contained in one file to modify another of those files.

File New adds an empty worksheet as a new file to the one(s) you already have open. See **New Worksheet**.

Related: **Multiple Sheets**
New Worksheet
Erase Worksheet
File Choices (contains a list of cross-references)

Example 1: Create two worksheets with data, then create a third that adds together the numbers in the first two worksheets.

Create a file for the East Division

You: Create this worksheet:

	A	B
1	EAST DIVISION EXPENSES	
2		
3	Rent	5000
4	Salary	3000
5	Supplies	450
6	Other	85
7		
8	TOTAL	8535

You: Type **/ F S EASTDIV** ↵   *to save this worksheet*

If **Cancel Replace Backup** appears, tap **R** to replace the file on disk. If you don't want to replace it, tap **C** *Cancel* or **B** *Backup*.

Create a file for the West Division

You: Create this worksheet:

	A	B
1	WEST DIVISION EXPENSES	
2		
3	Rent	200
4	Salary	300
5	Supplies	80
6	Other	20
7		
8	TOTAL	600

You: Type **/ F S WESTDIV** ↵   *to save this worksheet*

If it exists, type **R** to replace it or **C** to cancel without replacing it.

Create a file for the entire company

You: Create this worksheet:

	A	B
1	CORPORATE EXPENSES	
2		
3	Rent	
4	Salary	
5	Supplies	
6	Other	
7		
8	TOTAL	

You: Type **/ F S CORPEXP** ↵   *to save this worksheet*

If it exists, type **R** to replace it or **C** to cancel without replacing it.

Enter formulas in the third file that are linked to the first two files

You: Highlight cell B3.

Type **+<<EASTDIV>>B3+<<WESTDIV>>B3** ←⏎

Note: This adds the contents of B3 in EASTDIV plus the contents of B3 in WESTDIV and puts the answer in cell B3 of the current worksheet.

You: Type **/ C** ←⏎ **. ↓ ↓ ↓ ↓ ↓** ←⏎   *to copy this formula down*

Highlight cell B7.

Type **/ R E** ←⏎   *to erase the contents of cell B7*

1-2-3:

	A	B
1	CORPORATE EXPENSES	
2		
3	Rent	5200
4	Salary	3300
5	Supplies	530
6	Other	105
7		
8	TOTAL	9135

You: Type **/ F S CORPEXP** ←⏎   *to save this worksheet*

Type **R** to replace it or **C** to cancel without replacing it.

Example 2: Open three worksheet files and quickly switch between them.

You: Type **/ F R CORPEXP** ←⏎   *to retrieve the file CORPEXP that you created in the last example*

You: Type **/ F O B EASTDIV** ←⏎   *File Open Before, to open (retrieve) the file EASTDIV that you created in the last example*

You: Type **/ F O B WESTDIV** ⏎   *File Open Before to open (retrieve) the file WESTDIV that you created in the last example*

You: Type **/ W W P** *Worksheet Windows Perspective*

1-2-3:   All three files appear.

You: Hold **Ctrl** and tap **PgDn** or **PgUp**

1-2-3:   The cell pointer moves to one of the opened files on the screen.

You: Tap the **F5** key   *the GoTo key.*
            Tap the **F3** key   *the Name key*

            Highlight one of the file names that appear, such as **<<CORPEXP>>**

            Tap ⏎

1-2-3:   The cell pointer moves to the indicated file.

You: Hold the **Alt** key and tap **F6**   *Zoom*

1-2-3:   The file you are in zooms out to fill the screen.

You: Hold the **Alt** key and tap **F6**   *Zoom*

1-2-3:   The file you are in zooms back to its smaller size.

Multiple Sheets

Commands: / **Worksheet Insert Sheets**
/ **Worksheet Window Perspective**
/ **Worksheet Global Group**

Note: Multiple sheets are multiple layers contained in one file; the multiple layers create a three-dimensional effect. Multiple sheets may be used for multiple spreadsheets in one file or for one three-dimensional spreadsheet.

Use for multiple spreadsheets:

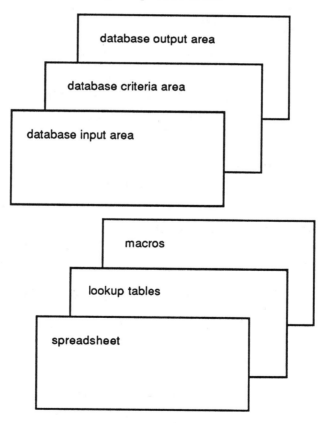

When used in this way, multiple sheets offer greater protection when you make global changes. For example, if you insert a row in the first sheet, it will not affect any other sheet, unless **GROUP** is at the bottom of the screen. You may also use multiple files to hold separate spreadsheets, databases, and macros.

Use for three-dimensional spreadsheets:

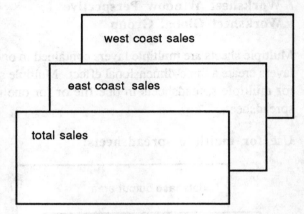

When used in this way, each sheet is a different layer of one spreadsheet. / **File Combine** is an older alternative and may still be used if the combined file is too big to fit into memory. Another alternative is linking multiple files.

Related: **Multiple (Linked) Files**
File Choices (contains a cross-reference)

Example 1:   Create a multiple sheet file for eastern division and western division sales, and then combine the totals on a third sheet for corporate sales.

You: Save your current worksheet. Reminder: / **F S** *File Save* etc.

You: Type / **W E Y** *Worksheet Erase Yes to clear the worksheet area*

Insert two additional sheets

You: Type / **W I S A 2** ←┘ *Worksheet Insert Sheet After 2-sheets*

Look at three sheets simultaneously

You: Type / **W W P** *Worksheet Window Perspective*

Turn on Group mode

> **You:** Type / **W G G E** *Worksheet Global Group Enable*

> *1-2-3:* **GROUP** appears at the bottom of the screen.

In the second sheet (sheet B)

> **You:** Hold **Ctrl** and tap **PgUp** *to switch to the second (B) sheet*

> **You:** Create this worksheet:

B	A	B
1	EAST DIVISION SALES	
2		
3	Widgets	300
4	Gadgets	400
5	Games	500
6		
7	TOTAL	1200

In the third sheet (sheet C)

> **You:** Hold **Ctrl** and tap **PgUp** *to switch to the third (C) sheet*

> **You:** Create this worksheet:

C	A	B
1	WEST DIVISION SALES	
2		
3	Widgets	20
4	Gadgets	30
5	Games	40
6		
7	TOTAL	90

In the first sheet (sheet A)

> **You:** Hold **Ctrl** and tap **PgDn** twice *to switch to the first (A) sheet*

You: Create this worksheet:

A	A	B
1	CORPORATE SALES	
2		
3	Widgets	
4	Gadgets	
5	Games	
6		
7	TOTAL	

You: Highlight cell B3 in sheet A.

           Type **+B:B3+C:B3** ←┘

Note: This adds the value in sheet B cell B3 plus the value in sheet C cell B3 and puts it in the current sheet (sheet A) cell B3.

You: Type **/ C** ←┘ **. ↓ ↓ ↓ ↓** ←┘   *to copy this formula down*

           Highlight cell B6.

           Type **/ R E** ←┘   *to erase the contents of cell B6*

1-2-3:

A	A	B
1	CORPORATE SALES	
2		
3	Widgets	320
4	Gadgets	430
5	Games	540
6		
7	TOTAL	1290

Turn on Group mode

You: Type **/ W G G E** *Worksheet Global Group Enable*

Warning: In Group mode, the formatting you do in one sheet affects the other sheets.

1-2-3:   **GROUP** appears in the lower-right corner.

Improve the appearance—widen columns and format cells

> **You:** Highlight cell A1.
>
> Type / **W C S 14** ↵ *Worksheet Column Set, to widen to 14*
>
> Highlight cell B7.
>
> Type / **R F C 2** ↵ ↵ *Range Format Currency 2 decimals*

1-2-3:

A	A	B
1	CORPORATE SALES	
2		
3	Widgets	320
4	Gadgets	430
5	Games	540
6		
7	TOTAL	$1,290

> Sheets B and C are similarly changed because **GROUP** mode is on.

Turn off Group mode

> **You:** Type / **W G G D** *Worksheet Global Group Disable*
>
> *1-2-3:* **GROUP** disappears from the bottom line.

Save

> **You:** Type / **F S MULTI** ↵ *save this worksheet*
>
> Type **R** to replace it or **C** to cancel without replacing it.

> **Example 2:** Create a multiple sheet file for database processing. Put the input area on sheet **A**, put the criterion on sheet **B** and put the output area on sheet **C**.
>
> **You:** Save your current worksheet. Reminder: / **F S** *File Save* etc.
>
> Type / **W E Y** *Worksheet Erase Yes, to clear the worksheet area*

Insert two additional sheets

      You: Type **/ W I S A 2** ↵   *Worksheet Insert Sheet After 2-sheets*

Look at three sheets simultaneously

      You: Type / **W W P** *Worksheet Window Perspective*

Turn on Group mode

      You: Type / **W G G E** *Worksheet Global Group Enable*

      1-2-3: **GROUP** appears in the lower-right corner.

In the first sheet (sheet A), put the input area

      You: Hold **Ctrl** and tap **PgDn**   *to switch to the first (A) sheet*

      You: Enter this
            information:

A	A	B	C
1	NAME	SALARY	DEPT
2	Adams	400	HQ
3	Davis	200	DP
4	Jones	300	CR
5	Smith	500	HQ
6	Ray	100	DP
7	Rauth	250	HQ
8	Abdill	250	MD

In the second sheet (sheet B), put the criteria area

      You: Hold **Ctrl** and tap **PgUp** *to switch to the second (B) sheet*

      You: Enter this
            information:

B	A	B	C
1	NAME	SALARY	DEPT
2			HQ
3			

      Note: HQ is the criterion for the records we will extract.

In the third sheet (sheet C), put the output area

      You: Hold **Ctrl** and tap **PgUp** *to switch to the third (C) sheet*

You: Enter this
information:

C	A	B	C
1	NAME	SALARY	DEPT
2			
3			

Turn on Group mode

You: Type / **W G G E** *Worksheet Global Group Enable*

Warning: In Group mode, the formatting you do in one sheet affects the other sheets.

1-2-3: **GROUP** appears in the lower-right corner.

Improve the appearance—widen columns and format cells

You: Highlight cell A1.

Type / **W C S 12** ↵ *Worksheet Column Set, to siden to 12*

Highlight cell B2.

Type / **R F , Ø**   *Range Format comma Ø decimals*

Tap **PgDn** ↵ ↵   *to paint the column*

·Turn off Group mode

You: Type / **W G G D** *Worksheet Global Group Disable*

1-2-3: **GROUP** disappears from the bottom line.

Extract all the HQ rows in sheet A to the output area in sheet C

You: Type / **D Q I A:A1..A:C8** ↵ *Data Query Input in sheet A*

Type **C B:A1..B:C2** ↵   *Criteria in sheet B*

Type **O C:A1..C:C1** ↵   *Output in sheet C*

Type **E Q** *Extract Quit*

1-2-3: The extracted output appears in sheet C:

C	A	B	C
1	NAME	SALARY	DEPT
2	Adams	400	HQ
3	Smith	500	HQ
4	Ray	100	DP
5			

Look at the output in sheet C using zoom

You: Tap **F5**

Type **C:** ←┘

Hold the **Alt** key and tap **F6** *to zoom out*

1-2-3: Sheet C appears full screen.

You: Hold the **Alt** key and tap **F6** *to zoom in*

Save

You: Type **/ F S MULTDB** ←┘   *to save this worksheet*

If **Cancel Replace Backup** appears, tap **R** to replace the file on disk. If you don't want to replace it, tap **C** *Cancel* or **B** *Backup*.

New Worksheet

Command: **/ Worksheet Erase**
/ File New

Note: When you are finished using a worksheet, you may erase it and start a new one using **Worksheet Erase**. If you want to keep your current file(s) open, use **File New** to open an additional empty file.

Warning: SAVE before using **Worksheet Erase**, or you may lose the entire worksheet you are currently working on, including any changes since the last time you saved. While 1-2-3 does warn you if you haven't saved your changes, it does not automatically save anything.

Note: **Worksheet Erase** removes all the open files you might have (see **Multiple Files**). **File New** adds another open file to what you already have open.

The **Worksheet Erase** command returns your worksheet to its initial settings—empty cells, column width of 9, cell format of General, and label alignment of left. **Worksheet Erase** does not affect files on disk. **File New** adds a new place-holder file on disk. However, if you don't subsequently **File Save** your new file, it is removed from disk.

Related: **Erase**
File Erase
Erase Worksheet
Save a File

Example 1: Erase the current worksheet and start a new worksheet.

You: Save your current worksheet if you don't want to lose it.

Save your current worksheet. Reminder: **/ F S** *File Save*

If **Cancel Replace Backup** appears, tap **R** to replace the file on disk. If you don't want to replace it, tap **C** *Cancel* or **B** *Backup*.

You: Type **/ W E Y**   *Worksheet Erase Yes*

Result: An empty worksheet appears.

Example 2:   Add a new worksheet to the one(s) you are working on. We will use **Worksheet Window Perspective** so we can see several open files. This is not necessary, it just helps our understanding of the process.

You: Type **/ W W P**   *Worksheet Window Perspective*

1-2-3:   It looks like three worksheets are on the screen. Actually, unless the borders show row numbers and column letters, they aren't really worksheets. The worksheet towards the bottom of the screen is the *first* one.

You: Type **/ F N A NEWTEST** ←┘   *File New After*

If **Cancel Replace Backup** appears, tap **R** to replace the file on disk. If you don't want to replace it, tap **C** *Cancel* or **B** *Backup*.

1-2-3:   Notice that the cell pointer is now in the second or third worksheet of the three on the screen.

Note: To switch between open files, hold **Ctrl** and tap **PgDn** or **PgUp**. Alternatively, tap **F5** (*the GoTo key*), then **F3** (*the Name key*), then highlight the desired file name you wish to go to.

When you have multiple files in memory and you save using **/ File Save**, 1-2-3 displays **[ALL MODIFIED FILES]** in place of the file name. Tap ←┘ to choose that option and save all the open files that have been changed since they were last saved. Otherwise, when you use **File Save**, it only saves the one file your cell pointer is in.

Numeric Entries

Note: There are two types of cell entries:

1. Values—numbers and formulas.

2. Labels—textual information, or numbers that are *not* to be used in computations, like ZIP codes and phone numbers.

Numbers start with one of these characters:

Ø 1 2 3 4 5 6 7 8 9 + - . (*or* $

Numbers may *not* have any spaces.

Numbers may *not* have commas, unless you have formatted those cells as **Automatic**. See **Formatting Numbers**, Chapter 2.

Numbers may end with a % to indicate a percentage.

Numbers can be entered in scientific notation, as shown below:

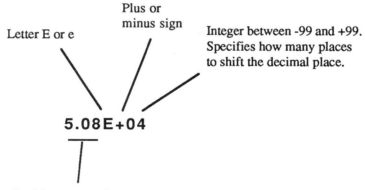

Letter E or e

Plus or minus sign

Integer between -99 and +99. Specifies how many places to shift the decimal place.

5.08E+04

Positive or negative number

Related: **Formatting Numbers**
Column Width
Label Entries
Designing Spreadsheets

Example: Enter 3 million dollars in cell B1.

You: Highlight cell B1.

Type **3000000**   *no commas or spaces*

Tap ←┘

1-2-3:

	A	B	C
1		3000000	
2			

To show dollar signs and commas and format the number

You: Type   **/ R F C Ø** ←┘ ←┘   *Range Format Currency zero*

1-2-3:

	A	B	C
1		********	
2			

The asterisks indicate the column isn't wide enough.

You: Type   **/ W C S** → → → ←┘   *Worksheet Column Set-Width*

1-2-3:

	A	B	C
1		$3,000,000	
2			

OS/2

Note: Lotus 1-2-3 Release 3.1 does not run under OS/2.

Yes, I know there are several references to OS/2 in the Lotus 1-2-3 Release 3.1 documentation, but two separate Lotus Pormpt Hotline support people have assured me that Release 3.1 does not run under 0S/2, and, as of December 1990, there are no plans to change that.

To run 1-2-3 under OS/2, use 1-2-3 Release 3.0, which runs under either DOS or OS/2. Better yet, use 1-2-3G which is a significantly enhanced version that runs under the OS/2 Presentation Manager.

Lotus 1-2-3 Release 3.1 does run successfully under Windows 3.0.

Related: **Windows 3.0**

Printing—Basics

Command: **/ Print Printer**

Note: Basic printing, as described below, produces a simple report, which is satisfactory most of the time. The next over twenty sections give possibilities for wide variety and expression.

To stop the print command and return to **READY** mode, as with any other command, hold the **Ctrl** key and tap the **Break** key, or tap the **Esc** key repeatedly. However, this will *not* stop the actual printing, because printing takes place in the background. To cancel printing, see **Printing—Cancel Printing**.

To print graphs see **Graphs**.

With large worksheets you may wish to use options described in the printing sections that follow this one.

Large worksheets: If your worksheet is so large that it won't fit across the printed page, 1-2-3 prints it in strips. You then get tape and scissors and reassemble it. You can choose sideways printing, if the spreadsheet is wide and not very long and your printer has graphic capabilities (such as dot matrix and laser printers).

Related: **Graphs**

Example: Print a spreadsheet or database that is on your worksheet.

You: Turn on your printer, and be sure it is ready (on-line). If you use continuous feed paper, before turning on the printer, align the perforation just above the print head, even with the top of the ribbon.

If you are printing on a laser printer, do the section **Printing— Laser Printers**, then continue here.

Tap **/ P P**   *Print Printer*

1-2-3:   **Range   Line   Page   Options   Clear   Align   Go   Image
Sample   Hold   Quit**   *the Print Menu*

You: Type   **R A1..F15** ←┘   *Range, to set the range to be printed*

Note: Specify the range you want printed. If any text overlaps into adjacent cells, include those columns in your range.

You: Type   **A G P Q**   *Align Go Page Quit*

Note: If your printer has continuous form paper, type **A G P P Q** instead of **A G P Q.**

Page tells the printer to print the last line and eject the sheet of paper. With continuous feed paper, tap **P** twice to eject the paper so that the next perforation is accessible.

1-2-3:   The printer prints the specified range of your worksheet.

You: Do not adjust the printer, just detach your printed worksheet.

Printing—Blank Lines Removed

Command: **/ Print Printer Options Other Blank-Header Suppress**

Note: 1-2-3 actually leaves three blank lines at the top of each page for a header and three lines at the bottom for a footer, even if there is no header or footer. You may wish to remove those blank lines if you have no header or footer text. With continuous feed paper, this permits you to print to the very edge of each sheet. With laser printers, you usually cannot print to the edge of the paper because of the printer's limitations.

Example: Print your worksheet with the six blank lines removed.

You: Create and save a long worksheet over 66 lines long.

Type **/ P P O O B S**   *Print Printer Options Other Blank-Header Suppress*

Type **H**   *Header*

If you see any header text, tap **Backspace** to remove it.

Tap ↵

Type **F**   *Footer*

If you see any footer text, tap **Backspace** to remove it.

Tap ↵

Type **Q Q**   *Quit Quit*

Print as usual (see **Printing—Basics**).

To print blank lines at the top and and bottom again

You: Type **/ P P O O B P Q Q**   *Print Printer Options Other Blank-Header Print Quit Quit*

Print as usual (see **Printing—Basics**).

Printing—Borders

Command: **/ Print Printer Options Borders**

Note: Borders are similar to headers and can be used in addition to headers and footers.

Borders cause specified rows and/or columns to be printed on every page, above or to the left of the print range.

Borders are useful when the worksheet is so large that it prints on multiple pages, and you want certain column or row headings to be repeated on each page.

Example: Print the following worksheet with borders (assume it is too big to print on one sheet of paper):

	A	B	C	D	E	F	G	H	I	J	K	L	M
1	expenses												
2		Jan	Feb	Mar	Apr	May	Jun	Jul	Aug	Sep	Oct	Nov	Dec
3	Phone	xxx	xxx	xxx	xxx	xxx	xxx	xxx	xxx	xxx	xxx	xxx	xxx
4	Rent	xxx	xxx	xxx	xxx	xxx	xxx	xxx	xxx	xxx	xxx	xxx	xxx
5	Salary	xxx	xxx	xxx	xxx	xxx	xxx	xxx	xxx	xxx	xxx	xxx	xxx
78	Interest	xxx	xxx	xxx	xxx	xxx	xxx	xxx	xxx	xxx	xxx	xxx	xxx
79	Magazines	xxx	xxx	xxx	xxx	xxx	xxx	xxx	xxx	xxx	xxx	xxx	xxx
80	Misc	xxx	xxx	xxx	xxx	xxx	xxx	xxx	xxx	xxx	xxx	xxx	xxx

For comparison, let's look at printing without borders

You: Type **/ P P**   *Print Printer*
Type **C B**   *Clear Borders—in case they were set before*
Type **R A1..M80** ⏎ *Range to print*
Type **A G P Q** *Align Go Page Quit—Tap **P** (Page) twice if you have continuous feed paper*

1-2-3 prints:

on the first page:

```
expenses
         Jan  Feb  Mar  Apr  May  Jun  Jul  Aug
Phone    xxx  xxx  xxx  xxx  xxx  xxx  xxx  xxx
Rent     xxx  xxx  xxx  xxx  xxx  xxx  xxx  xxx
Salary   xxx  xxx  xxx  xxx  xxx  xxx  xxx  xxx
                             *
                             *
                             *
```

the second page:

```
                             *
                             *
                             *
Interest    xxx  xxx  xxx  xxx  xxx  xxx  xxx  xxx
Magazines   xxx  xxx  xxx  xxx  xxx  xxx  xxx  xxx
Misc        xxx  xxx  xxx  xxx  xxx  xxx  xxx  xxx
```

the third page:

```
  Sep  Oct  Nov  Dec
  xxx  xxx  xxx  xxx
  xxx  xxx  xxx  xxx
  xxx  xxx  xxx  xxx
        *
        *
        *
```

the fourth page:

```
        *
        *
        *
  xxx  xxx  xxx  xxx
  xxx  xxx  xxx  xxx
  xxx  xxx  xxx  xxx
```

Note: Page 4 shows numbers, but we have no idea what month or expense they belong to. Pages 2 and 3 are not much better.

Let's set up some borders and print again

You: Type **/ P P**   *Print Printer*

Type **R B3..M80** ⟵   *Range*

Note: This time the range does NOT include column A nor rows 1 and 2 because they will be borders.

You: Type **O B C A1** ⟵ **B R A1..A2** ⟵**Q**   *Options   Borders*
Column A1 Borders
Row A1..A2 Quit

Note   This last command set the borders. To set a border column, you need only choose one cell in that column. To make column A a border column, chose any cell in that border. In this case, A1 was chosen. Likewise, to make rows 1 and 2 into border rows, choose a range that includes cells from both rows. In this case, I chose A1..A2.

You: Type **A G P Q**   *Align Go Page Quit*

1-2-3 prints: *on the first page:*

expenses								
	Jan	Feb	Mar	Apr	May	Jun	Jul	Aug
Phone	xxx	xxx	xxx	xxx	xxx	xxx	xxx	xxx
Rent	xxx	xxx	xxx	xxx	xxx	xxx	xxx	xxx
Salary	xxx	xxx	xxx	xxx	xxx	xxx	xxx	xxx
				*				
				*				
				*				

the second page:

expenses								
	Jan	Feb	Mar	Apr	May	Jun	Jul	Aug
				*				
				*				
				*				
Interest	xxx	xxx	xxx	xxx	xxx	xxx	xxx	xxx
Magazines	xxx	xxx	xxx	xxx	xxx	xxx	xxx	xxx
Misc	xxx	xxx	xxx	xxx	xxx	xxx	xxx	xxx

the third page:

```
            Sep Oct Nov Dec

Interest    xxx xxx xxx xxx
Magazines   xxx xxx xxx xxx
Misc        xxx xxx xxx xxx
                     *
                     *
                     *
```

the fourth page:

```
            Sep Oct Nov Dec
                 *
                 *
                 *
Interest    xxx xxx xxx xxx
Magazines   xxx xxx xxx xxx
Misc        xxx xxx xxx xxx
```

Note: Notice that each printed page has appropriate information from column A and rows 1 and 2.

To remove border setting

You: Type **/ P P C B Q** ◄━┘   *Print Printer Clear Borders Quit*

Save your worksheet.

Printing—Cancel Printing

Command: / **Print Cancel**

Note: How you cancel your printer from printing depends partly on your hardware and systems software.

The **Print Cancel** command will stop 1-2-3 from sending information to be printed.

However, you may have a print spooler (can be software or hardware) that holds the rapid flood of information coming to it and slowly passes it on to your printer. In this case, follow the print cancel instructions that came with your spooler. A spooler could be holding hundreds of pages by the time you tell 1-2-3 to stop sending information to be printed. These pages would continue to print even after you issue the **Print Cancel** command.

Also, your printer has a temporary holding area, called a print buffer, that may hold several lines up to half a page of information waiting to be printed. While you could turn the printer off and on to cancel that, you are usually better off just printing the extra information.

Example: Cancel printing.

You: Tap **Esc** until **READY** appears.

Type / **P C** *Print Cancel*

Note: Even without a spooler, the printer may continue printing another half page or so. If you have a spooler, it may already be holding dozens of pages waiting to send them to the printer. You have not cancelled your spooler yet.

Follow the print cancel instructions that came with your spooler to cancel the rest of the printout.

Printing—Cell Formulas

Command: / **Print Printer Options Other Cell-Formulas**

Note: Printing cell formulas is one way to check formulas for accuracy. 1-2-3 prints each formula on a separate line, so what you see printed looks nothing like your worksheet. A printout of cell formulas is, nevertheless, still very useful.

Example: Print the cell formulas in the following worksheet:

	A	B	C
1	DEPARTMENT	AMOUNT	PERCENT OF TOTAL
2	Personnel	30000	15%
3	Accounting	15000	8%
4	Production	120000	60%
5	Sales	35000	18%
6			
7	TOTAL	200000	

You: Create the above worksheet using these hints:

Highlight cell B1.
Type **/ W C S 10** ↵   *to set column width to 10*

Highlight cell C1.
Type **/ W C S 17** ↵   *to set column width to 17*

Highlight cell B7.
Type **@SUM(B2..B5)** ↵   *to add the column of numbers*

Highlight cell C2.
Type **+B2/$B$7** ↵   *to calculate percentage*
Type **/ C** ↵ **.↓ ↓ ↓** ↵   *to copy the formula down*
Type **/ R F P Ø** ↵ **↓ ↓ ↓** ↵   *to format as percentages*

Type **/ P P**   *Print Printer*

You: Type **R B2..C7** ↵   *Range*

Note: In an attempt to reduce the number of lines printed, the range specified does not include the entire spreadsheet, just the cells that may contain formulas

You: Be sure the printer is "ready" and on-line

Type **O O C Q** *Options Other Cell-Formulas Quit*

Type **A G P Q** *Align Go Page Quit*

Result: The following is printed:

```
A:B2: [W10]  30000
A:C2: (P0) [W17]  +B2/$B$7
A:B3: [W10]  15000
A:C3: (P0) [W17]  +B3/$B$7
A:B4: [W10]  120000
A:C4: (P0) [W17]  +B4/$B$7
A:B5: [W10]  35000
A:C5: (P0) [W17]  +B5/$B$7
A:B7: [W10]  @SUM(B2..B5)
```

The printout shows cells that contain either formulas or information. Empty cells are not printed. Each value (**30000, 15000,** etc.) and formula (**+B2/$B$7**) is displayed one per line.

The [**W10**] and [**W17**] show columns that were set using **Worksheet Column Set-Width.** Global Column widths, set using **Worksheet Global Column-Width**, are not indicated.

The (**P0**) indicates this cell was formatted with **Range Format.** (**P0**) stands for Percent, zero decimal places. You might also see (**,2**) - comma with two decimal places; (**C2**) - Currency with two decimal places; (**F0**) - Fixed with zero decimal places; (**G**) - General; etc.

Printing—Compressed Type

Command: **/ Print Printer Options Advanced Layout Print Compressed**

/ Print Printer Options Advanced Layout Line-Spacing Compressed

Note: Compressed print causes your printer (if it is capable) to print in smaller letters and numbers.

Compressed line spacing causes your printer to print more lines per inch than it usually does. Many printers print six lines per inch. This command could change it to print eight lines per inch.

You probably will not like the look of both pitch and line spacing compression, so choose one or the other.

There is no need to change your margins, as 1-2-3 will automatically accommodate the increased number of characters per line, and the increased number of lines per page.

Example: Print a worksheet, compressing the appearance of the output.

You: Create a worksheet.

To compress characters (print smaller letters and numbers)

You: Type / **P P O A L P C Q Q Q Q** *Print Printer Options Advanced Layout Print Compressed Quit Quit Quit Quit*

To compress the line spacing (print more lines per inch)

You: Type / **P P O A L L C Q Q Q Q** *Print Printer Options Advanced Layout Line-Spacing Compressed Quit Quit Quit Quit*

Print as usual (see Printing—Basics)

Printing—Date and Time

@Function: **@NOW**

Command: **/ Print Printer Options Header/Footer**

Note: An at sign—@—can be entered in the header or footer and will print the current date at the top or bottom of your printout. See **Printing—Headers and Footers**.

Alternatively, type **@NOW** into a cell in your worksheet. In this case, follow these instructions:

- Highlight desired cell for date or time.
- Type **@NOW** in a cell in your worksheet.
- Format this cell as a date or time (see the example below).
- Include this cell in your print range.

Example 1: Enter today's date into a worksheet in such a way that it will change to tomorrow's date tomorrow, etc.

You: Highlight cell C1.

Type **@NOW** ↵   *or type @TODAY* ↵

1-2-3:

	A	B	C	D
1			32021.78	

You: Type **/ R F D 1** ↵ *Range Format Date 1st choice*

1-2-3:

	A	B	C	D
1			*********	

You: Type **/ W C S 10** ↵ *to widen the column to 10*

Result: The following appears (assuming that today is Sep 1, 1987):

	A	B	C	D
1			01-Sep-87	

This date only changes when the worksheet is recalculated.

Example 2:   Enter the current time into a worksheet.

You: Highlight cell D1.

Type **@NOW** ↵

1-2-3:

	A	B	C	D
1				32021.78

You: Type **/ R F D T 1** ↵   *Range Format Date Time 1st choice*

1-2-3:

	A	B	C	D
1				********

You: Type **/ W C S 12** ↵   *to widen the column to 12*

Result: The following appears (assuming it is 11:32 am and 30 seconds):

	A	B	C	D
1				11:32:30 AM

This time only changes when the worksheet is recalculated.   You
may need to tap the **F9** key, the **Calc** key, to see the updated time.

You: Tap the **F9** key just before printing this worksheet.

Printing—Fonts

Command: / **Print Printer Options Advanced Fonts**

Note: A font is the style of the letters and numbers.

This sentence is using a serif font. Notice the tiny little lines and shadings on each letter, especially on the capital letters.

This is bold serif printing. It is good for emphasis and for titles.

This sentence is in italic serif printing. It is also good for emphasis and for book titles.

The printing in this sentence is sans serif. Notice how plain these letters look.

This is bold sans serif printing. It is excellent for titles.

1-2-3 provides a sample printout to show you what is available on your printer for the way it was installed. See **Printing—Sample.**

During the installation of 1-2-3, depending on your printer, specific fonts may have been installed. The fonts you can use in 1-2-3 depends on what was installed into 1-2-3, in addition to the fonts available with your printer. For example, when you install fonts for an Apple LaserWriter Plus, you can choose either Bookman/Avant Garde or Times/Helvetica fonts. In either case, you get eight fonts installed—four serif fonts (Bookman or Times) and four sans serif fonts (Avant Garde or Helvetica). For another example, if you install an HP LaserJet II with no cartridge, even if you have a Z (or other) cartridge, 1-2-3 will not use it, and you will be limited to regular and bold serif fonts.

Here are the 8 font choices:

1 - regular serif	5 - regular sans serif
2 - bold serif	**6 - bold sans serif**
3 - *italic serif*	7 - *italic sans serif*
4 - ***bold/italic serif***	8 - ***bold/italic sans serif***

You always have all eight choices, but if your printer doesn't support a particular font, 1-2-3 will choose something else. For example, if you choose font 3 (italic serif) but 1-2-3 doesn't think your printer supports italic serif, then 1-2-3 may substitute regular serif. In this case, choosing either 1 or 3 would result in the same font being printed. See **Printing—Sample** to see which fonts 1-2-3 will use on your printer for the eight font choices.

Use the **Print Printer Options Advanced Fonts** command to set different fonts for each of these areas of your printed worksheet: specified range, headers/footers, border areas, and frame.

Example: Print a worksheet with bold sans serif header and italic serif range.

You: Create or retrieve a worksheet to be printed.

Type **/ P P O A F** *Print Printer Options Advanced Fonts*

Type **H 6** *Header/Footer 6—for bold sans serif font choice*

Type **R 3** *Range 3—for italic serif choice*

Type **Q Q Q Q** *Quit Quit Quit Quit*

Print your worksheet as usual.

Printing—Headers and Footers

Command: / **Print Printer Options Header/Footer**

Note: A header is a single line of text that appears at the top of each printed page. It might be the title of the worksheet, the name of your company, the date, your name, the page number, or other information.

A footer is a single line of text that appears at the bottom of each printed page, with similar information.

1-2-3 gives you right, left, and centering capabilities, as well as the ability to print the current date and keep track of page numbers in your header and footer.

Type a # in the header or footer to have a page number printed.

Type an @ in the header or footer to have the date appear.

Tap the ¦ (broken bar key, usually the shifted Backslash key) to separate the left-aligned, centered, and right-aligned segments of your header and footer. Here are some examples:

You Type	**Printed Result**		
	left	*center*	*right*
WIDGETS	WIDGETS		
¦ WIDGETS		WIDGETS	
¦¦ WIDGETS			WIDGETS
WIDGETS¦@¦#	WIDGETS	9/15/87	3
@¦¦ page #	9/15/87		page 3

Example: Print a spreadsheet with a header and footer.

You: Create a worksheet and save it.

Type **/ P P O H**   *Print Printer Options Header*

1-2-3:   **Enter Header Line:**

You: Type **WIDGETS, INC. ¦¦ page   #** ⟵ *type a space before #*

Type **F ¦ written by Mary Morrisson ¦ @** ⟵ *Footer*

Type **O F Q Q**   *Other Formatted Quit Quit*

Print as usual (see **Printing—Basics**).

Result: The following appears:

```
WIDGETS, INC.                                      page 1

~~~~  ~~~~  ~~  ~~  ~~  ~~~  ≈  ≈
~~~~  ~~~~  ~~  ~~  ~~  ~~~  ≈  ≈
~~~~  ~~~~  ~~  ~~  ~~  ~~~  ≈  ≈
~~~~  ~~~~  ~~  ~~  ~~  ~~~  ≈  ≈
~~~~  ~~~~  ~~  ~~  ~~  ~~~  ≈  ≈
~~~~  ~~~~  ~~  ~~  ~~  ~~~  ≈  ≈
~~~~  ~~~~  ~~  ~~  ~~  ~~~  ≈  ≈
~~~~  ~~~~  ~~  ~~  ~~  ~~~  ≈  ≈
~~~~  ~~~~  ~~  ~~  ~~  ~~~  ≈  ≈
~~~~  ~~~~  ~~  ~~  ~~  ~~~  ≈  ≈

                        written by Mary Morrisson   9/15/87
```

Note: You will NOT see the footer until after you type P for page. If you manually release the paper, your footer will NOT BE PRINTED.

Printing—Laser Printers

Command: / **Print Printer Options Pg-Length**

Note: 1-2-3 assumes a page length that won't work with certain printers, especially most laser printers. Check your printer manual for details.

Check the help screen. From **READY**, tap the **F1** key (**Help**) and choose **Printer Information** for information about various printers.

Example: Set the page length for an HP LaserJet printer with no cartridge.

You: Type **/ P P O P**   *Print Printer Options Pg-Length*

Type **60** ←⏎

For other printers, choose a number from this chart:

Printer	Portrait	Landscape
Apple LaserWriter	63	47
HP DeskJet	60	45
HP Laserjet, cartridge F	72	45
HP Laserjet, cartridge J	72	45
HP Laserjet, cartridge Z	72	45
HP Laserjet, no cartridge	**60**	45

You: Type **Q Q**   *Quit Quit*

To align your laser printer: Take it off-line by pressing On-Line, then press Form Feed, and press On-Line.

Print as usual (see **Printing—Basics**).

Printing—Margins

Command: **/ Print Printer Options Margins**

Note: This command sets the margins for the printed page. It is important to know your printer in order to set margins.

The top, bottom, right, and left margins can be set. Except for the right margin, the other margins are measured from the corresponding edge of the paper (i.e., the top margin is the distance from the top of the paper to the printed text). The exception is the right margin, because it is measured from the left edge of the paper, instead of the right edge. Here is a diagram with sample settings:

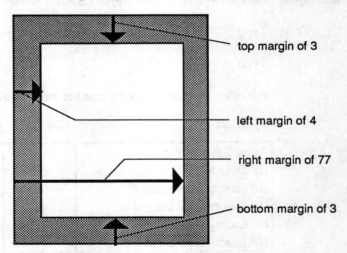

- top margin of 3
- left margin of 4
- right margin of 77
- bottom margin of 3

Tip: If you subtract the left margin from the right margin (subtract 4 from 77) you get the number of characters that the printer will print on one line (73, in this case).

1-2-3 adds an additional three lines to the top and bottom for headers and footers, even if there aren't any. To eliminate these six extra lines, see **Printing—Blank Lines Removed.**

The right margin setting must be less than or equal to the maximum number of characters your printer can print on one line. Many dot matrix printers can print 80 regular size characters per line and 132 characters in compressed mode. For instructions to inform your printer to use compressed mode, see **Printing—Compressed**. Do not adjust the margins for compressed printing, 1-2-3 will do that automatically.

For sideways (landscape) printing, the right margin and page length, need to be adjusted (see **Printing—Sideways—Landscape**).

Many dot matrix wide carriage printers can print 132 regular size characters per line and over 200 characters in compressed mode.

Thimble and daisy wheel printers have different elements that print different sizes. 10 pitch permits 10 characters per inch. 12 pitch permits 12 characters per inch.

Top or bottom margin settings of six give a one-inch margin (unless your printer is set to eight lines per inch).

If you use continuous feed paper, align the perforation just above the print head, even with the top of the ribbon.

Example: Set the print margins to the following:

left	10	characters
right	75	characters
top	6	lines
bottom	6	lines

You: Create and save a worksheet as usual.

Type **/ P P O**   *Print Printer Options*

Type **M R 75** ↵   *Margins Right*

Type **M L 10** ↵   *Margins Left*

Type **M T 6** ↵   *Margins Top*

Type **M B 6** ↵   *Margins Bottom*

Type **Q Q**   *Quit Quit*

Print as usual (see **Printing—Basics**).

Printing—Nonadjacent Columns

Command: / **Worksheet Column Hide**
           / **Worksheet Column Display**

Note: All we do is hide the columns we don't want printed, then print the
        worksheet. When finished, we can re-display the hidden columns if
        we wish. You may also be interested in **Printing—Nonadjacent
        Ranges.**

Example: Print the following worksheet without printing columns B through I:

	A	B	C	D	E	F	G	H	I	J	K	L	M
1	expenses												
2		Jan	Feb	Mar	Apr	May	Jun	Jul	Aug	Sep	Oct	Nov	Dec
3	Phone	xxx	xxx	xxx	xxx	xxx	xxx	xxx	xxx	xxx	xxx	xxx	xxx
4	Rent	xxx	xxx	xxx	xxx	xxx	xxx	xxx	xxx	xxx	xxx	xxx	xxx
5	Salary	xxx	xxx	xxx	xxx	xxx	xxx	xxx	xxx	xxx	xxx	xxx	xxx

*
*
*

	A	B	C	D	E	F	G	H	I	J	K	L	M
78	Interest	xxx	xxx	xxx	xxx	xxx	xxx	xxx	xxx	xxx	xxx	xxx	xxx
79	Magazines	xxx	xxx	xxx	xxx	xxx	xxx	xxx	xxx	xxx	xxx	xxx	xxx
80	Misc	xxx	xxx	xxx	xxx	xxx	xxx	xxx	xxx	xxx	xxx	xxx	xxx

Hide columns

You: Type / W C H B1..I1 ↵ *Worksheet Column Hide*

1-2-3:

	A	J	K	L	M
1	expenses				
2		Sep	Oct	Nov	Dec
3	Phone	xxx	xxx	xxx	xxx
4	Rent	xxx	xxx	xxx	xxx
5	Salary	xxx	xxx	xxx	xxx

*
*
*

	A	J	K	L	M
78	Interest	xxx	xxx	xxx	xxx
79	Magazines	xxx	xxx	xxx	xxx
80	Misc	xxx	xxx	xxx	xxx

Columns B through I have disappeared from the screen.

You: Print as usual (see **Printing—Basics**).

Result: This is printed:

```
expenses
              Sep  Oct  Nov  Dec
Phone         xxx  xxx  xxx  xxx
Rent          xxx  xxx  xxx  xxx
Salary        xxx  xxx  xxx  xxx

                    *
                    *
                    *

Interest      xxx  xxx  xxx  xxx
Magazines     xxx  xxx  xxx  xxx
Misc          xxx  xxx  xxx  xxx
```

To re-display the hidden columns

You: Type **/ W C D**   *Worksheet Column Display*

1-2-3:

	A	B*	C*	D*	E*	F*	G*	H*	I*	J	K	L	M
1	expenses												
2		Jan	Feb	Mar	Apr	May	Jun	Jul	Aug	Sep	Oct	Nov	Dec

The hidden columns are temporarily displayed with asterisks.

You: Type B1..I1 ↵   *or highlight cells in desired columns*

1-2-3:

	A	B	C	D	E	F	G	H	I	J	K	L	M
1	expenses												
2		Jan	Feb	Mar	Apr	May	Jun	Jul	Aug	Sep	Oct	Nov	Dec

Printing—Nonadjacent Ranges

Command: **/ Print Printer**

Note: In the **Range** option of the **Print** command, you may specify multiple ranges, separating these ranges with commas.

Related: **Printing—Nonadjacent Columns**

Example: Print rows 1-3, 11-13, and row 18 of the following worksheet:

	A	B	C	D	E	F	G	H	I	J	K	L	M
1			BUDGET FOR 1990										
2		Jan	Feb	Mar	Apr	May	Jun	Jul	Aug	Sep	Oct	Nov	Dec
3	EXPENSES												
4	Phone	xxx	xxx	xxx	xxx	xxx	xxx	xxx	xxx	xxx	xxx	xxx	xxx
5	Rent	xxx	xxx	xxx	xxx	xxx	xxx	xxx	xxx	xxx	xxx	xxx	xxx
6	Salary	xxx	xxx	xxx	xxx	xxx	xxx	xxx	xxx	xxx	xxx	xxx	xxx
7	Books	xxx	xxx	xxx	xxx	xxx	xxx	xxx	xxx	xxx	xxx	xxx	xxx
8	Interest	xxx	xxx	xxx	xxx	xxx	xxx	xxx	xxx	xxx	xxx	xxx	xxx
9	Misc	xxx	xxx	xxx	xxx	xxx	xxx	xxx	xxx	xxx	xxx	xxx	xxx
10	Travel	xxx	xxx	xxx	xxx	xxx	xxx	xxx	xxx	xxx	xxx	xxx	xxx
11	TOTAL	xxx	xxx	xxx	xxx	xxx	xxx	xxx	xxx	xxx	xxx	xxx	xxx
12													
13	INCOME												
14	sales	xxx	xxx	xxx	xxx	xxx	xxx	xxx	xxx	xxx	xxx	xxx	xxx
15	interest	xxx	xxx	xxx	xxx	xxx	xxx	xxx	xxx	xxx	xxx	xxx	xxx
16	consulting	xxx	xxx	xxx	xxx	xxx	xxx	xxx	xxx	xxx	xxx	xxx	xxx
17	training	xxx	xxx	xxx	xxx	xxx	xxx	xxx	xxx	xxx	xxx	xxx	xxx
18	TOTAL	xxx	xxx	xxx	xxx	xxx	xxx	xxx	xxx	xxx	xxx	xxx	xxx

You: Type **/ P P R A2..M4,A12..M14,A19..M19 Q** ↵
Print Printer Range Quit

Print as usual (see **Printing—Basics**). The following is printed:

BUDGET FOR 1990												
Jan	Feb	Mar	Apr	May	Jun	Jul	Aug	Sep	Oct	Nov	Dec
EXPENSES												
TOTAL	xxx	xxx	xxx	xxx	xxx	xxx	xxx	xxx	xxx	xxx	xxx	xxx
INCOME												
TOTAL	xxx	xxx	xxx	xxx	xxx	xxx	xxx	xxx	xxx	xxx	xxx	xxx

Printing—Page Breaks

Command: / **Worksheet Page**

Note: Worksheet Page inserts a blank row and puts ¦ : : (broken bar and two colons) into a cell in the row to mark the page break. Any data you put in that row will not be printed.

Warning: This command inserts a blank row across all 256 columns of your worksheet. There may be information you don't want separated that will be separated by this blank row. You could just type the ¦ : : yourself into a cell on the left edge of the print range.

Example: Insert a page break in the following worksheet prior to printing.

	A	B	C	D	E	F	G	H	I	J	K	L	M
1		BUDGET FOR 1991											
2		Jan	Feb	Mar	Apr	May	Jun	Jul	Aug	Sep	Oct	Nov	Dec
3	EXPENSES												
4	Phone	xxx	xxx	xxx	xxx	xxx	xxx	xxx	xxx	xxx	xxx	xxx	xxx
5	Rent	xxx	xxx	xxx	xxx	xxx	xxx	xxx	xxx	xxx	xxx	xxx	xxx
6	Salary	xxx	xxx	xxx	xxx	xxx	xxx	xxx	xxx	xxx	xxx	xxx	xxx
7	Books	xxx	xxx	xxx	xxx	xxx	xxx	xxx	xxx	xxx	xxx	xxx	xxx
8	Interest	xxx	xxx	xxx	xxx	xxx	xxx	xxx	xxx	xxx	xxx	xxx	xxx
9	Misc	xxx	xxx	xxx	xxx	xxx	xxx	xxx	xxx	xxx	xxx	xxx	xxx
10	Travel	xxx	xxx	xxx	xxx	xxx	xxx	xxx	xxx	xxx	xxx	xxx	xxx
11	TOTAL	xxx	xxx	xxx	xxx	xxx	xxx	xxx	xxx	xxx	xxx	xxx	xxx
12													
13	INCOME												
14	Sales	xxx	xxx	xxx	xxx	xxx	xxx	xxx	xxx	xxx	xxx	xxx	xxx
15	Interest	xxx	xxx	xxx	xxx	xxx	xxx	xxx	xxx	xxx	xxx	xxx	xxx
16	Consulting	xxx	xxx	xxx	xxx	xxx	xxx	xxx	xxx	xxx	xxx	xxx	xxx
17	Training	xxx	xxx	xxx	xxx	xxx	xxx	xxx	xxx	xxx	xxx	xxx	xxx
18													

You: Highlight cell A12.

Type   / **W P** *Worksheet Page*

1-2-3:

	A	B	C	D	E	F	G	H	I	J	K	L	M
1						BUDGET FOR 1991							
2		Jan	Feb	Mar	Apr	May	Jun	Jul	Aug	Sep	Oct	Nov	Dec
3	EXPENSES												
4	Phone	xxx	xxx	xxx	xxx	xxx	xxx	xxx	xxx	xxx	xxx	xxx	xxx
5	Rent	xxx	xxx	xxx	xxx	xxx	xxx	xxx	xxx	xxx	xxx	xxx	xxx
6	Salary	xxx	xxx	xxx	xxx	xxx	xxx	xxx	xxx	xxx	xxx	xxx	xxx
7	Books	xxx	xxx	xxx	xxx	xxx	xxx	xxx	xxx	xxx	xxx	xxx	xxx
8	Interest	xxx	xxx	xxx	xxx	xxx	xxx	xxx	xxx	xxx	xxx	xxx	xxx
9	Misc	xxx	xxx	xxx	xxx	xxx	xxx	xxx	xxx	xxx	xxx	xxx	xxx
10	Travel	xxx	xxx	xxx	xxx	xxx	xxx	xxx	xxx	xxx	xxx	xxx	xxx
11	TOTAL	xxx	xxx	xxx	xxx	xxx	xxx	xxx	xxx	xxx	xxx	xxx	xxx
12	::												
13													
14	INCOME												
15	Sales	xxx	xxx	xxx	xxx	xxx	xxx	xxx	xxx	xxx	xxx	xxx	xxx
16	Interest	xxx	xxx	xxx	xxx	xxx	xxx	xxx	xxx	xxx	xxx	xxx	xxx
17	Consulting	xxx	xxx	xxx	xxx	xxx	xxx	xxx	xxx	xxx	xxx	xxx	xxx
18	Training	xxx	xxx	xxx	xxx	xxx	xxx	xxx	xxx	xxx	xxx	xxx	xxx

Note: Notice that a blank row was inserted into the worksheet.

You: Print as usual (see **Printing—Basics**).

Result: When you print, rows 1 through 12 will print on the first page, and rows 13 on down will print starting on the second page.

Printing—Page Length

Command: / **Print Printer Options Page-Length**

Note: Standard page length is 11 inches, which translates to 66 lines of output (if your printer is set to 6 lines per inch). Lotus 1-2-3 can specify a page length of 1 to 1000 lines.

For laser printers, use the special settings for your printer. Several settings are mentioned in **Printing—Laser Printers**. Alternatively, in **READY**, tap the **F1** (Help) key and select the option **Printer Information**.

Related: **Printing—Laser Printers**
Printing—Margins

Example: Print on legal-size continuous-feed paper (8.5 inches by 14 inches), 6 lines per inch.

You: Create or retrieve a worksheet.

Type **/ P P** *Print Printer*

Type **O P 84** ←⏎ *Options Pg-Length 84*

Note: At 6 lines per inch, 14 inch paper holds 6 times 14, or 84 lines.

You: Type **Q Q** *Quit Quit*

Print as usual (see **Printing—Basics**).

Result: The worksheet will be printed on paper 14 inches long with appropriate page breaks.

Printing—Printer Control Characters (Setup and Broken Bar)

Command: / **Print Printer Options Setup**

Note: Printer control characters, also called printer codes or escape character sequences, are used to print italics and compressed (smaller) print, underlines, enhanced (darker) print, and double and triple spacing, and so on. With Release 3, there are special commands and options for most of these printing needs. See the various "**Printing—**" topics.

If none of these commands meet your needs, then welcome to the deep dark mystery of **Setup** strings and broken bar control characters.

Printer codes are special numbers and letters sent from the computer to the printer. The code sets a feature in the printer. The printer remains set until you turn it off or until the computer sends another code to the printer that removes that feature. Once your computer has sent a code, such as underlining, that feature remains turned on, even after you quit 1-2-3 and turn off your computer.

Not all printers recognize the same codes, so look up the proper codes in your printer manual. Here are some common codes for Epson dot matrix and compatible printers:

compressed mode	\015
turn off compressed mode	\018
enhanced (darker)	\027\069
turn off enhanced	\027\070

If you put one of these codes in the middle of your worksheet it will be sent to the printer half way through the printing and will take affect at that point. Codes put in the setup string are sent to the printer before your worksheet is printed.

If you change the character size or line spacing using these printer codes, you will need to reset the right and bottom margins and page lengths yourself. If there is an appropriate 1-2-3 command, use it instead of using printer codes or the Setup option. See **Printing—Fonts** or **Printing—Compressed**, so that 1-2-3 will manage your line and character counts for you.

Example 1: Print a worksheet in compressed mode (small typeface) on an Epson dot matrix or compatible printer.

You: Create and save a worksheet

Type **/ P P O S** *Print Printer Options Setup*

If there is already a setup string, tap **Esc** once to remove it.

Type **\ Ø15** ←┘ *Backslash Ø15—this is your printer code*

Type **Q Q** *Quit Quit*

Adjust the right margin. See **Printing—Margins** for details.

Print as usual (see **Printing—Basics**).

Result: Your worksheet is printed in compressed (small) typeface.

Example 2: Print the body of a worksheet in compressed mode (small typeface), and print the title in enhanced (dark) typeface on an Epson dot matrix or compatible printer.

You: Create a worksheet similar to the following and save it.

	A	B	C	D	E
1					
2			BUDGET FOR 1987		
3					
4		Jan	Feb	Mar	Apr
5	EXPENSES				
6	Phone	xxx	xxx	xxx	xxx
7	Rent	xxx	xxx	xxx	xxx
8	Salary	xxx	xxx	xxx	xxx
9	Books	xxx	xxx	xxx	xxx
1 0	Interest	xxx	xxx	xxx	xxx
1 1	Misc	xxx	xxx	xxx	xxx
1 2	Travel	xxx	xxx	xxx	xxx
1 3	TOTAL	xxx	xxx	xxx	xxx
1 4					

Replace the xxx's with any numbers you wish.

Set the setup string

You: Type / **P P O S** *Print Printer Options Setup*

If there is a Setup String, tap the **Esc** key to remove it.

Type \Ø18\Ø27\Ø69 ↵   *to turn compressed off and turn enhanced on*

Type **Q Q** *Quit Quit*

Embed the printer codes for small typeface into your worksheet

You: Highlight cell A3

Type / **W I R** ↵ *Worksheet Insert Row*

Type ¦¦ \Ø27\Ø70\Ø15 ↵   *to turn enhanced off and turn compressed on*

1-2-3:

	A	B	C	D	E
1					
2			BUDGET FOR 1987		
3	¦¦\027\070\015				
4					
5		Jan	Feb	Mar	Apr
6	EXPENSES				
7	Phone	xxx	xxx	xxx	xxx
8	Rent	xxx	xxx	xxx	xxx
9	Salary	xxx	xxx	xxx	xxx
10	Books	xxx	xxx	xxx	xxx
11	Interest	xxx	xxx	xxx	xxx
12	Misc	xxx	xxx	xxx	xxx
13	Travel	xxx	xxx	xxx	xxx
14	TOTAL	xxx	xxx	xxx	xxx

contents of cell A3:

¦¦\027\070\015

Note: The ¦¦ permits embedded printer codes in the worksheet. Put it in the first column—the left side—of the range to be printed. Do not put any other information in that row, as it will not be printed. The code **\027\070\015** turns enhanced mode off and turns compressed (smaller) typeface on.

You: Turn the printer off and on, to clear any previous settings.

Print as usual (see **Printing—Basics**).

Result: The following is printed:

	BUDGET FOR 1987					
	Jan	Feb	Mar	Apr	May	Jun
EXPENSES						
Phone	xxx	xxx	xxx	xxx	xxx	xxx
Rent	xxx	xxx	xxx	xxx	xxx	xxx
Salary	xxx	xxx	xxx	xxx	xxx	xxx
Books	xxx	xxx	xxx	xxx	xxx	xxx
Interest	xxx	xxx	xxx	xxx	xxx	xxx
Misc	xxx	xxx	xxx	xxx	xxx	xxx
Travel	xxx	xxx	xxx	xxx	xxx	xxx
TOTAL	xxx	xxx	xxx	xxx	xxx	xxx

Printing—Sample

Command: / **Print Printer Sample**

Note: 1-2-3 provides a sampler of the fonts, colors, pitches, line spacings, graphs, graphics, and so on that your printer is capable of printing. *This is very useful.*

Example: Print a sampler for your printer.

You: If you have a laser printer, see **Printing—Laser Printer** and follow those instructions first. Then continue with the next step.

You: Type / **P P S A G Q**   *Print Printer Sample Align Go Quit*

1-2-3:   A multiple page sampler is printed.

Printing—Sideways—Landscape

Command: **/ Print Printer Options Advanced Layout Orientation Landscape**

Note: Landscape mode means printing sideways on the paper. You need to adjust your margins and page length prior to printing. Most dot matrix, laser, and ink jet printers can print sideways. Daisy wheel and thimble printers cannot print landscape mode.

Example: Print your worksheet sideways on 8 1/2 by 11 inch paper.

You: Create and save a worksheet that you want printed sideways.

Type **/ P P O A L O L Q Q** *Print Printer Options Advanced Layout Orientation Landscape Quit Quit*

Type **M R 101 ←** *Margins Right*

Note: Choose a number appropriate for the right margin on your printer. With paper 11 inches wide, at 10 characters per inch, you could print a maximum of 110 characters. Giving a margin of 9 characters leaves the 101 that we specified. See **Printing—Margins** for more information on margins.

You: Type **P 45 ←** *Options Pg-Length 45*

Note: Choose the number of lines that fit in 8 1/2 inches of paper. If you have a laser printer, see the section on **Printing—Laser** for the number you should use for the page length. 45 is good for HP LaserJet printers.

You: Type **Q Q** *Quit Quit*

Print as usual (see **Printing—Basics**).

Printing—Suspend and Resume

Command: / **Print Suspend Quit**
/ **Print Resume Quit**

Note: Suspend and Resume allow you to temporarily halt and restart printing of very large worksheets.

Example 1: Temporarily halt the printer (suspend printing) while it is printing.

You: Type / **P S Q** *Print Suspend Quit*

1-2-3: 1-2-3 stops sending printed material to the printer. The printer may not pause right away because it is still printing what was already sent. If you have a print spooler, the printer may not pause for a long time.

Example 2: Resume printing after you suspended it.

You: Type / **P R Q** *Print Resume Quit*

1-2-3: 1-2-3 starts sending printed material to the printer again.

Printing—Wysiwyg

Note: Wysiwyg makes printing so much easier. Wysiwyg supports many different printers, which means never needing to set the page length or the setup string for the particular printer you have.

Be sure Wysiwyg is active before trying these examples. Depending on whether or not you have a mouse, do the first or the second example.

Example 1: Printing with Wysiwyg without a mouse.

You: Load and Invoke Wysiwyg, if not yet done.

Tap **:** *a colon (a shifted semicolon) brings up the Wysiwyg menu*

1-2-3: This is the Wysiwyg menu:
Worksheet Format Graph Print Display Special Text Named-Style Quit Column Row Page

You: Tap **P R S** *Print Range Set*

1-2-3: **Range to Print:**

You: Type **A1..F15** ↵ *or any range you want printed. If text overlaps into adjoining cells, include them in the range*

1-2-3: The range A1..F15 is printed.

Example 2: Printing with Wysiwyg using the mouse.

You: Load and Invoke Wysiwyg, if not yet done.

Hold the **Ctrl** key.

Using the left button, click in cell A1 and drag to cell F15.

1-2-3: The range A1 .. F15 is highlighted   *If text overlaps into adjoining cells, include them in the range*

You: Move the mouse about a half inch above the worksheet area.

You: Click the right mouse button until the Wysiwyg menu appears.

1-2-3:   This is the Wysiwyg menu:
        Worksheet Format Graph Print Display Special Text Named-Style Quit
        Column Row Page

You: Move the mouse over **Print** and click with the left button.

1-2-3:   The print options screen appears.

You: Move the mouse over **Range** and click with the left button.

You: Move the mouse over **Set** and click with the left button.

1-2-3:   The range you highlighted is now chosen.

You: Move the mouse over **Go** and click with the left button.

1-2-3:   The range A1..F15 is printed.

Protecting Cells

Commands: / **Worksheet Global Protection**
/ **Range Protect**
/ **Range Unprotect**
/ **File Admin Seal File**

Note: You can protect specific cells in your worksheet to prevent the contents from being accidentally changed.

In most worksheets there are areas that you plan to change, like expense and income figures, and areas that should not be changed, like titles and formulas. We are all human and occasionally we type information into the wrong cell and clobber its previous contents. Protect your worksheet to avoid that.

Cell protection does not prevent information from being intentionally destroyed. It also does not prevent the entire file from being erased. The best bet to avoid disaster is to make backup copies of your files and then lock up the diskettes or tape cartridges that contain the backups. Keep a current backup copy in a separate building (see **Backups**).

Protecting cells is a two-step process:

1. Protect the entire worksheet, using / **Worksheet Global Protection Enable.**

2. Carve out specific ranges in the worksheet that you do not want protected, using / **Range Unprotect**. Use / **Range Protect** if you unprotected too much with / **Range Unprotect.**

Changing protected cells is a three step process:

1. Use /**Worksheet Global Protection Disable** to remove cell protection.

2. Make your changes to the worksheet.

3. Use / **Worksheet Global Protection Enable** to return the worksheet to the protected status.

Alternate way to change just a few protected cells:

1. Use **Range Unprotect** to remove cell protection on a few selected cells or a range.

2. Make your change to the worksheet.

3. Use / **Range Protect** to re-protect those cells.

Once you have set all your cell formatting, cell protection, etc., you may wish to seal your settings. Use **File Admin Seal File** to seal your settings with a password so others can retrieve and use the file, but they can't change your formatting, cell protection status, network reservation settings, named ranges, named graphs, and so on. Your unprotected cells, however, still can be erased or changed.

Example 1: Protect the titles and formulas in the following worksheet from accidental destruction:

	A	B	C
1	DEPARTMENT	AMOUNT	PERCENT OF TOTAL
2	Personnel	3000	15%
3	Accounting	15000	8%
4	Production	120000	60%
5	Sales	35000	18%
6			
7	TOTAL	200000	

You: Create the above spreadsheet

Note: Once this spreadsheet is created, the only cells that should be changed are in the range B2..B5. All other cells contain title/label information or formulas and should be protected.

Type / **W G P E** *Worksheet Global Protection Enable*

1-2-3: **READY**

Note: At this point, the entire worksheet is protected. You cannot type anywhere and change the contents of a cell. **/ Range Erase** will not work. However, **/ Worksheet Erase** *will* erase everything, if you try it.

You: Highlight cell B2.

Type **/ R U** ↓ ↓ ↓ ↵   *Range Unprotect*

1-2-3: **READY**

Note: The range B2..B5 appears brighter, or is colored differently, than the rest of the worksheet. The range B2..B5 is now unprotected.

Result: You may now change the contents of the range B2..B5

Example 2: Seal your worksheet settings with a password.

You: Create your worksheet. Protect desired cells.

Type **/ F A S F** *File Admin Seal File*

Type a password that you will remember.

Tap ↵

1-2-3: Asterisks instead of the password appear on the screen.

You: Type your password again, for verification.

Tap ↵

Save your current worksheet. Reminder: **/ F S** *File Save* etc.

Range

What is a range?

A range is a rectangular group of one or more cells. Many commands use ranges as part of the command. A range name address specifies the cell names in two diagonal corners of the range. For example **B3..D4**, or **B4..D3**, or **D3..B4**, or **D4..B3** specifies the range of the six cells highlighted below.

A	A	B	C	D	E
1					
2					
3		██	██	██	
4		██	██	██	
5					

In 1-2-3 Release 3, ranges frequently begin with the sheet number. So this range can also be written as: **A:B3..A:D4** because it is in sheet A.

Here are some examples of differently sized ranges—all rectangular:

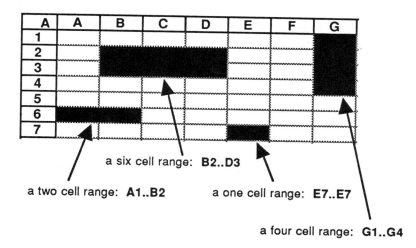

a six cell range: **B2..D3**

a two cell range: **A1..B2**

a one cell range: **E7..E7**

a four cell range: **G1..G4**

Each of these ranges may be written with the sheet number, for example: A:B2..A:D3 is the same as B2..D3 in the A sheet.

When do I specify a range?

In the middle or end of many of 1-2-3's commands you are asked to specify a range. For example, after typing **/ C** (which starts the **Copy** command), you enter a range (in this case, the range of cells you wish to copy). The **Print, Range, Move, Data,** and other commands also ask you for ranges.

When a command asks you for a range, it also provides a suggested range that you can accept or change. The suggested range could be the cell you highlighted before starting the command or a remembered range from the last time you used that command. Sometimes it is just a single cell (which isn't a range at all).

Different ways to change the suggested range:

- If you see a single cell, you can tap the period (.) key to make it a range, then tap the arrow keys to paint the range.

- If you see a range, just tap the arrow keys to paint a larger or smaller range.

- You can just type another range. Your typing will replace 1-2-3's suggestion.

- If the wrong range is highlighted, tap the Backspace key to change the range to a single cell. Tap the arrow keys to move the cell pointer. Tap the period (.) key. Then tap arrow keys to paint the desired range.

- To change a single cell to a range, tap the period (.) key.

- In a multicelled range, you can change the active painting corner by tapping the period.

What if the command does not give me a range?

If the command only gives you a single cell address, such as **A:B5,** you can change that to a range by tapping a period (don't type the word period, just tap **.**). **A:B5** becomes **A:B5..A:B5**

What if the command gives me a range I don't want?

Tap the **Backspace** key. Then tap any arrow or other cursor positioning key to move the one highlighted cell. When you are within your range, tap the period key and paint your range using arrow keys. Of course, You can always type in the desired range. Your typing will replace the range displayed on line 2 of the control panel, but it usually won't highlight any cells on the worksheet.

The following diagrams illustrate four typical range situations:

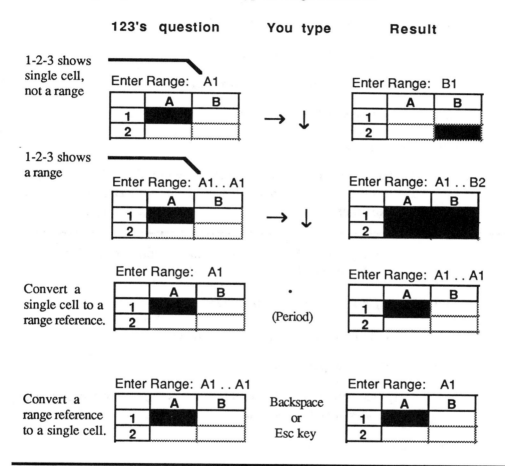

Example 1: Let's try manipulating a range within a command. This example illustrates range manipulation, but doesn't accomplish anything, because we never complete the command.

You: Save your current worksheet (start by typing / **F S** and so on).

Type / **W E Y** *Worksheet Erase Yes, to clear your worksheet*

Type / **P P R** *Print Printer Range*

Note: On line 2, 1-2-3 is requesting a range, but only a single cell is displayed. We will now convert that single cell—**A:A1** to a range.

You: Tap **.** *tap the period key*

Note: Now a range appears—**A:A1..A:A1**

You: Tap ↓ ↓ ↓ → → →   *to paint the range*

Tap ↵   *to end the range specification*

Note: Always tap ↵ to end a range.

You: Type **Q** *to Quit*

Result: We have illustrated the use of a range within the **Print** command. **Print** is one of the commands that remembers the last range you set. The next time you use **Print,** this painted range will appear.

Example 2: This example also illustrates range manipulation—converting a range to a single cell, and back again with a different range.

You: Type **/ P P R** *Print Printer Range*

Note: The last range we used appears highlighted.

You: Tap the **Backspace** key.

Note: Only one cell appears highlighted. It is the cell we highlighted before we started the command.

You: Tap ↓ ↓ ↓ → → →

Note: The cell pointer moves, but we are not painting any ranges.

You: Tap **.** *tap the period key*

Note: Now a one-celled range appears—**A:A1..A:A1**

You: Tap ↓ ↓ ↓ → → →   *to paint a new range*
Tap ↵ *to end the range specification.*
Type **Q** *to Quit*

Range Names

Commands: / **Range Name Create**
             / **Range Name Labels**
             / **Range Name Table**
             / **Range Name Delete**
             / **Range Name Reset**
             / **Range Name Note Create**
             / **Range Name Note Table**
             / **Range Name Note Delete**
             / **Range Name Note Reset**

Note: If you plan to use the same range over and over, it is useful to give it a meaningful name, like SALES or OUTPUT. These range names can be used in commands that ask for a range, such as / **Print Printer**, / **Data Query Input**, / **Copy**, or in functions that refer to ranges. Range names are used frequently with macros.

A range name identifies the first cell of the macro. These macro range names are frequently just a Backslash followed by a single letter (for example: \ A or \ G), although with Release 3 they can now be up to 15 characters long.

/ **Range Name Create** and / **Range Name Labels** create range names. / **Range Name Labels** can create many names at a time and is widely used with macros.

/ **Range Name Table** is used to put a list of your range names on your worksheet. This list is not updated until you issue this command again.

/ **Range Name Delete** and / **Range Name Reset** are used to remove range names. They do not delete the contents of cells; they just remove the meaningful names you gave to certain ranges. / **Range Name Delete** deletes one name. / **Range Name Reset** deletes all the names, without any confirmation message.

Use / **Range Name Note** commands to document the purpose of your range names.

If you use / **Range Name Create** to create a name that already exists, the named range is automatically painted and you can see the existing definition, and, if desired, change it.

Rules for range names

A range name may be up to 15 characters long. It should *not* start with a number, and it should *not* contain the following characters:

+ - / & < > @ #

The letters may be either upper- or lowercase. 1-2-3 will display lowercase as uppercase.

Instead of remembering what you can't do, I suggest you only use letters, numbers, and the underscore "_" character.

Example 1: Name some ranges in a worksheet.

You: Create the following worksheet:

	A	B
1	Phones	55
2	Rent	555
3	Travel	5
4	Misc	5
5		
6	Total	620

Create range names

You: Highlight cell A1.

Type / **R N L R** ↓ ↓ ↓ ↓ ↓ ↵   *Range Name Labels Right*

1-2-3: **READY** appears.

It looks like nothing happened, but in fact you just created five range names for the five data-containing cells in column B.

Use range names

You: Tap the **F5** key   *the GoTo key*

Tap the **F3** key *the Name key*

1-2-3: **Misc   Phones   Rent   Total   Travel**

These are the five names you just created in alphabetical order (other names may also be there, if they were created earlier).

You: Highlight the name **Rent** on line 3 above the worksheet.

Tap ↵

Note: The cell B2 is highlighted, proving that it has a name—Rent. You may use these range names in formulas and commands.

Use a range name in a command

You: Type **/ C RENT** ↵ **C2** ↵   *Copy*

1-2-3:

	A	B	C
1	Phones	55	
2	Rent	555	555
3	Travel	5	
4	Misc	5	
5			
6	Total		

Notice that 555, in cell B2 (with the name RENT) was copied to cell C2.

Example 2:   Give a range name to a range of cells.

You: Create the following worksheet:

	A	B
1	Phones	5 5
2	Rent	5 5 5
3	Travel	5
4	Misc	5
5		
6	Total	

Create a range name

You: Type / R N C   *Range Name Create*

Type **EXPENSES** ←┘ **B1..B4** ←┘

1-2-3: **READY** appears. It looks like nothing happened, but in fact the range B1..B4 is now named EXPENSES

Using a range name

You: Highlight cell B6.

Type **@SUM(EXPENSES)** ←┘

Result:

	A	B
1	Phones	55
2	Rent	555
3	Travel	5
4	Misc	5
5		
6	Total	620

We used the new range name instead of specifying B1..B4

Example 3: Document your range names.

You: Use the worksheet created above, which already has some range names.

Highlight cell A1.

Type / R N L R ↓ ↓ ↓ ↓ ↓ ←┘   *Range Name Labels Right*

Note: Each cell in column B now has a range name using the names in column A. That is, Rent is now the range name of B1..B1

You: Type / R N N C   *Range Name Note Create*

Tap **F3** *the name key*

Highlight the name **Rent**

Tap ←⏎

Type **Rent for 3 rooms** ←⏎

Type **C** *Create*

Highlight the name **Travel**

Tap ←⏎

Type **Local travel** ←⏎

Type **Q** *Quit*

Note: You have now documented two range names, Rent and Travel. You may continue documenting the other names if you wish.

You: Highlight cell E1 *be sure columns E, F, and G are empty.*

Type **/ R N N T** ←⏎ **Q** *Range Name Note Table Quit*

Highlight cell F1.

Type **/ W C S 11** ←⏎ *Worksheet Column Set-Width to 11*

1-2-3:

	A	B	C	D	E	F	G
1	Phones	55			Expenses	A:B1..A:B4	
2	Rent	555	555		Misc	A:B4..A:B4	
3	Travel	5			Phones	A:B1..A:B1	
4	Misc	5			Rent	A:B2..A:B2	3 rooms
5					Total	A:B6..A:B6	
6	Total	620			Travel	A:B3..A:B3	Local travel

Example 4: Display the range names and the ranges they define, without the notes.

You: Use the worksheet created above, which already has some range names.

Highlight an empty cell, such as cell E8.

Type **/ R N T** ←⏎ *Range Name Table*

Result: The following appears:

	A	B	C	D	E	F	G
1	Phones	55			Expenses	A:B1..A:B4	
2	Rent	555	555		Misc	A:B4..A:B4	
3	Travel	5			Phones	A:B1..A:B1	
4	Misc	5			Rent	A:B2..A:B2	3 rooms
5					Total	A:B6..A:B6	
6	Total	620			Travel	A:B3..A:B3	Local travel
7							
8					Expenses	B1..B4	
9					Misc	B4..B4	
10					Phones	B1..B1	
11					Rent	B2..B2	
12					Total	B6..B6	
13					Travel	B3..B3	

The range names and the corresponding ranges they define are listed
in columns E and F.

Relative and Absolute Cell References

Relative and absolute cell references are used in formulas that are copied or moved. The concepts behind relative and absolute cell references are best explained with some examples.

Assume you have the following spreadsheet, and you need to write formulas for the cells outlined in dark lines: the item totals, grand total, and percent of the grand total:

	A	B	C	D	E	F	G	H
1							Item	Percent of
2	Item	Mon	Tue	Wed	Thur	Fri	Totals	Grand Total
3								
4	Phone	15	3	12	6	2		
5	Supplies	30	0	0	0	0		
6	Travel	80	2	2	2	2		
7	Salary	0	0	0	0	200		
8	Rent	0	0	0	0	180		
9	Other	0	9	6	0	7		
10								
11	Grand Total ->							

You could type the following formulas into the cells indicated (but we have a shortcut coming up):

G4	@SUM(B4..F4)	H4	+G4/G11
G5	@SUM(B5..F5)	H5	+G5/G11
G6	@SUM(B6..F6)	H6	+G6/G11
G7	@SUM(B7..F7)	H7	+G7/G11
G8	@SUM(B8..F8)	H8	+G8/G11
G9	@SUM(B9..F9)	H9	+G9/G11
G11	@SUM(G4..G9)		

Notice that the cell references in the formulas in **G4** through **G9** change as the row changes. That is, the formula in the fourth row (in **G4**) refers to the fourth row and the formula in the fifth row (in **G5**) refers to the fifth row, and so on.

Notice, however, that the cell references for the denominator in column H do not change as the row changes. The denominator is always **G11**, no matter which row the formula is in.

Instead of typing in each formula, we could have entered one formula in cell **G4** and copied it to cells **G5..G9** to have produced the same result in those cells because the cell references in the formula are relative to the row they are in. The Copy command will change them depending on the row they are copied to.

But if we tried to copy the formula in **H4** down the column, the denominator would have changed from **G11** to **G12** to **G13** and so on.

Let us consider the other type of cell reference—the **absolute cell reference**.

An **absolute cell reference** is used in formulas when two things are true:

      1. The formula is to be copied or moved.

      2. A cell reference in the formula must not change.

When writing a formula with absolute cell references, a **$** is placed in front of the row and/or column of the cell reference, for example: **+$B$6/$C$8**

When you copy or move a formula, 1-2-3 does not change the absolute cell references.

You can combine absolute and relative cell references. For example: **+B10+$D$2**

To make a range name absolute, precede the name with a **$**
      For example: **$RATE.**
When highlighting cells to create a formula, tap the **F4** (absolute) key so that 1-2-3 will add the **$**

Returning to the "Percent of Grand Total" (column H) in the above spreadsheet, we could have typed in cell H4:   **+G4 / $G$11**   and then copied this formula to cells **H5** through **H9**. In this case, the denominator would not have changed during the copy process.

      Tips: If there is *more than one occurrence* of a value (for example: in the above spreadsheet there are lots of items), *use relative cell references* to reference them.

              If there is *only one occurrence* of a value, and you plan to copy, move, or use in a condition a formula that refers to that value (for example: in the above spreadsheet there is only one TOTAL—in

G11—and the formula in H4 refers to that cell), *use an absolute cell reference* to reference it.

If you do not plan to copy or move a formula or use it in a condition, then use relative cell references. (For example: in the above worksheet, we initially typed each formula separately in column H.)

Related: **Conditions**
 Copy
 Formulas
 Functions
 Move

Example: Calculate percentages of a total.

You: Create the following worksheet:

	A	B	C
1	DEPARTMENT	AMOUNT	PERCENT OF TOTAL
2	Personnel	30000	
3	Accounting	15000	
4	Production	120000	
5	Sales	35000	
6			
7	TOTAL		

You: Highlight cell B7.

Type   **@SUM(B2..B5)** ↵

1-2-3:

	A	B	C
1	DEPARTMENT	AMOUNT	PERCENT OF TOTAL
2	Personnel	30000	
3	Accounting	15000	
4	Production	120000	
5	Sales	35000	
6			
7	TOTAL	200000	

You: Highlight cell C2.

Type   +B2/$B$7   ↵

Note: This formula divides the amount by the total to get percent of total.

Here is an alternate method to enter the formula:
Tap   + ← / ← ↓ ↓ ↓ ↓ ↓
Tap   the **F4** key   *the absolute key*
Tap   ↵

1-2-3:

	A	B	C
1	DEPARTMENT	AMOUNT	PERCENT OF TOTAL
2	Personnel	30000	0.15
3	Accounting	15000	
4	Production	120000	
5	Sales	35000	
6			
7	TOTAL	200000	

Cell C2 is still highlighted.

You: Type / C ↵ . ↓ ↓ ↓ ↵   *to copy the formula down*

1-2-3:

	A	B	C
1	DEPARTMENT	AMOUNT	PERCENT OF TOTAL
2	Personnel	30000	0.15
3	Accounting	15000	0.075
4	Production	120000	0.6
5	Sales	35000	0.175
6			
7	TOTAL	200000	

You: Type / R F P Ø ↵ ↓ ↓ ↓ ↵   *Range Format Percent, to convert the fractions in column C to percentages*

Result:

	A	B	C
1	DEPARTMENT	AMOUNT	PERCENT OF TOTAL
2	Personnel	30000	15%
3	Accounting	15000	8%
4	Production	120000	60%
5	Sales	35000	18%
6			
7	TOTAL	200000	

If you highlight cells C2, C3, C4 and C5, one at a time, you will see the following in the top-left corner of the screen:

$$C2 \quad +B2/\$B\$7$$
$$C3 \quad +B3/\$B\$7$$
$$C4 \quad +B4/\$B\$7$$
$$C5 \quad +B5/\$B\$7$$

Notice that while the numerator (a relative cell reference) has changed on each row, the denominator, $B$6 is the same, in spite of being copied. That is because the denominator has a $, which makes that cell reference into an absolute cell reference.

Tips: Note that there are many amounts (i.e., B2, B3, B4, B5), but there is only one total (B6). Therefore, in the formula to be copied, B2 is a relative cell address, and B6 is an absolute cell address.

If there is *only one occurrence* of a value (the total in this example), and you plan to copy, move, or use in a condition a formula that refers to that value, *use an absolute cell reference* to reference that value.

If there is *more than one occurrence* of a value (the amounts in this example), *use relative cell references* to reference those values.

Recalculation and the Calc Key

Command: / **Worksheet Global Recalculation**

Note: Usually, when you change a value, all the affected formulas are recalculated, and you see the new answers. This is called **automatic recalculation.** With large worksheets, a red or white **CALC** indicator may momentarily appear in the status line at the bottom of the screen while this is occurring. You may continue to work while the automatic recalculation is being done. There is no need to change to manual recalculation with Release 3, as there was with earlier releases of 1-2-3. With manual recalculation, formulas are not recalculated until the **F9 (Calc)** key is tapped.

Example: Change recalculation to manual, enter some data, then recalculate the worksheet.

You: Create the following worksheet:

	A	B
1	ITEM	COST
2		
3	Desk	199.95
4	Chair	49.95
5	Lamp	12.55
6		
7	TOTAL	

You: Highlight cell B7.

Type   **@SUM(B3..B5)** ↵

1-2-3:

	A	B
1	ITEM	COST
2		
3	Desk	199.95
4	Chair	49.95
5	Lamp	12.55
6		
7	TOTAL	262.45

Notice that the total is correct

Turn off automatic recalculation

You: Type **/ W G R M** *Worksheet Global Recalculation Manual*

You: Highlight cell B3.

Type **450.55** ↩

1-2-3:

	A	B
1	ITEM	COST
2		
3	Desk	450.55
4	Chair	49.95
5	Lamp	12.55
6		
7	TOTAL	262.45

Notice that the total is *not correct* and that **CALC** appears at the bottom of your screen in blue or black on white. This indicates that some formulas may need to be recalculated and that you are in manual recalculation mode.

You: Tap the **F9** key *the Calc key*

1-2-3:

	A	B
1	ITEM	COST
2		
3	Desk	450.55
4	Chair	49.95
5	Lamp	12.55
6		
7	TOTAL	513.05

Turn automatic recalculation on

You: Type **/ W G R A** *Worksheet Global Recalculation Automatic*

Restore

Note:	You should make backup copies of all your important worksheets. Important worksheets are any that you don't want to type in again. For more information, see the section on **Backups**.
	You only need to restore a worksheet file if you destroyed your hard disk version.
	If you have destroyed files on your hard disk version and you used DOS BACKUP to back up those files to diskette, then DOS RESTORE is the only way to get them back.

Example:	Use the DOS RESTORE command to restore worksheets backed up with the DOS BACKUP command.
You:	Exit from 1-2-3 and get to the DOS prompt.
DOS:	**C>** or **C:\123R3>** *or similar prompt*
You:	Put a backup diskette into drive A: (see **Backups** in Chapter 2 to create a backup diskette)
	Type **RESTORE A: C:\123R3\xxxx.??3** ←┘ *where xxxx is the name of a worksheet to be restored. ??3 will become WK3 and FM3 for your worksheet and Wysiwyg files.*
DOS:	**Insert backup diskette 01 in drive A:** **Strike any key when ready**
You:	Tap ←┘ *to proceed with restore*
Result:	You have restored one worksheet.
Important:	DOS RESTORE only works with diskettes backed up with the DOS BACKUP command (see **Backups**).

Retrieve a File

Command: / **File   Retrieve**

Note: Retrieving a file means finding it on your hard disk or floppy diskette and creating a working copy that you can view and work on. At this point, you have two identical copies of the information, one on disk, and the other in memory, which is your current worksheet. They remain identical until you start changing the current worksheet. Use file open for the second worksheet when you want two worksheets in memory simultaneously.

If you change the worksheet in memory, save it every 15 minutes (see **Save a File**). Also, save before experimenting. If you do destroy your current worksheet, do not save it. Instead, retrieve a fresh copy from the disk.

When you have multiple files in memory (see **Multiple (Linked) Files**), and you use / **File Retrieve** to retrieve a file, the file you retrieve replaces the current file in memory. The current file is the one in which the cell pointer is located. Other files in memory are not affected.

You can retrieve 1-2-3 files from earlier releases, but it may take a little longer because 1-2-3 is actually converting them to Release 3 format as it retrieves them.

Related: **Combining 1-2-3 Files**
Import Data into 1-2-3
File Choices (a list of cross-references)
Directories
Multiple (Linked) Files
Database 9—dBASE Input

Example: Retrieve or load an existing file.

You: Tap / **F R**   *File Retrieve*

1-2-3:   **Name of file to retrieve: XXXXXX ?**

   The names of some files on your disk appear on the third line of the screen.

You: Tap the **F3** key   *the Name key*

1-2-3:   The names of all the 1-2-3 files in the current directory of your disk appear on the screen.

You: Tap → *or* ↓ until the desired file name is highlighted.

   Tap ↵   *to select the highlighted file*

1-2-3:   **WAIT** then **READY** appear in the upper-right corner.

Result: Your worksheet appears in the spreadsheet window.

Row Height with Wysiwyg

Command: **: Worksheet Row Set-Height**
              : Worksheet Row Set-Height
              Mouse control

Note: Use these commands to adjust the height to be visually pleasing.

          Height is measured in points. There are 72 points to an inch. Normal height is approximately 14 points.

Example 1:   In your worksheet, set the height of row 1 to A to 36 points.

    You: Type **: W R S** *Worksheet Row Set-Height*

             Highlight cell A1 *or any cell in row 1*

  1-2-3: **Select the rows to set height to: A:A1 . . A:A1**

    You: Tap ⏎

  1-2-3: **Enter row height (1..255): 14** *might not be 14*

    You: Tap ↓ until the row is 36 points high.

   Note: You could just type 36 but then you lose the flexibility of watching the row height as it is adjusted.

  1-2-3: **Enter row height (1..255):   36**

    You: Tap ⏎

  1-2-3:

A	A	B	C	D	E
1					
2					
3					

Look for **READY** in the upper-right corner to be sure you are finished. If it isn't there, you forgot the ← to end the command.

Example 2:   Change the height of a row by dragging the mouse.

You: Move the mouse arrow so that the point is between the 1 and 2 row names, as shown in this diagram:

	A	B	C	D
1				
2				

Click and hold down the left mouse button.

1-2-3:   The mouse arrow becomes like a cross.

You: Keep holding down the mouse button and drag down. Release the button.

1-2-3:   Row 1 is taller.

Save a File

Command: / **File Save**

Note: Save stores your current worksheet on a disk. If you are saving to a new diskette (floppy disk), format it first (see **Formatting Diskettes**).

SAVE EVERY 15 MINUTES.
SAVE BEFORE YOU EXPERIMENT.

If you don't save, everything you typed could be lost in an instant. Lotus 1-2-3 provides *no* automatic save. Essentially, your worksheet is in RAM, which means Random Access Memory, but more importantly, RAM is the work space in the computer—the community room—where information and programs get together to do some work. RAM is not your disk. If you lose electric power, RAM is wiped clean. And so is your worksheet. But, if you saved your worksheet, there is a copy on disk, which you can retrieve.

When saving a file that already exists on disk, you get three choices: **Cancel Replace Backup.** **Replace** is your usual choice because that replaces the existing file with your updated worksheet. Choose **Backup** if you wish to keep the disk file and still save your worksheet. The old disk file will be renamed so that it ends in **.BAK** instead of **.WK3** as most 1-2-3 files do. If you don't want to save your file (that is, you changed your mind), tap **C** for **Cancel**.

This Backup option is **not** a substitute for regularly backing up your disks. See **Backup** for more information.

You can save your worksheets as Release 2 or 2.01 files by specifying the extension **.WK1** at the end of your file name when you save it. This only works with single sheet files. Also it won't work with files sealed with the **File Admin Seal** command (see **Protecting Cells**). If the file contains data or functions, etc., that are incompatible with Release 2, 1-2-3 will save the file, but it will also tell you that some information was lost.

When you have multiple files in memory and you save using / **File Save**, 1-2-3 displays **[ALL MODIFIED FILES]** in place of the file name. Tap ←┘ to choose that option and save all the open files that have been changed since they were last saved.

Related: **Backup**
eXtract Data to 1-2-3 Files
File Choices (a list of cross-references)
Directories
Formatting Diskettes

Example 1: Save a worksheet for the first time (creates a new file on disk).

You: Tap **Esc** if **READY** is not in the upper-right corner.

You: Tap / **F S** *File Save*

1-2-3: **Enter name of file to save: C:\123R3\FILEØØØ1.WK3**

Note: 1-2-3 gives you a sample name that you can use if you wish. The name includes the drive (**C:**), the directory (**\123R3** on the C: disk), a file name (**FILEØØØ1**), and file extension (**.WK3**).

You: Type a one- to eight-character file name, with no spaces. I recommend using only letters and numbers, even though DOS permits other symbols in file names. It doesn't matter whether you use upper- or lowercase letters for the file name.

You: Tap ←┘

1-2-3: **WAIT** then **READY** appear in the upper-right corner.

Result: Your worksheet (on the screen) is now saved to disk. In other words, the information is now in two places.

Example 2: Save changes to a file already existing on disk.

You: Tap / **F S** *File Save*

1-2-3: **Enter name of file to save: C:\123R3\XXXXX.WK3**
where your file name appears instead of XXXXX

Note: You need not retype the file name because it is already there. .WK3 is an extension that 1-2-3 Release 3 adds to the file name, therefore, you never need to type .WK3 while in 1-2-3 Release 3.

You: Tap ←⏎

Note: If **Cancel Replace Backup** appears, you tap **R** to replace the file on disk. If you don't want to replace it, tap **C** *Cancel* or **B** *Backup.*

You: Tap **R**   *To Replace the disk file with the newest version*

Note: Backup creates two versions on disk. The latest, ending in .WK3, and the second latest, ending in .BAK

1-2-3: **WAIT** then **READY** appear in the upper-right corner.

Example 3: Save a worksheet using a different file name to create two copies of the file on disk, so that one can be modified.

You: Tap / **F S** *File Save*

1-2-3: **Enter name of file to save: C:\123R3\XXX.WK3**
where XXX is your file name

You: Type a one- to eight-character file name, with no spaces.

Tap ←⏎

1-2-3: **WAIT** then **READY** appear in the upper-right corner.

Result: Another file on disk contains a copy of your current worksheet.

Search

Command:	/ Range Search

Note:	Search is a wonderful alternative to the database command / **Data Query Find,** which takes a number of keystrokes to set up. Search will find any set of keystrokes in any part of a cell within a specified range.

Related:	**Database**

Example: Find all the "Pat"s in the following worksheet:

	A	B
1		
2	Smith, Pat	Patterson, NJ
3	Patrick, Jane	
4	Sympathetic	

You: Create the above worksheet.

Highlight cell A1.

Type **/ W C S 17** ↵   *Worksheet Column Set-Width to 17*

Type **/ R S A2..B4** ↵ **PAT** ↵ **B F**   *Range Search Both Find*

1-2-3: Cell A2 is highlighted. It found Pat in the middle of the cell.

You: Type ↵ *chooses Next*

1-2-3: Cell A3 is highlighted. It found Pat as part of Patrick.

You: Type ↵ *chooses Next*

1-2-3: Cell A4 is highlighted. It found pat in the middle of Sympathetic.

You: Type ↵ *chooses Next*

1-2-3: Cell B2 is highlighted. It fount Pat as part of Patterson.

You: Type ↵ *chooses Next*

1-2-3: Beeps, and **ERROR** appears in the upper-right corner because there aren't any more PATs.

You: Tap ↵ *to end and return to* **READY** *mode.*

Solver

Note: Solver is an add-in that solves "what-if" questions. It is especially useful when your problem has several possible answers. Solver helps you find the best answer for your needs.

For example, assume you want to maximize your business profits. Solver can show you different combinations of increased income (sales) and reduced expenses (like salary and rent) to achieve a profit.

For another example, say you want to produce a product and make the price as low as possible. Therefore you want to reduce the cost of the raw materials by buying in bulk, while still being able to store the material, etc. Solver can find the best combination of buying.

An add-in must be loaded before it can be used. Example 1 shows how to load Solver. Example 2 uses Solver.

OVERVIEW OF STEPS

1. Create or load your worksheet.

2. Load the Solver add-in.

3. Invoke the Solver add-in.

4. Use the Solver menu.

5. Quit the Solver add-in.

TERMS YOU SHOULD KNOW

Adjustable cell—This is the cell containing a value that Solver can change when calculating answers. The adjustable cell must be one of the components of a formula and it must be a number, not a formula or a label. For example, when looking for optimal profit, an adjustable cell could contain monthly entertainment costs. You may specify as many adjustable cells as you wish.

Answer—This is the solution. There are three possible answers:

Best answer—This is the best answer Solver found, given the values you put in the adjustable cells. It may or may not be the mathematical optimum.

Optimal answer—This is the mathematical optimum.

Sample answer—These are additional answers that Solver found that are not the best or optimal answers, but you may like one of them better for your particular situation.

Answer number—Solver numbers the answers it finds. Number one is the optimal answer.

Attempt—This is the best solver can do. Solver only provides you with attempts when it can't find an answer. It means your constraints are so limiting that there is no answer to your problem.

Constraint cell—This is a cell with a formula that limits the answers you will be happy with. For example, a constraint cell could limit the rent you will pay, or specify the minimum salary you desire to be paid. There are three kinds of constraints:

Binding constraint—This is a constraint that is satisfied at its most limiting condition. For example, assume B10 is the maximum rent you will pay, and a constraint formula is +B10<=2000. If an answer found by Solver pushed this constraint to its maximum (i.e., $2000) than this constraint is said to be binding for that answer.

Inconsistent constraint—This is a constraint that Solver tried to meet, but couldn't .

Unused constraint—This is a constraint that Solver gave up on and just ignored for the answer it found. For example, assume B15 is the minimum salary you desire and the constraint formula is +B15>=50000. If the answer from Solver contains 40000, than Solver didn't use this constraint in finding this answer.

Optimal cell—This is the cell that you want to be maximized or minimized. For example, this could be your profits cell, that you want to maximize.

Cell reports—These are little windows that show how Solver used various cells in finding the answer.

Guess value—When Solver has trouble figuring out the answer, it may ask you for an educated guess.

Problem cells—No, these are not the bad guys. Problem cells are all the cells Solver uses to find the answer to the problem, including adjustable cells, constraint cells, the optimal cell, etc.

What-if limit—This is the approximate range of values that you can have in an adjustable cell and still satisfy all your constraints, assuming the other constraint cells don't change.

Related: **Add-Ins**
       Backsolver
       Functions
       Multiple Files

Example 1: Load Solver from the **C:\ADDINS** directory.

You: Hold the **Alt** key and tap **F10**. Release the **Alt** key.

   Type **L** *Load*

1-2-3: The following appears:
    Specify an add-in to read into memory: C:\123R3*.PLC

You: Tap **F3**

1-2-3: A list of files appears.

You: If you see **SOLVER.PLC**
Highlight **SOLVER.PLC**
Tap ←┘

If you do not see **SOLVER.PLC**
Tap **Backspace**
Highlight **ADDINS**
Tap ←┘   *hopefully you now see SOLVER.PLC*
Highlight **SOLVER.PLC**
Tap ←┘   *wait—it takes a while to load this product*

If you still do not see **SOLVER.PLC**
Try another directory, or another drive.
Or, perhaps you need to install it.   Add-ins are installed separately from the main 1-2-3 software.

1-2-3: No-Key 1 2 3

You: If these choices appear, you can type a **1**, **2**, or **3** so that later you will be able to activate this add-in with a function key.

Or, if you don't wish to use functions keys, tap **N**   *for No-Key.*

Note: Activating an add-in key with a function key is convenient if you will be using it repeatedly.   Otherwise, choose No-Key.

You: **Q** ←┘ *Quit*

Result: It may look like nothing happened, but now you are ready to Invoke Solver—see Example 2.

Note: Once you have loaded an add-in, do not load it again, unless you quit 1-2-3.

You can make an add-in load automatically when 1-2-3 is started. See Example 3 below.

Example 2: Use Solver to determine the most expensive house you can buy. Assume you can adjust the bank loan and the down payment somewhat. The next figure shows the adjustable cells, the optimal cell, and the constraints.

	A	B
1	Determine the most expensive house I can buy	
2		
3	bank loan	$64,141
4	down payment	$20,000
5		
6	purchase price	$84,141
7		
8	monthly payment	$660
9	loan interest rate	12.0%
10	loan term (years)	30
11		
12	existing debt payments	$5,000
13	yearly mortgage payments	$7,917
14	real estate taxes (2%)	$1,683
15	home insurance	$400
16	total annual debt	$15,000
17		
18	maximum debt: $15,000	1
19	max down payment: $20,000	1
20	down pay at least 20% of price	1

adjustable cells (rows 3–4)

optimal cell (row 6)

constraint cells (rows 18–20)

The adjustable cells are filled in by Solver.

The optimal cell is the one we want to maximize.

The constraint cells contain our constraints:
Maximum debt cannot exceed $15,000 (that's all we can afford).
Maximum down payment is $20,000 (that's all the cash we have).
The down payment must be at least 20% of the price (this could be a bank loan requirement).

You: Start with an empty spreadsheet (see **New Worksheet** in Chapter 2 for details, if necessary).

Move cursor to A1. Type **/ W C S 30** ↵   *to set width to 30*
Move cursor to B1. Type **/ W C S 15** ↵   *to set width to 15*
Type in the information shown below:

	A	B
1	Determine the most expensive house I can buy	
2		
3	bank loan	
4	down payment	
5		
6	purchase price	
7		
8	monthly payment	
9	loan interest rate	
10	loan term (years)	
11		
12	existing debt payments	
13	yearly mortgage payments	
14	real estate taxes (2%)	
15	home insurance	
16	total annual debt	
17		
18	maximum debt: $15,000	
19	max down payment: $20,000	
20	down pay at least 20% of price	

You: Highlight cell B3.   Type **60000** ←

Highlight cell B4.   Type **20000** ←

Highlight cell B6.   Type **+B3+B4** ← *to add the bank loan plus down payment*

Highlight cell B8.   Type **@PMT(B3,B9/12,B10*12)** ←
to calculate the monthly payment (see
***Functions** for details on @PMT)*

Highlight cell B9.   Type **0.12** ← *12% interest rate annually*

Highlight cell B10.   Type **30** ← *30 year loan*

Highlight cell B12.   Type **5000** ← *assume we owe 5000 in credit cards, etc.*

Highlight cell B13.   Type **+B8*12** ← *monthly payment times 12 months / year*

Highlight cell B14.   Type **+B6*.02** ← *2% real estate tax on purchase price*

Highlight cell B15.   Type **400** ← *assumed a flat amount here*

Highlight cell B16.   Type **@SUM(B12..B15)** ← *add up debt*

You: Highlight cell B18.   Type   **+B16<15000** ↵ *a condition. See*
                                   Conditions in Chapter 2
          Highlight cell B19.   Type   **+B4<=20000** ↵
          Highlight cell B20   Type   **+B4>=0.2*B6** ↵ *.02 is 20%*

          Type   **/ R F C Ø** ↵ **B3..B16** ↵ *to format as currency*
          Type   **/ R F P 1** ↵ **B9** ↵ *to format as a percentage*
          Type   **/ R F G** ↵ **B1Ø** ↵ *to format as general*

1-2-3:   You have created the following worksheet:

	A	B
1	Determine the most expensive house I can buy	
2		
3	bank loan	$60,000
4	down payment	$20,000
5		
6	purchase price	$80,000
7		
8	monthly payment	$660
9	loan interest rate	12.0%
10	loan term (years)	30
11		
12	existing debt payments	$5,000
13	yearly mortgage payments	$7,917
14	real estate taxes (2%)	$1,683
15	home insurance	$400
16	total annual debt	$15,000
17		
18	maximum debt: $15,000	1
19	max down payment: $20,000	1
20	down pay at least 20% of price	1

The 1's in cells B18, B19, and B20 indicate true. A Ø would indicate false. In lay terms, if Solver causes a Ø to appear in any of your constraint cells, then it was not able to meet that constraint. A 1 means Solver is able to satisfy that constraint. As we haven't yet run Solver, the 1's mean that our guesses in cells B3 and B4 do satisfy our constraints, although probably not with the optimum answer.

You: Invoke Solver as follows:

If you assigned a function key to Solver :

Hold **Alt** and tap that function key

Otherwise:

Hold the Alt key and tap **F10**
Type **I**   *Invoke*
Tap **F3**   *to show the list of loaded add-ins*
Highlight **SOLVER**
Tap ↵

1-2-3:   The Solver menu appears:

Define	Solve	Answer	Report	Options	Quit
Adjustable		Constraints	Optimal	Quit	

You: Type   **D A B3..B4** ↵   *Define Adjustable cells*

Type   **C B18..B20** ↵   *Constraint cells*

Type   **O X B6** ↵   *Optimal cell maXimize*

Type   **Q**   *Quit, to quit defining cells*

Type   **S P**   *Solve Problem*

Wait

Type   **A O**   *Answer Optimal*

1-2-3:   The following spreadsheet appears:

	A	B
1	Determine the most expensive house I can buy	
2		
3	bank loan	$64,141
4	down payment	$20,000
5		
6	purchase price	$84,141
7		
8	monthly payment	$660
9	loan interest rate	12.0%
10	loan term (years)	30
11		
12	existing debt payments	$5,000
13	yearly mortgage payments	$7,917
14	real estate taxes (2%)	$1,683
15	home insurance	$400
16	total annual debt	$15,000
17		
18	maximum debt: $15,000	1
19	max down payment: $20,000	1
20	down pay at least 20% of price	1

The most expensive house I can purchase, with these constraints, is $84,141, shown in cell B6.

You: If this answer doesn't suit you, type **F N P** *or* **L** *First, Next, Previous, or Last* and see if any of those answers suit you better.

You: If you want separate reports, type **R**   *Report*

Try these choices for a variety of information from Solver:

Type **A**   *Answers*

Type **H**   *How*

Type **W T** *What-if Table*

Type **I T** *Inconsistent Table*
A beep is good. It means there are no inconsistencies.

Type **U T** *Unused Table*

1-2-3: Each time you type a choice, a new spreadsheet with additional information appears. These are separate spreadsheets with names such as ANSWERØ2.WK3 and CELLSØØ1.WK3.

You: When finished, type **Q** *Quit*

If not at **READY**, again type **Q** *Quit*

If you requested separate reports, you now have multiple files open. Hold **Ctrl** and tap **Page Down** or **Page Up** to scroll through each report. To get back to your original worksheet, hold **Ctrl** and tap **Page Down** repeatedly until it appears.

Save your current worksheet. Reminder: **/ F S** *File Save* etc.

Example 3: Customize 1-2-3 so that Solver automatically loads whenever you start 1-2-3.

You: Start 1-2-3 as usual.

Hold the **Alt** key and tap **F10**

Type **S S S**   *Settings System Set*

Tap **F3**

Note: The aim of these next key strokes is to find **SOLVER.PLC**. It could be in any of several directories.

You: If you see **SOLVER.PLC**
            Highlight **SOLVER.PLC**
            Tap ↵

If you don't see **SOLVER.PLC**
            Tap **Backspace**
            Highlight **ADDINS**   Tap ↵
            Highlight **SOLVER.PLC**   Tap ↵

Note: If you want to assign a function key to Solver, type 1, 2, or 3 instead of N in the following line.

You: Type **Y N U Q Q** *Yes No-key Update Quit Quit*

Result: From now on, every time you start 1-2-3, Solver will also start. You just need to wait a few seconds longer.

Example 4:   Remove Solver from memory and prevent it from automatically loading when you start 1-2-3.

You: Hold the **Alt** key and tap **F10**

Type **S S C**   *Setting System Cancel*

Highlight **SOLVER**   *to remove it from memory*

Tap ↵

Type **U Q R**   *Update Quit Remove*

Highlight **SOLVER**   *to remove it from the automatic load list*

Tap ↵

Type **Q**   *Quit*

Result: From now on, when you start 1-2-3, Solver will not automatically start.

Sort

Command: **/ Data Sort**

Note: You may sort columns in a database, or you may sort any column of labels or values that appear on a worksheet.

Sorting means putting rows of information in order. It does not mean searching for, or extracting, specified information. (That is, you never *sort* a database on New York State, although you can *search* a database for NY state records.) To search, see **Database**.

The area that contains the rows you sort is called the **Data-Range**. It differs slightly from the input area of a database, because it need not contain field names (column labels). Field names may exist in the row above the Data-Range.

If sort is done incorrectly, you could end up with fields being mismatched with other fields on the same row. Therefore, we recommend saving your worksheet as a precaution prior to sorting. You can also Enable Undo, and undo any disastrous sort results.

OVERVIEW OF STEPS

- Save your worksheet.

- Create a Data-Range.

- Specify the primary or main sort key.

- Specify Ascending or Descending order.

- Optionally specify a secondary sort key and Ascending or Descending, and up to 253 more sort keys.

- Sort.

DESIGN OF DATABASE

The design of a database is very important. You decide what information is in each column. You are limited to 256 fields (columns) because that is the physical limit of a 1-2-3 worksheet. Here are some considerations for database design:

If you have names in a database and you want the rows in order by last name, but you want to display first then last name, they should be in separate columns, as shown:

	A	B
3	FIRST	LAST
4	Jane	Smith
5	Joe	Rosa
6	Ann	Hankins
7	Jack	Hankins

As your data becomes more fragmented into additional columns and rows, it uses more memory and disk space. It also takes more keystrokes, and therefore time, to enter the information. If information does not need to be divided into separate columns, keep it in the same column (for example, street number and name). As much as possible, try to bunch the information toward the upper-left corner of your worksheet.

Tip: You do not need column headers, but they are useful in documenting your data. You may leave blank rows between the headers and data.

However, check the rules for database input areas if you plan to find or extract data or use database functions because, while **Sort** has no rules for column headers, database functions and **Data Query** commands have very specific rules (see **Database**).

Related: **Database**

Example 1: Sort the following database on LAST and FIRST names.

	A	B	C	D
3	FIRST	LAST	NUMBER	STREET
4	Jane	Smith	44	Lexington
5	Joe	Rosa	117	Atlantic
6	Ann	Hankins	55	West 18
7	Jack	Hankins	55	West 18

Create your worksheet

You: Create the worksheet shown above.

Save your current worksheet. Reminder: **/ F S** *File Save* etc. See **Save** for details.

Start the sort command

You: Type **/ D S D** *Data Sort Data-Range*

Identify the Data-Range

1-2-3: **Enter Data-Range:** *some cell or range appears*

You: Type **A4..D7** ↵ *Note that row 3 is NOT included*

Note: *All four columns* are included, even though you are only sorting columns A and B. It is very important to include *all* of your columns.

Identify the primary key (Last name)

You: Tap **P** *Primary-key*

Type **B1** ↵ *or any cell in column B, to make LAST the primary key*

1-2-3: **Primary sort key: B1 Sort order (A or D):** *a letter appears*

You: Type **A** ↵ *Ascending order*

Note: Ascending order is like a phone book; the names are in alphabetical order. Descending order is like reading a phone book backward— the Z names are first.

Identify the secondary key   (First name)

You: Tap **S** *Secondary-key*

You: Type **A1** ↵ *or any cell in column A, so that FIRST name is the secondary key*

You: Type **A** ↵ *Ascending order*

Sort the records

You: Tap **G Q** *Go Quit*

1-2-3: Did you blink? If so, you missed it. The records are all sorted.

Result:

	A	B	C	D
3	FIRST	LAST	NUMBER	STREET
4	Ann	Hankins	55	West 18
5	Jack	Hankins	55	West 18
6	Joe	Rosa	117	Atlantic
7	Jane	Smith	44	Lexington

Example 2: Sort the following database on CITY, STATE, and COUNTRY, using the extra keys available in Release 3 and up.

	A	B	C	D
1	COUNTRY	STATE	CITY	CLIMATE
2				
3	USA	New York	Buffalo	snowy
4	USA	New York	Albany	hot & cold
5	CANADA	Quebec	Quebec	colder
6	CANADA	Ontario	Toronto	pleasant
7	USA	Georgia	Alanta	hot

Create your worksheet

> **You:** Create the worksheet shown above.
>
> Save your current worksheet. Reminder: **/ F S** *File Save* etc. See **Save** for details.

Start the sort command

> **You:** Type **/ D S D** *Data Sort Data-Range*

Identify the Data-Range

> **You:** Type **A3..D7** ↵ *Note that row 2 is NOT included.*
>
> Note: *All four columns* are included, even though you are only sorting columns A, B, and C.

Identify the three keys

> **You:** Type **P A1** ↵ **A** ↵ *Primary-key Ascending order*
>
> Type **S B1** ↵ **A** ↵ *Secondary-key Ascending order*

Type **E 1** ↵ **C1** ↵ **A** ↵   *Extra-key # 1 Ascending order*

Sort the records

You: Tap **G Q**   *Go Quit*

1-2-3: Did you blink. If so, you missed it. The records are all sorted.

Result:

	A	B	C	D
1	COUNTRY	STATE	CITY	CLIMATE
2				
3	Canada	Ontario	Toronto	pleasant
4	Canada	Quebec	Quebek	colder
5	USA	Georgia	Alanta	hot
6	USA	New York	Albany	hot & cold
7	USA	New York	Buffalo	snowy

Status

Command: / **Worksheet Status**
            / **Worksheet Global Default Status**

Note: The **Worksheet Status** command displays information about your worksheet. The **Worksheet Global Status Default** command displays additional status information.

Example: Display the status of a worksheet.

You: Create or retrieve desired worksheet.

       Type   / **W S**

1-2-3:   A screen of status information appears.

You: Tap ↵

1-2-3:   Your worksheet reappears.

You: Type   / **W G D S** *Worksheet Global Default Status*

1-2-3:   Another screen of additional status information appears.

You: Tap ↵

1-2-3:   Your worksheet reappears.

Titles

Command: **/ Worksheet Titles**

Note: The **Titles** command enables you to keep certain rows and/or columns on the screen, no matter how far down or to the right you scroll. Using the titles option is very useful for large spreadsheets and databases.

Related: **Windows**
Hiding Columns

Example: Set titles in the following spreadsheet:

	A	B	C	D	E	F	G	H	I	J	K	L	M
1	expense												
2		Jan	Feb	Mar	Apr	May	Jun	Jul	Aug	Sep	Oct	Nov	Dec
3	Phone	xxx	xxx	xxx	xxx	xxx	xxx	xxx	xxx	xxx	xxx	xxx	xxx
4	Rent	xxx	xxx	xxx	xxx	xxx	xxx	xxx	xxx	xxx	xxx	xxx	xxx
5	Salary	xxx	xxx	xxx	xxx	xxx	xxx	xxx	xxx	xxx	xxx	xxx	xxx
6	Books	xxx	xxx	xxx	xxx	xxx	xxx	xxx	xxx	xxx	xxx	xxx	xxx
7	Interest	xxx	xxx	xxx	xxx	xxx	xxx	xxx	xxx	xxx	xxx	xxx	xxx
8	Misc	xxx	xxx	xxx	xxx	xxx	xxx	xxx	xxx	xxx	xxx	xxx	xxx
9	Travel	xxx	xxx	xxx	xxx	xxx	xxx	xxx	xxx	xxx	xxx	xxx	xxx

You: Create the above worksheet. Use any numbers for *xxx*. Assume it continues down for at least 30 additional lines.

To set Titles

You: Highlight cell B3.

1-2-3:

	A	B	C	D	E	F	G	H	I	J	K	L	M
1	expense												
2		Jan	Feb	Mar	Apr	May	Jun	Jul	Aug	Sep	Oct	Nov	Dec
3	Phone	xxx	xxx	xxx	xxx	xxx	xxx	xxx	xxx	xxx	xxx	xxx	xxx
4	Rent	xxx	cxx	xxx	xxx	xxx	xxx	xxx	xxx	xxx	xxx	xxx	xxx
5	Salary	xxx	xxx	xxx	xxx	xxx	xxx	xxx	xxx	xxx	xxx	xxx	xxx
6	Books	xxx	xxx	xxx	xxx	xxx	xxx	xxx	xxx	xxx	xxx	xxx	xxx
7	Interest	xxx	xxx	xxx	xxx	xxx	xxx	xxx	xxx	xxx	xxx	xxx	xxx
8	Misc	xxx	xxx	xxx	xxx	xxx	xxx	xxx	xxx	xxx	xxx	xxx	xxx
9	Travel	xxx	xxx	xxx	xxx	xxx	xxx	xxx	xxx	xxx	xxx	xxx	xxx

For Titles to work, you highlight the cell below and to the right of the desired titles. Row 2 and column A are the desired titles; therefore, cell B3 is highlighted.

You: Type **/ W T B** *Worksheet Titles Both*

Tap → → → → → → → → *and so on*

1-2-3:

	A	D	E	F	G	H
1	expenses					
2		Mar	Apr	May	Jun	Jul
3	Phone	xxx	xxx	xxx	xxx	xxx
4	Rent	xxx	xxx	xxx	xxx	xxx
5	Salary	xxx	xxx	xxx	xxx	xxx
6	Books	xxx	xxx	xxx	xxx	xxx
7	Interest	xxx	xxx	xxx	xxx	xxx
8	Misc	xxx	xxx	xxx	xxx	xxx
9	Travel	xxx	xxx	xxx	xxx	xxx

column A is still   note the missing columns here
on the screen

You: Similarly, tap the **PgDn** key. *Rows 1 and 2 remain on the screen.*

Tap the **Home** key.

1-2-3: Cell B3, not cell A1, is highlighted.

Turn off Titles

You: Type **/ W T C** *Worksheet Titles Clear*

Translate Data

Translate is a command in the 1-2-3 Access Menu, which is a separate menu from the menus in the 1-2-3 worksheet. If you start 1-2-3 by typing **123**, you go immediately to a worksheet. If you start 1-2-3 by typing **LOTUS**, you go to the Access Menu, which has these four commands:

      1-2-3   Install   Translate   Exit

Choose 1-2-3 to get a worksheet. Choose Translate to Import or export data (see **File Choices**).

Import into 1-2-3 means to take data (information), usually from another type of software (such as WordPerfect or dBASE) and bring it into a worksheet.

Exporting means to take data currently in a worksheet and write it to disk in a form acceptable to another type of software (such as to dBASE, WordPerfect, Symphony, and so on).

For a cross-reference of topics, see **File Choices** in Chapter 2. To use the Translate command, see **Translate Data to Word Processing**, or **Translate dBASE Data to 1-2-3**.

      Related: **File Choices** (a list of cross-references)

Undo Mistakes

COMMANDS: **/ Worksheet Global Default Other Undo Enable**
/ Worksheet Global Default Other Undo Disable

Note: Sometimes you make a mistake. Use **Undo** to undo it. **Undo** removes only the last mistake.

Undo has two steps. The first step enables the undo and it must be done before you make your mistake.

1. **/ Worksheet Global Default Other Undo Enable Update Quit.** This command is only done once. It activates the undo environment so that you can undo your actions.

2. Hold **Alt** and tap **F4**. This is the actual undo. Do it in **READY** mode, after you made your mistake.

Tip: Enabling Undo (step 1), will slow down the worksheet slightly. Use the second command to turn it off (disable it) when your worksheet is complete.

Warning: Several commands, especially those affecting files on disk and printing operations, cannot be undone. In this case, **Undo** will undo the most recent operation that it can undo, even though it isn't the last one. Also, you cannot undo the **Undo** command. That is, you can't redo an operation by issuing the **Undo** a second time.

Example: Use Undo to remove a mistake.

You Type **/ W G D O U E U Q** *Worksheet Global Default Other Undo Enable Update Quit*

In any cell, type **ABCD** ↵ *This is your mistake*

Hold **Alt** and tap **F4** *the Undo key*

Type **Y** *Yes*

1-2-3: The cell contents ABCD are removed.

Windows

Commands: / Worksheet   Windows Horizontal
            / Worksheet   Windows Vertical
            / Worksheet   Windows Sync
            / Worksheet   Windows Unsync
            / Worksheet   Windows Clear

Note: Sometimes you want to see two separate areas of your worksheet simultaneously. The **Worksheet Titles** or the **Worksheet Column Hide** commands are also quite useful. The **Worksheet Windows** command does permit simultaneous scrolling (moving) through two separate areas of your worksheet.

Tap the **F6** key, the **Windows** key, to move from one window to the other.

You may split your screen horizontally or vertically.

Unless you choose **Unsync**, your windows will scroll together as follows:

- If you split horizontally (sideways), the two windows will move simultaneously as you scroll sideways.

- If you split vertically (up and down), the two windows will move simultaneously as you scroll up and down.

Related: **Hiding Columns**
           Titles

Example: Create two windows, for a spreadsheet and a macro (assuming you will put other information in cell AA1).

	A	B	C	D	E	F
1	salary	250.55				
2	interest	123.45				
3	dividends	27.58				
4						
5	total	401.58				

You: Tap **Home**

Highlight cell C1   *or any cell in column C*

Type / **W W V**   *Worksheet Windows Vertical*

1-2-3:

	A	B		C	D	E
1	salary	250.55	**1**			
2	interest	123.45	**2**			
3	dividends	27.58	**3**			
4			**4**			
5	total	401.58	**5**			

Notice that cell B1 is highlighted.

If you use the positioning keys to move around, you will find that you cannot move out of the left window.

To switch between windows, tap the F6 key, the Window key

You: Tap the **F6** key   *the window key*

1-2-3:

	A	B		C	D	E
1	salary	250.55	**1**			
2	interest	123.45	**2**			
3	dividends	27.58	**3**			
4			**4**			
5	total	401.58	**5**			

Now you are in the window on the right side. By tapping the **F6** key, you can move back and forth between the windows.

You: Tap the **F5** key *the GoTo key*

Type AA1 ←┘

1-2-3:

	A	B			A A	A B	A C	A D
1	salary	250.55		1				
2	interest	123.45		2				
3	dividends	27.58		3				
4				4				
5	total	401.5		5				

Now the right window shows cell AA1 etc., and you can type in a macro, or other data, and view both your worksheet and your macro. Alternatively, consider hiding columns C thru Z.

Remove the right window

You: Type **/ W W C** *Worksheet Windows Clear*

Result: The following appears:

	A	B	C	D	E	F
1	salary	250.55				
2	interest	123.45				
3	dividends	27.58				
4						
5	total	401.58				

Windows 3.0

Note: Windows 3.0 is a Microsoft product that is a sophisticated extension of the DOS operating system. When used, Windows runs under DOS, and applications such as 1-2-3 run under Windows. Without Windows, 1-2-3 runs directly under DOS.

You have a choice of three different modes in which to run Windows 3.0: Real, Standard, and 386 Enhanced. Lotus 1-2-3 Release 3.1 runs successfully under all three modes of Windows.

Real mode runs on practically every IBM or compatible computer that 1-2-3 release 3.0 does.

For Standard mode, you need an Intel 80286 processor or higher.

For 386 Enhanced mode, you need an Intel 80386 processor or higher and 2 Megabytes or more of memory.

Windows 3.0 uses an additional 6 to 8 Megabytes of your hard disk.

In order to use 1-2-3 under Windows, you need to further customize your system after 1-2-3 Release 3.1 has been installed.

Example 1: Customize 1-2-3 and Windows for Real or Standard modes.

Note: There are two ways to tell Windows where the 1-2-3 directory is located. One way (using PATH) is described in the Lotus 1-2-3 documentation. The other way involves using the PIF Editor under Windows.

You: Tap **Home**

Example 2: Customize 1-2-3 and Windows for 386 Enhanced mode.

You: Tap **Home**

Example 3:   Start 1-2-3 under windows.

You: Tap **Home**

Wysiwyg

Note: Wysiwyg (What You See Is What You Get) is probably the reason you upgraded to Release 3.1. Wysiwyg is an add-in that provides sophisticated graphics and mouse capabilities.

Once you load Wysiwyg (see Example 1 below), you can continue to use all the usual 1-2-3 commands (starting with /) while you use all the additional Wysiwyg commands (starting with :). Therefore, I recommend that you have Wysiwyg load automatically when you start 1-2-3 (see Example 2 below).

There seem to be limited reasons not to automatically load Wysiwyg:

1. You never want boxes, graphics, or other report enhancements, and you don't have a mouse.

2. You can't stand the bright white background (you can change that).

3. You can't wait for the few extra seconds for Wysiwyg to load.

Some of Wysiwyg's features include:

- Altering screen colors

- Many fonts

- Bold and italic text

- lines, boxes, and shaded boxes

- Printer control

- Printing data, paragraphs of text, charts, and graphics on the same page

- Changing row height as well has column width

- Use of a mouse for cell, range, and menu selections.

Related: See the individual Wysiwyg commands: **Worksheet, Format, Graph, Print, Display, Special, Text,** and **Named-Style.**

Example 1:   Load and use Wysiwyg.

    You: Start 1-2-3 as usual.

            Hold the **Alt** key and tap **F10**

            Type **L**   *Load*

            Highlight **WYSIWYG.PLC**

            Tap ←┘

            Type **Q**   *Quit*

    1-2-3:   The spreadsheet turns white.

Example 2:   Customize 1-2-3 so that Wysiwyg automatically loads whenever you start 1-2-3.

    You: Start 1-2-3 as usual.

            Hold the **Alt** key and tap **F10**

            Type **S S S**   *Setting System Set*

            Highlight **WYSIWYG.PLC**

            Tap ←┘

            Type **Y N U Q Q**   *Yes No-key Update Quit Quit*

    1-2-3:   The spreadsheet turns white.

    Result: From now on, every time you start 1-2-3, Wysiwyg will also start. You just need to wait a few seconds longer.

Example 3:   Use the Wysiwyg menus.

    You: Tap **:**   *The colon, which is a shifted semicolon*

            Or, move the mouse pointer above the spreadsheet into the menu area. If the Wysiwyg menu doesn't appear, click the right mouse button.

1-2-3: The Wysiwyg main menu appears:

Worksheet Format Graph Print Display Special Text Named-Style Quit

You: To choose one of these options:
Use the mouse to click on the option of your choice
Or, tap the first letter of the option
Or, tap the arrow keys to highlight your choice and tap ←⏎

Example 4: Remove Wysiwyg from memory and prevent it from automatically loading when you start 1-2-3.

You: Start 1-2-3 as usual.

Hold the **Alt** key and tap **F10**

Type **S S C**   *Setting System Cancel*

Highlight **WYSIWYG**

Tap ←⏎

Type **U Q R**   *Update Quit Remove*

Highlight **WYSIWYG**

Tap ←⏎

Type **Q**   *Quit*

1-2-3: The spreadsheet turns white.

Result: From now on, every time you start 1-2-3, Wysiwyg will also start. You just need to wait a few seconds longer.

Viewer

Note: Viewer is an add-in that lets you rapidly view the contents of files without loading them. It's a wonderful feature.

OVERVIEW OF STEPS

2. Load the Viewer add-in.

3. Invoke the Viewer add-in.

4. Use the Viewer menu.

5. Quit the Viewer add-in.

Related: **Add-Ins**
Multiple Files

Example 1: Load Viewer from the **C:\ADDINS** directory.

You: Hold the **Alt** key and tap **F10**. Release the **Alt** key.

Type **L** *Load*

1-2-3: The following appears:
Specify an add-in to read into memory: C:\123R3*.PLC

You: Tap **F3**

1-2-3: A list of files appears.

You: If you see **VIEWER.PLC**
Highlight **VIEWER.PLC**
Tap ←

If you do not see **VIEWER.PLC**
Tap **Backspace**
Highlight **ADDINS**
Tap ← *hopefully you now see VIEWER.PLC*

Highlight **VIEWER.PLC**
Tap ←⏎   *wait—it takes a while to load this product*

If you still do not see **VIEWER.PLC**
Try another directory, or another drive.
Or, perhaps you need to install it. Add-ins are installed separately from the main 1-2-3 software.

Wait. Don't tap ←⏎ again, until instructed.

1-2-3:   **No-Key 1 2 3**

You: If these choices appear, you can type a **1, 2**, or **3** so that later you will be able to activate this add-in with a function key.

Or, if you don't wish to use functions keys, tap **N** *for No-Key.*

Note: Activating an add-in key with a function key is convenient if you will be using it repeatedly. Otherwise, choose No-Key.

You: Q←⏎ *Quit*

Result: It may look like nothing happened, but now you are ready to Invoke Viewer—see Example 2.

Note: Once you have loaded an add-in, do not load it again, unless you quit 1-2-3.

You can make an add-in load automatically when 1-2-3 is started. See Example 3 below.

Example 2: Use Viewer to view files.

You: Invoke Viewer as follows:

If you assigned a function key to Viewer:

Hold **Alt** and tap that function key

Otherwise:

> Hold the **Alt** key and tap **F10**
> Type **I**   *Invoke*
> Tap **F3**   *to show the list of loaded add-ins*
> Highlight **VIEWER**
> Tap ↵

1-2-3:   The Viewer menu appears:

Retrieve Open Link Browse
View and retrieve file (.WK1, .WKS, .WR1, .WRK, .WK3)

You: Type **B** *Browse*

Tap **F2** *to reset any settings. To keep the settings, don't tap F3.*

To view a file, tap ↑ or ↓

1-2-3:   If you highlight a file on the left, you will see its contents on the right. Not all files have meaningful contents.   If you highlight a directory on the left, you will see on the right a list of all the files with size, date and time beside them. Directories are represented within <directory>

You: Keep tapping ↓ until you see some 1-2-3 worksheet files.

1-2-3:   The contents of the highlighted file appears on the right.

You: To change to a higher level directory, tap ←   *left arrow*

To see the files in a directory, tap →   *right arrow*

To end Viewer tap ↵   or **Esc**

Example 3:   Customize 1-2-3 so that Viewer automatically loads whenever you start 1-2-3.

You: Start 1-2-3 as usual.

Hold the **Alt** key and tap **F10**

Type **S S S**   *Settings System Set*

Tap **F3**

Note: The aim of these next key strokes is to find **VIEWER.PLC**. It could be in any of several directories.

You: If you see **VIEWER.PLC**
      Highlight **VIEWER.PLC**
      Tap ↵

      If you don't see **VIEWER.PLC**
      Tap **Backspace**
      Highlight **ADDINS**   Tap ↵
      Highlight **VIEWER.PLC**   Tap ↵

Note: If you want to assign a function key to Viewer, type **1**, **2**, or **3** instead of **N** in the following line.

You: Type **Y N U Q Q**   *Yes No-key Update Quit Quit*

Result: From now on, every time you start 1-2-3, Viewer will also start. You just need to wait a few seconds longer.

Example 4: Remove Viewer from memory and prevent it from automatically loading when you start 1-2-3.

You: Hold the **Alt** key and tap **F10**

      Type **S S C**   *Setting System Cancel*

      Highlight **VIEWER**   *to remove it from memory*

      Tap ↵

      Type **U Q R**   *Update Quit Remove*

      Highlight **VIEWER**   *to remove it from the automatic load list*

      Tap ↵

      Type **Q**   *Quit*

Result: From now on, when you start 1-2-3, Viewer will not automatically start.

Zero Suppression

Command: / **Worksheet Global Zero Yes**
            / **Worksheet Global Zero Label**

Note: Zero suppression means that zero values appear blank. This is useful when you have formulas that often give zero values and you don't want all those zeros cluttering up the worksheet.

Unlike earlier releases of 1-2-3, Release 3 remembers how you set **Zero Suppression** in between uses of the file.

Example 1:   Suppress zeros in the following worksheet:

	A	B	C	D	E	F	G
1	VOUCHER						
2							
3		MON	TUES	WED	THUR	FRI	TOTAL
4	TRAVEL	250.45				250.45	$500.90
5	MEALS		30.00		25.00		$55.00
6	LOCAL TRAVEL						$0.00
7	MISCELLANEOUS						$0.00
8	==============	=======	=======	=======	=======	=======	=======
9	TOTAL	$250.45	$30.00	$0.00	$25.00	$250.45	$555.90

You: Type / **W G Z Y** *Worksheet Global Zero Yes*

Result: The following appears:

	A	B	C	D	E	F	G
1	VOUCHER						
2							
3		MON	TUES	WED	THUR	FRI	TOTAL
4	TRAVEL	250.45				250.45	$500.90
5	MEALS		30.00		25.00		$55.00
6	LOCAL TRAVEL						
7	MISCELLANEOUS						
8	==============	=======	=======	=======	=======	=======	=======
9	TOTAL	$250.45	$30.00		$25.00	$250.45	$555.90

Notice that cells D8, G5, and G6 do not show zeros.

Example 2: Replace zero values with the word "None".

You: Use the worksheet created in the previous example.

Type / W G Z L None ↵ *Worksheet Global Zero Label None*

Result: The following appears:

	A	B	C	D	E	F	G
1	VOUCHER						
2							
3		MON	TUES	WED	THUR	FRI	TOTAL
4	TRAVEL	250.45				250.45	$500.90
5	MEALS		30.00		25.00		$55.00
6	LOCAL TRAVEL						None
7	MISCELLANEOUS						None
8	===============	=======	=======	=======	=======	=======	=======
9	TOTAL	$250.45	$30.00	None	$25.00	$250.45	$555.90

Chapter 3

Problems and Solutions

How to Use This Chapter

This chapter contains an alphabetized list of typical problems with suggested solutions. To use this chapter, follow these suggestions:

- Look around the screen. Are there any messages? Look at the top for messages such as **EDIT**. Look at the bottom for messages such as **NUM** or **CIRC**. Look in the cell for messages such as **ERR**. Start by looking up these messages in this chapter.

- State your problem: For example, "I can't get Copy to work." Then rephrase your statement, putting the subject first. Restated, the problem becomes "Copy doesn't work...." Look up this phrase.

Hints and Tips

Many errors are just the result of extra keystrokes, such as:

1. You typed a space when you shouldn't have.

2. You tapped ←⟃ when you shouldn't have.

3. You typed an apostrophe when you shouldn't have.

4. You pressed down and held a key until you saw results. Consequently, the key started repeating, giving undesired results. Remember—just tap a key.

Additional Help

1-2-3 offers help on your computer. Tap the **F1** key for **help** (see **Help** in Chapter 2).

Chapter 5 of the *Lotus 1-2-3 Release 3.1 Reference* book includes 30 pages on troubleshooting.

As a last resort, use the backup copy of your worksheet. You *did* remember to make backups, didn't you? (See **Backups** in Chapter 2.)

$A:$C$5 doesn't work

You may only have two dollar signs in an absolute or mixed cell reference. Remove one $. See **Relative and Absolute Cell References** in Chapter 2.

A> prompt appears

See: **DOS prompt appears.**

Apostrophes appear in the cell when they shouldn't

Highlight the offending cell. Look at the upper-left corner of the screen. Do you see these two opposing accent marks: ´` ?

If so, tap **F2**, tap the **Home** key, tap →, tap the **Del** key, and tap ←⏎

In the future use the apostrophe immediately to the right of the letter L; don't use the one under the ~ or any other accent mark that may appear on your keyboard.

Arrow keys don't work

Does **NUM** appear in the lower-right corner? If so, you are in Number mode instead of Arrow mode. Tap the **Num Lock** key once, and **NUM** will disappear.

Does **MENU** appear in the upper-right corner? If so, you are in the middle of a command. Tap the **Esc** key several times until **READY** appears.

Does **CMD** appear on the screen? If so, you are in the middle of an executing Macro. Either wait until the macro finishes or hold the **Ctrl** key and tap the **Break** key (probably the Scroll Lock key) to terminate the macro.

Does **SCROLL** appear at the bottom of the screen? If so, tap the **Scroll Lock** key once to remove the message.

Are you in **EDIT** mode? Look at the upper-right corner of the screen. If **EDIT** appears, tap the **Esc** key several times to return to **READY** mode.

Asterisks ******** fill some cells

Widen your columns. The numbers are there but are too long to be displayed.

B> prompt appears

See: **DOS prompt appears.**

Blank screen

Did your screen suddenly go blank? Try tapping the **Home** key. Then tap the **Esc** key or hold the **Ctrl** key and tap the **Scroll Lock** key. You may have hit the **F10** key (the graph key) by mistake.

Are you trying to graph something? If your monitor doesn't support graphics, then you can't graph anything. If you try, your screen will go blank. If your monitor does support graphics, then something may be wrong with your graph settings. See the error message **Graph doesn't display** for more information.

If your monitor does support graphics but you have never successfully displayed a graph, perhaps you have the wrong drivers installed. You may need to run the Install program again. Follow the instructions in your Lotus 1-2-3 documentation.

Also, check all your cables and wires. Make sure everything is plugged in and that nothing is loose.

C> prompt appears

See: **DOS prompt appears.**

CALC appears at the bottom right of the screen

This is not an error. If it appears momentarily and then disappears, just ignore it. It means automatic recalculation is occurring in the background. You can continue your work as usual. If CALC persists on the screen and is blue or black on a white background, then your spreadsheet has been set to manual recalculations. In this case, tap the **F9** key (the **Calc** key) to recalculate the formulas in the worksheet (see **Recalculation Modes and the Calc Key**).

CIRC appears at the bottom right of the screen

Except for rare intentional situations, **CIRC** means you have an error, usually **disastrous**, in some formula in your worksheet. When you fix the incorrect formula, the **CIRC** message goes away. First you need to find which formula is incorrect. Type **/ W S** *Worksheet Status* and look at the cell mentioned on the "Circular Reference" row. This is the cell causing the **CIRC**.

CIRC means that a formula contains a reference to itself (a circular reference). For example if cell **C7** contains +C5+C7, it contains a reference to itself, which is almost always incorrect. See **Formulas** in Chapter 2 for more details.

Commands do not work right

The commands given do not produce the results they should. This will occur if you hold down a letter or the ←┘ key, causing it to automatically repeat.

Always tap your keys and take your fingers off the keys as fast as possible, then wait, with your hands off the keyboard, even if nothing seems to be happening. Some commands take a minute or more to be processed. Most computers let you type ahead, meaning, you can momentarily be typing faster than the computer is processing your keystrokes.

You may be striking ←┘ too frequently. For instance, if the instructions are:
         type / F R COSTS ←┘
only tap ←┘ after COSTS and not after the **F** or **R**.

Copy doesn't copy anything

You tried to copy cell A14 across the row but the result looks like this, with nothing changed:

	A	B	C	D	E
1 4	xxxxx				

You specified an incorrect FROM range. The FROM range is only one cell. Tap ←┘ *before* you begin painting. For example, type / C A14 ←┘   B14..E14 ←┘

See the section on **Copy** in Chapter 2 for details.

Copy only copies one cell

You tried to copy cell A14 across the row, but the result looks like this, with nothing in any cell except the first (A14) and last ones (E14).

	A	B	C	D	E
1 4	xxxx				xxxx

You forgot the PERIOD, when specifying the TO range. See the section on **Copy** in Chapter 2 for details.

Data Fill doesn't fill in any numbers

If you want an *increasing* series of numbers (for example: 1, 2, 3, 4, 5, ... or 1980, 1981, 1982, 1983, ...), check the following:

- Make sure your start value is *correct* (for example, 1 or 1980).

- Make sure your step value is *positive* (for example, 1).

- Make sure your stop value is *large* enough (for example, 10 or 1990 or better yet 99999). It's quite acceptable if it is too large.

- Make sure the stop value is *larger* than the start value.

If you want a *decreasing* series of numbers (for example, 100, 99, 98, 97, ...), check the following:

- Make sure your start value is *correct* (for example, 100).

- Make sure your step value is *negative*, with a minus sign (for example, -1).

- Make sure your stop value is *small* enough (for example, 0 or -9999).

- Make sure the stop value is *smaller* than the start value.

If these values are okay, perhaps your range isn't big enough. Type **/ D F** and look at the range now highlighted. If you don't see a range highlighted, then that is the problem. Tap ↓ or → until the desired range is highlighted, and continue with your command. See **Data Fill** in Chapter 2 for details.

Date appears as ✱✱✱✱✱✱✱✱✱✱✱ no matter how wide I make the column

Did you type too many days for the month? For example typing **2/31/88** will give all asterisks, because February doesn't have 31 days. Make sure February only has 28 days (29 in leap years, which are all the years divisible by 4 except the year 2000). Make sure April, June, September, and November have no more than 30 days.

Date appears as a funny number

Does the cell contain a number between **1** and **73050**? If so, you just need to format it as a date. Highlight the cell and type **/ R F D 1** ← If asterisks appear, widen the column by typing **/ W C S 10** ← For more information, see **Dates** in Chapter 2.

Date error using @DATE

@DATE takes three numbers: year, month, and day. For example @DATE(89,6,30) is 1989, June, 30. Remember that some months have only 30 days (April, June, September, and November). 1-2-3 puts ERR in the cell if you try 31 days in those months. Also, February usually has only 28 days. Once every 4 years it has 29 (except the year 2000).

Disk Full

This message appears when you try to save a worksheet and the diskette or hard disk does not have enough room. Insert a blank formatted diskette and try saving again. Try File Erase to erase unnecessary files and free up some disk space. See Formatting Disks and File Erase in Chapter 2 for details.

Disk is write-protected appears in the lower-left corner of the screen

The diskette you are trying to save to, extract to, or file print is write protected. If it is a 5-1/4 inch diskette, either it does not have a write protect notch, or the notch is covered with tape. Tape is put over the notch to prevent the computer from changing its contents or adding new files. If you are sure you want to write to that diskette, remove the tape covering the write-protect notch. If the disk has no notch, it is probably for good reason. Think twice before you decide to cut a notch in the disk. Otherwise, put another diskette in the drive.

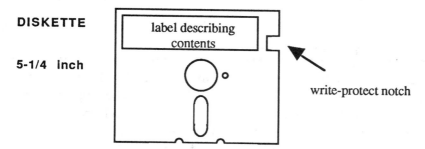

DISKETTE

5-1/4 inch

label describing contents

write-protect notch

If the diskette is a 3-1/2 inch diskette, you slide the plastic to close the hole to permit writing to diskette. Slide the plastic to open the hole to write-protect the diskette.

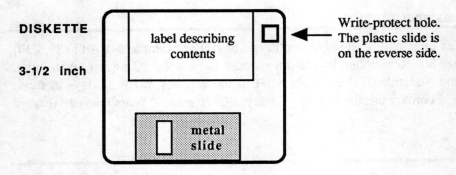

DISKETTE

3-1/2 inch

label describing
contents

Write-protect hole.
The plastic slide is
on the reverse side.

metal
slide

DOS prompt appears

Lotus 1-2-3 is not active. Somehow you have activated DOS.

      First, try typing **EXIT** ←⏎

If EXIT works, it means that somehow, you typed **/ S** for System. And, best of all—
you probably didn't lose anything.

If you are running under Windows, try holding the **Ctrl** key and tapping **Esc**. To rotate
through the active programs and icons under Windows, keep Holding **Ctrl** and tapping
Esc. Stop when 1-2-3 appears, or when you have seen all the programs.

If that doesn't work, follow your instructions for starting Lotus 1-2-3. See **Getting
Started** in Chapter 1. You may need to restart your computer. This is a last resort
technique, but here it is: hold down the **Ctrl** and **Alt** keys, and then tap the **Del** key.
Release all keys, and wait.

EDIT appears in the upper-right corner

If you type something into a cell that 1-2-3 initially thinks is a number, but really isn't,
1-2-3 puts you into **EDIT** mode, expecting you to fix it. If it should be a number, then
remove all blanks, commas, dollar signs, and nonnumeric characters and tap ←⏎ . If it
isn't a number, tap **home**, type an apostrophe ('), then tap ←⏎ . If you just want out,
tap **Esc**, which will get rid of that information. See **Numeric Entries** or **Label
(Text) Entries** in Chapter 2.

ERROR is flashing in the upper-right corner

Look in the lower-left corner for an error message, such as **Disk is write-protected**,
Disk full, or **Memory Full**. Tap the **F1** Key, which will produce a 1-2-3 help screen
specific to the error that occurred. After reading the help provided, tap the **Esc** key twice

(once to get out of help, and once to clear the error message). You will probably *not* be in **READY** mode, so look at the upper-left corner to see where you are. If confused, just keep tapping Esc until **READY** appears. Look up the error message in this section.

EXTRACT In / Data Query Extract didn't extract anything

There are several possible solutions:

1. Make sure the column headings are identical for the input, criteria, and output areas. See **Database 2** and **Database 3** for details.

2. Be sure the textual information in your input area is spelled identically to the textual information in your criteria.

3. Textual information must have the same number of spaces and periods etc. in order for a match to be found. Different capitalization doesn't matter.

4. Make sure there are no blank lines between the column headers (field names) and the data rows. See **Delete a Row** or **Move** to remove blank lines.

5. Check your criteria conditions for accuracy.

6. Make sure any criteria cells that look empty really are empty. Use / **Range Erase** on all apparently empty cells in the criteria.

7. Make sure your input, criteria, and output areas are correct. Refer to **Database 4, 5, 6,** or **7** for instructions to check these areas. Each area must include the column headings (field names) at the top of the range. Both Input and Criteria areas must be at least two rows long. Input is probably much longer. The output range should be either only one row (the column header row) or long enough for the maximum number of rows that will be extracted.

8. Check your numbers. Either none of them should have label prefixes (' " or ^) or all of them should have label prefixes, in which case your numbers are really text (labels) and cannot be used in arithmetic calculations.

9. Check your dates. Either none of them should have label prefixes (' " or ^) or all of them should have label prefixes, in which case they are really text (labels).

10. If your criteria formula refers to cells within the input area, do not use $ in the cell addresses (*avoid* **$D$5**, use **D5** instead). If your criteria refers to cells outside the

input area range, precede the row and column with $ (for example, G5 becomes $G$5). This makes the cell reference absolute (see **Relative and Absolute Cell References** in Chapter 2).

11. If all the rows are extracted to your output area, it means your criteria probably has a blank row, or the condition is incorrect or missing.

12. If you use numeric comparisons, make sure the cells in the formulas refer to the first row of data, not the field names in the input area. That is, if your input area starts in row three with the field names, the criteria should refer to row four, where the actual data starts. Better yet, use the column name instead of the cell address, as shown in the examples in **Database 2—Criteria**.

File is missing. I can't retrieve it. I know I saved it, but it isn't there.

Perhaps you forgot to type the name when you saved it, and 1-2-3 provided a substitute name. At the **READY** mode, type / **F R** *File Retrieve.* Tap the F3 key. Do you see a lot of names that look like **FILE0001.WK3 FILE0002.WK3 FILE0003.WK3** and so on? Let's retrieve the last one (the one with the highest number), by typing / **F R FILE0057** ⟵ *File Retrieve,* assuming the highest number is 57. Is this your file? If not, try some other numbers. When you find your file, save it with the correct name (see **Save a File** in Chapter 2.) Another possibility is that you saved it in a different directory or disk (see **Directories** in Chapter 2.)

Graph doesn't display

When you try to view the graph the screen goes blank. There are several common reasons for this:

1. Your monitor doesn't support graphics. Many monochrome monitors, especially IBM monochrome monitors, do not support graphics. Several hundred dollars for a special monitor graphics adaptor board (hardware) and a new monitor can correct this situation.

2. Your monitor does support graphics, but you have the wrong screen driver installed. Run the install program again, specifying the correct hardware configuration for your computer. See your Lotus 1-2-3 manual for details.

3. You didn't define any data ranges, or you accidentally reset them all. See **Graphs** for instructions to set the ranges correctly. See below for resetting specific ranges

4. You have specified a range or legend incorrectly. Check each desired range as follows:

   Tap the **Esc** key until **READY** appears in the upper-right corner.

Type **/ G X**	*Look at the highlighted X range. Is it correct ?*	Type ↵
Type **A**	*Look at the highlighted A range. Is it correct?*	Type ↵
Type **B**	*Look at the highlighted B range. Is it correct?*	Type ↵
Type **C**	*Look at the highlighted C range. Is it correct?*	Type ↵
Type **D**	*Look at the highlighted D range. Is it correct?*	Type ↵
Type **E**	*Look at the highlighted E range. Is it correct?*	Type ↵
Type **F**	*Look at the highlighted F range. Is it correct?*	Type ↵

   You should now see **TYPE X A B C D E F** *etc.*

   For each range you do *not* use, type the following:
   Type **R F** ↵   *to reset the F range so that it is not used*
   Type **E** ↵   *to reset the E range so that it is not used*
   Type **D** ↵   *to reset the D range so that it is not used*
   Type **C** ↵   *to reset the C range so that it is not used*
   Type **B** ↵   *to reset the B range so that it is not used*
   Type **Q V** *Quit View*

   You should now see a graph.

5. You selected manual scaling (**/ Graph Options Scale Y-scale Manual**) and set the lower limit higher than the upper limit, or you forgot to set both limits.

6. For line graphs, you may have selected **/ Graph Options Format Graph Neither**, which hides both lines and symbols. Type **/ G O F G B Q V** *Graph Options Format Graph Both Quit View*.

Graph doesn't print

The **PrtScrn** key cannot be used to print graphs. However, it can be used to determine whether the printer is working. Tap the **PrtScrn** key (on older keyboards, hold the **shift** key while you tap **PrtScrn**). Does anything print? If not, then your printer is not working. In this case, refer to: **Printer doesn't print**.

If your printer works otherwise, except for graphics, check the following:

- Does your printer support graphics? Most daisy wheel and thimble letter-quality printers do not print graphics.

- Perhaps when 1-2-3 was installed, the printer was incorrectly specified for graphics. You may need to run the install program again, specifying the correct hardware configuration for your computer. See your Lotus 1-2-3 manual for details.

See **Graphs** in Chapter 2 for further information.

Green Cells after using Auditor

Unless you choose **Options Reset Highlight Quit** before quitting the Auditor, various cells on your spreadsheet will be left green (or bright) because they have been marked U for Unprotected. One way to fix this is to highlight the green (or bright) cell, and type **/ R P** ↩ *for Range Protect*. This turns the Protect mode on, which is usually what you want.

GROUP is on. Columns or rows get deleted from multiple sheets

Group mode is very powerful. It permits you to do something in one sheet of a multiple sheet worksheet and have that same action affect *all* the other sheets at the same time. This includes formatting numbers, changing column widths, and inserting and deleting columns and rows. Whenever Group mode is on, **GROUP** appears at the bottom of the screen. To turn it off, type **/ W G G D** for Worksheet Global Group Disable. **GROUP** disappears, and your actions will be restricted to the sheet your cell pointer is in.

Incorrect answer for a formula

Does **CIRC** appear at the bottom right of the screen? If so, see **CIRC** in this section.

Does **CALC** appear at the bottom right of the screen? If so, see **CALC** in this section.

Check your formula. Are all the cell references correct? Do the cells you refer to have the correct contents?

You may have omitted necessary parentheses in your formula. Parentheses change the order of calculation. For example:

1+2/4 equals 1.5 because 2 is divided by 4, giving 0.5, then 1 is added to the 0.5

(1+2)/4 equals .75 because 1 is added to 2 giving 3, then the 3 is divided by 4

If your formula appears correct, check the cells referenced by the formula. Do these cells have values or labels in them? Numbers that are in label instead of value format will give you wrong answers. Also, 1-2-3 sometimes treats text as if it were a zero, or **ERR** may appear in the cell containing your formula. There are two ways to check for incorrect use of labels.

1. Highlight, one at a time, each cell referenced. As you highlight each cell, look at the top left of the screen to see the true cell contents. If you see an apostrophe or **(L)**, then 1-2-3 is treating this cell as a label.

2. Type **/ W W M E** *Worksheet Windows Map Enable*. All columns become 2 characters wide. Every cell with a number has a **#**. Every cell with a formula has a **+**. Every cell with a label has a **''**   Make sure the cells you use in your numeric calculations do not have a **''**   Type **/ W W M D** *Worksheet Windows Map Disable* to make your worksheet appear normal.

If you have labels where you should have values, you need to know the Global format in order to know how to fix the problem. Type **/ W S** *Worksheet Status*. Look for your Global Format.

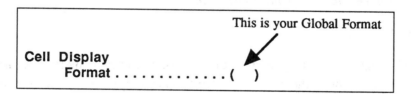

If your global format is **(L)** fix this problem as follows:

1. Type **/ W G F , 2** ↵   *Worksheet Global Format comma 2*, to change the global format to comma with two decimal places. You probably don't ever want the global format to be **(L)**, which stands for **Label**.

2. Highlight the cell that contains the apostrophe.

3. Tap the **F2** key *the Edit key*.

4. Tap the **Home** key.

5. Tap the **Del** key *to remove the apostrophe*.

6. Tap ↵

If your global format is (A) fix this problem as follows:

1. Highlight the cell that contains the apostrophe.

2. Type / **R F R** ↵ *Range Format Reset —to remove the range formatting.*

3. Retype the number that is in the cell. Only type the number and decimal point. Do not type commas, dollar signs, or spaces. Tap ↵

If your global format is anything else, fix this problem as follows:

1. Highlight the cell that contains the apostrophe.

2. If you see (L), type / **R F R** ↵   *Range Format Reset—to remove the range formatting as a label.*

3. Tap the **F2** key *the Edit key.*

4. Tap the **Home** key.

5. Tap the **Del** key *to remove the apostrophe.*

6. Tap ↵

If the machine beeps and **EDIT** appears in the upper-right corner, there is an invalid character in the cell. Remove the invalid character, or tap the **Esc** key twice and retype the intended contents.

Examine any apparently empty cells referenced in your formula. If any have an apostrophe, this could be the problem. Highlight the offending cell and type / **R E** ↵ *Range Erase* (see **Erase** in Chapter 2).

If you used functions, check the range(s) used in the function.

Is the answer just slightly off?   Refer to the section on **Functions**, and look at the examples for the functions **@ROUND** and **@INT**. Perhaps they can help.

Invalid cell or range address—Press F1 for help

Are you using a range address? If so, then the name you are using is not known to 1-2-3. Tap the **F5** key then the **F3** key. Do you see the name? Tap **Esc** several times to back out to **READY** . If you do not see the name, you need to recreate the name. If you do see the name, then you probably typed it with a space at the beginning, in the middle, or at the end. In this case, you also need to recreate the range name. See **Range Names** in Chapter 2.

Label does not overlap into the next cell

There is something in the cell to the right that has priority over the overlapped label. Even spaces have priority in their own cell. Highlight the cell to the right. If there is nothing you wish to keep, erase it by typing **/ R E** ↵

Mem flashing on the bottom line of the screen

This is a warning that you have very little memory remaining in your computer.

Memory Full appears in the lower-left corner

You attempted to create a worksheet that is too big for your computer's memory. Try to bunch all the data-containing cells in the upper-left corner of the worksheet. Tap the **End** key then the **Home** key to see the lower-right corner of the data-containing cells of your worksheet.

Menu keeps appearing when you type a Backslash or enter a macro

You are typing the **Forward Slash** instead (/), which does bring up the menu. If you are trying to type a **Backslash**, be sure it tilts left like \

If you are entering a macro, be sure to type an apostrophe before the slash, like this ' /

Mouse doesn't work

If you see an arrow, but clicking on the left button doesn't work, tap the ↵ key, Perhaps you hit the Pause key, which pauses the program, until ↵ or another key is depressed.

Number acts as if it has a value of zero

Two possible reasons. First, if the number is typed in as a label, that is, if you have a label prefix character at the beginning, it will be treated as a label. All labels have a numerical value of zero. To check this, highlight the number in question. Look at the upper-left corner. Do you see an apostrophe, caret, or quote mark at the beginning of the number? If so, remove it as follows: Tap the **F2** key (the **Edit** key), tap **Home**, tap the **Del** key, then tap ←⏎ If **EDIT** appears in the upper-right corner, follow the instructions for the **EDIT** error message.

The second possible reason is often the result of automatic formatting. To check this, highlight the number in question. Look at the upper-left corner. Do you see an **L** in parentheses (**L**) in front of the number? If so, the number has been formatted as a label. Reformat it as follows: Type / **R F R** ←⏎ *Range Format Reset*. Then retype the number correctly. See the warning at the end of **Formatting Numbers** in Chapter 2.

Only the last entry I typed appears; everything else disappears

Try tapping the **Home** key then tap the **PgDn** or the ⇆ key slowly to see if anything else is there. If not, you probably tapped ←⏎ after each entry, and essentially typed everything into the same cell. Each new entry completely replaced the last one.   Enter your information again (the old information is lost), this time tapping → or ↓ after each entry. Look at your screen to be sure information is going into the correct cells.

Printer doesn't work

While the **PrtScrn** key cannot be used to print graphs, it can be used to determine whether the printer is working. Tap the **PrtScrn** key (on older keyboards you may need to hold the **Shift**, tap the **PrtScrn** key, and then release the **Shift** key). Does anything print? If not, check the following:

- Is the printer on?

- Is it plugged into the electrical outlet?

- Does that outlet have power? Try plugging in a lamp to check the outlet.

- Is the printer cable plugged into the correct plug in the back of the computer?

- Are the connections between the printer and the computer firmly plugged in at each end?

- Is your printer ready? This is sometimes indicated by three green lights, or a nonflashing steady green or yellow light. Check your printer manual for proper light display for "ready" mode.

- Is there paper in the printer? Is it jammed?

- Is the ribbon used up?

- Is the cover closed? Some printers won't print unless the cover is completely closed.

If you are on a network, or running under Windows or DesqView, they may be preventing the printouts from getting to the printer. Are you using a print spooler (either software or hardware) that prints in the background. Any of these products may be halting the printing, so you may wish to check the manuals that came with these products for help.

If the printer works but your graphs aren't printing, see the problem **Graph doesn't Print** in this chapter.

Printer prints more than the range specified

You probably have a border set that is longer than the print range. You can set your borders again with this command: **/ Print Printer Options Borders Columns** *or* **Rows** etc. Or you can completely clear the borders with this command: **/ Print Printer Clear Borders.** See **Printing—Borders** in Chapter 2.

Printer prints worksheet multiple times

You probably held the **G** (Go) key down too long. Just tap it. Release your hand, and *wait* for your printout.

Printout is incorrect

If your header, or footer, doesn't align or center properly, or if your printer only prints on the left side of the paper, or if each line wraps around on the next line, it is probably because your margins are set incorrectly. See the section **Printing—Margins** in Chapter 2.

RD appears at screen bottom. Can't save file

See **Save won't work. Worksheet file has no reservation.**

Save won't work.   Worksheet file has no reservation

Do you see **RD** at the bottom of the screen?   When you are on a network with other people, and you are all using and updating the same worksheet file, only one of you is permitted to save the file at any given time. The person with that permission is said to have the *reservation*. This *reservation* is passed around from computer to computer on the network.   The **RD** means that you do not have the reservation. To get the reservation, type / **F A R G** *File Admin Reservation Get*. If someone else on the network has the reservation, you won't be able to get it. To play fair on the network, once you have saved your changes, release your reservation by typing / **F A R R** *File Admin Reservation Release*. If you aren't on a network, then don't release it. Releasing the reservation won't buy you anything, and will only give you grief.

Screen moves when I tap an arrow key, but the highlighted cell doesn't change

Do you see **SCROLL** at the bottom of the screen? If so, tap the **Scroll Lock** key to remove the message. Now your arrow keys should work the way you want them to.

Text does not overlap into the next cell

There is something in the cell to the right that has priority over the overlapped label. Even spaces have priority in their own cell. Highlight the cell to the right. If there is nothing you wish to keep, erase it by typing / **R E** ↵

Titles command just beeps, and won't work

Is cell A1 highlighted? If so, that's the problem.

If you want **Vertical Titles,** you cannot issue the command when any cell on the upper-most visible row is highlighted.

If you want **Horizontal Titles,** you cannot issue the command when any cell on the left-most visible column is highlighted.

If you want **Both** horizontal and vertical titles, you cannot issue the command when any cell in either the upper-most visible row or the left-most visible column is highlighted.

Highlight another cell. Then type / **W T** *Worksheet Titles etc.*

See **Titles** in Chapter 2 for details.

Total (sum) Is incorrect

Do you see **CIRC** at the lower-right corner of the screen? If so, see **Circ** in this chapter.

If **CIRC** does not appear, check the range used in the **@SUM** function.

If the range is correct, refer to **Functions** in Chapter 2, and look at the examples for **@ROUND** and **@INT**. Perhaps they can help.

Also, see **Incorrect Answer for a formula** in this chapter.

Worksheet file has no reservation. File Save command won't work.

See **Save won't work. Worksheet file has no reservation.**

Worksheet Range Copy Move... keeps appearing on line 2 of the screen

You are typing a **Forward Slash** (/) which brings up the menu.

If you are trying to type a **Backslash**, be sure it tilts left like \

If you are entering a macro, be sure to type an apostrophe before the slash, like this **' /**

Wrong answer for a calculation

See **Incorrect Answer for a formula** in this chapter.

Index

absolute cell addresses, 327-31
  copying formulas with, 87-88
Absolute key (F4), 202
Access Menu
  to exit from, 26
  Translate command in, 362
add-in programs, 44
addition, 198
adjustable cells, in Solver, 343
aligning labels (text), 13, 45-46
  with Wysiwyg, 47-48
allocation of funds spreadsheets, 153-55
Alt-F1 (Compose) key, 202
Alt-F2 (Record) key, 203
Alt-F3 (Run) key, 203
Alt-F4 (Undo) key, 203
Alt-F6 (Zoom) key, 203
AND condition, 81
  in criteria area of database, 105-6
apostrophe ('), 241
  problems with, 381
arguments, in IF statements, 204
arrow keys, problems with, 381
ASCII files, 177
  importing into 1-2-3, 236-38
asterisks (*), 73
  problems with, 381, 384
@ sign, 14
Auditor, 50-60
  circular references and, 54-56
  creating a sample worksheet for illustrative examples, 51-53
  dependent references and, 58-59
  green cells after using, 390
  loading, 53-54
    automatically, 59
  precedent references and, 56-57
  removing from memory, 60
  uses of, 50
audit range, defined, 51
automatically loading worksheets, 61-62
automatic recalculation, 332-33
@AVG function, 206
axes, 217-18

backing out of commands (escaping), 17, 20
  with a mouse (in Wysiwyg), 32
backing up files, 70-71
backslash (\), 241, 393
  aligning labels and, 45
Backsolver, 63-69
  adjustable cells in, 63
  creating a sample worksheet for use with, 64-65
  formula cells in, 63
  loading, 65-66
    automatically, 68-69
  removing from memory, 69
Backspace key, 5, 21
BACKUP command (DOS), 70-71
balance brought forward (YTD) spreadsheets, 158-63
bar charts, 221

blank lines removed, printing with, 280
blank screen, 382
borders
  printing with, 281-84
  of worksheet area, 8
broken bar (|), 241
  aligning labels and, 45
budget spreadsheets, 156-57
BUFFERS command, in CONFIG.SYS file, 84

CALC, 382
Calc key (F9), 202
caret label prefix (*), 241
cells
  defined, 2
  entering information into, 12-16
  fixing typing mistakes already in, 21
  protecting, 314-16
  screen display of, 8
centering text. See aligning labels
@CHOICE function, 95
@CHOOSE function, 209-10
CIRC, 382-83, 397
circular references, 199, 382-83
  Auditor and, 54-56
  defined, 50
clock display, 72
CMD, 381
colon (:), for Wysiwyg menu, 29
columns
  deleting, 149
  hidden
    printing with, 298-300
  hiding, 232
  inserting, 239
  nonadjacent, printing, 298-300
  screen display of, 8
column width, 73-74
  in databases, 99-100
  with Wysiwyg, 75-76
combining 1-2-3 files, 77-80, 190
commands
  backing out (escaping) from, 17, 20
    with a mouse (in Wysiwyg), 32
  examples of, 17
  problems with entering, 383
  ranges and, 17
  READY mode for starting, 17
  screen display of, 8, 18
  selecting, 18-19
    with a mouse (in Wysiwyg), 31-32
  to start, 17
  Worksheet versus Range versus File, 43
comments, hidden, 49
Compose key (Alt-F1), 202
compressed type, 288
conditions, 81-83
CONFIG.SYS file, 84
constraint cells, in Solver, 344
control panel, 7-8, 85
Copy command, steps of, 86

399

402   Fast Access/Lotus 1-2-3 (Release 3.1+)